Black Bondage
in the North

Black Bondage in the North

EDGAR J. McMANUS

SYRACUSE UNIVERSITY PRESS   1973

FIRST EDITION

Library of Congress Cataloging in Publication Data

McManus, Edgar J.

   Black bondage in the North.
   Bibliography: p.
   1. Slavery in the United States—New England.
2. Slavery in the United States—Middle Atlantic
States. I. Title.
E441.M16   301.44'93'0974   72-12425
ISBN 0-8156-0091-7

Manufactured in the United States of America

To J. E. M.

Edgar J. McManus is professor of history at Queens College, Flushing, New York. He received the B.S., M.A., and Ph.D. from Columbia University and the J.D. from New York University. His articles have appeared in *Journal of Negro History* and *New York Law Forum*. Dr. McManus is the author of *A History of Negro Slavery in New York*, published by Syracuse University Press in 1966.

Contents

Preface

For nearly two hundred years the North maintained a slave regime more varied and complex than the "peculiar institution" of the South. Unlike the South, which used slaves primarily for agricultural labor, the North trained and diversified its slave force to meet the needs of a complicated economy. From the seventeenth century onward, Negroes could be found in virtually every field of Northern economic life. They worked as carpenters, shiprights, sailmakers, printers, tailors, shoemakers, coopers, blacksmiths, bakers, weavers, and goldsmiths. In technical skill and versatility they spanned the whole range of free labor. Some became so expert in the skilled crafts that the free workers protested bitterly against their own loss of jobs and economic opportunities. That slavery for blacks could mean hardship for many whites sometimes became painfully clear to those who had to compete with the system.

There is currently no general history of Negro slavery in the North. A number of articles and monographs on individual states and local areas have appeared, but a comprehensive account of the Northern slave system has long been overdue. Ulrich B. Phillips devoted only a single chapter to the North in his study of American slavery, and subsequent treatments have continued to be cursory. For a slave system that lasted so long and had such bitter racial implications, these abbreviated accounts have proved inadequate. The full story deserves to be told, both to understand the role of blacks in the settlement and development of the North and to fill an obvious gap in the study of American colonial history.

This book examines the nature and operation of Northern slavery from its colonial beginnings until its demise in the late eighteenth century. The everyday life and working conditions of the slaves are described, and emphasis is placed on the ways in which bondsmen accommodated themselves to the system. Since their skills often gave them considerable bargaining power, some managed to obtain personal privileges and eventual freedom in return for efficient service. I have attempted to show how these concessions modified slavery from the automatic system of subordination prescribed by the slave codes. The codes themselves are analyzed from the standpoint of slave control and white security, and also for their impact on the legal status of Negroes. An effort has also been made to relate slave law to the socioracial prejudice that underpinned slavery and that persisted in the North after abolition. Finally, the study describes how black resistance to bondage undermined economic efficiency and turned the racial hegemony of the whites into a regime of mutual terror and repression.

An attempt has been made throughout to tell the story objectively with a minimum of generalization or interpretation. I have particularly avoided imposing a conceptual framework on the study and have resisted the temptation, often strong, to use the material as a forum for my own opinions. My goal has been to describe the actual operation of a slave system, not to generalize about the mainsprings of slavery and race relations. Since this is a pioneer study, it seemed more important to define factual boundaries than to plunge into theoretical thickets. My primary aim has been to provide hard data from which slavery may be viewed in fresher perspective and from which black-white relationships may be more soundly appraised.

Such an approach has tended to narrow the focus of the study and has precluded the ideological éclat that writers, and sometimes readers, find intellectually stimulating. But to have veered from course for philosophical forays, however tempting and interesting, would have compromised the purpose of the study. My aim throughout has been to provide factual groundwork, not to attempt a full-blown conceptualization of the subject.

This is not to say that Northern slavery lacks implications for other times and places. Quite the contrary, the enslavement of blacks was everywhere part of the same great racial confrontation that profoundly altered the history of this hemisphere. There was a much greater similarity in slave practices throughout the Americas than some comparative studies have suggested. What happened to blacks in New York and Massachusetts had its counterpart in Virginia and Brazil. Nevertheless, this aspect of slavery is subsidiary to the main purpose of the study and therefore has been deferred to a concluding chapter which does not disturb the descriptive emphasis of the book.

Although this study owes a heavy debt to regional and state monographs, particularly those of Lorenzo J. Greene and Edward R. Turner, archival and documentary sources have been relied upon throughout. Nothing reveals the practices and presumptions of the slave system more cogently than the records of the slaveholders themselves. For the sake of clarity and as a convenience to the reader, abbreviations in all quotations have been spelled out, and whenever it was possible to do so without changing the original sense or meaning, spelling and punctuation have been modernized. In all other respects, however, the quoted texts have been cited exactly in order to preserve the authenticity of the reference.

The preparation of this book benefited materially from the assistance of many groups and individuals. My greatest debt is to the American Council of Learned Societies for a fellowship that enabled me to devote an uninterrupted year to the project. The American Philosophical Society also provided generous support in the form of a research grant. A summer fellowship from the John Carter Brown Library facilitated my research in New England.

Librarians and archivists often helped beyond the ordinary call of duty. I am especially grateful to Mr. Albert Baragwanath of the Museum of the City of New York, Mr. Wilmer R. Leech, former curator of manuscripts of the New-York Historical Society, Mr. Leo Flaherty of the Massachusetts State Library, Mrs. Laurence Hardy and Mrs. Mary C. Thayer of the John Carter Brown Library in Providence, Mrs. Thyra Jane Foster of the Rhode Island Historical Society, Mr. John D. Kilbourne and Mr. Conrad Wilson, formerly of the Historical Society of Pennsylvania, and Mrs. Eleanor Mayer of the Friends Historical Library of Swarthmore College. I also wish to thank the staffs of the New York Public Library and its Schomburg Collection branch, the East Hampton Free Library, the New York Society Library, the Rhode Island

Historical Society, the Newport Historical Society, the American Philosophical Society, the Columbia University Library, the Historical Documents Collection of Queens College, the University of Pennsylvania Library, and the Friends Seminary of New York City. Their unfailing courtesy and helpfulness simplified many problems of research and greatly assisted the completion of this study.

My debt to historians and scholars is also great. Professors Kenneth Scott and Leo Hershkowitz of Queens College shared their specialized knowledge of early New York history with me, and another colleague, Professor Stanley P. Hirshson, turned up references in the course of his own researches. Professors Lorenzo J. Greene of Lincoln University, Benjamin Quarles of Morgan State College, and Arthur Zilversmit of Lake Forest College provided suggestions and insights that contributed significantly to this study. Professor Richard B. Morris of Columbia University furnished substantial assistance from the beginning, and I deeply appreciate his interest and encouragement. I am indebted to Professor Jerry Frost of Vassar College for numerous leads on Quakers and slavery, and to Mr. Peter Emmer of the University of Amsterdam for information on the Dutch slave trade. A note of thanks is also due to Mr. Nicholas Di Michael, an M.A. graduate of Queens College, and to Mrs. Elaine Weiss and Mr. Eugene Mohring, now doctoral candidates at the City University of New York, who served as my research assistants and helped me with the newspaper files of the colonial press. Mr. Edward Garvey of the Queens College administrative staff has my gratitude for his painstaking care in correcting and typing the manuscript.

Finally, I am grateful to my wife, Joan Thornton McManus, for numerous suggestions as to style and content. Her editorial assistance and encouragement contributed beyond measure to the completion of this volume. My sincere thanks to all who helped so generously in so many ways.

EDGAR J. McMANUS

Queens College
December 1972

Abbreviations Used in the Notes

AHR	*American Historical Review*
APS	American Philosophical Society, Philadelphia
CHS	Connecticut Historical Society
CSL	Connecticut State Library
CSM	Colonial Society of Massachusetts
HDC, QC	Historical Documents Collection, Queens College
HSP	Historical Society of Pennsylvania
JCBL	John Carter Brown Library, Providence
JNH	*Journal of Negro History*
LC	Library of Congress
LCP	Library Company of Philadelphia
MCNY	Museum of the City of New York
MHS	Massachusetts Historical Society
MSL	Massachusetts State Library
MVHR	*Mississippi Valley Historical Review*
NEQ	*New England Quarterly*
NHS	Newport Historical Society
NYHS	New-York Historical Society
PMHB	*Pennsylvania Magazine of History and Biography*
RIHS	Rhode Island Historical Society
SPG	Society for the Propagation of the Gospel in Foreign Parts
UPL	University of Pennsylvania Library
WMQ	*William and Mary Quarterly*

Black Bondage
in the North

1

Slavery and Settlement

The Northern colonies had every advantage that nature could bestow for successful settlement and development. From the Delaware estuary to Massachusetts Bay, an invigorating climate of alternating seasons set the stage for a balanced growth of industry and agriculture. Indigenous crops as well as those introduced from Europe grew readily in the large areas of arable land, relieving the settlers of dependence on outside sources of sustenance. In the northernmost region of settlement, where agriculture was less productive, the Atlantic fisheries supplemented the food supply and provided surpluses with which to pay for needed imports. There was plenty of timber for shipbuilding and commerce, abundant raw materials, fine harbors, and navigable rivers linking the coast with the interior. In all, the natural environment could not have been more favorable for colonization and development.

Only one serious obstacle impeded Northern colonial progress: an acute shortage of labor that everywhere retarded growth and hobbled the economy. A vast amount of work was required to exploit the resources of a new continent, and the supply was kept down by the refusal of workers to accept a permanent wage-earning status. The desire to acquire land or a trade that could be passed on to their children turned workers into entrepreneurs who hacked farms out of the wilderness or sought their fortunes in the towns as self-employed artisans and craftsmen. Land was so cheap that a hired man could easily save enough to obtain a start, and an enterprising laborer had no more difficulty setting himself up as an independent tradesman.[1] So completely did free settlers reject the wage system that every colony relied to some extent upon compulsory labor—indentured servitude for whites and slavery for blacks—to provide the day-to-day working force essential for economic progress.[2]

But slavery far more than indentured servitude gave the colonial labor system its essentially coercive character. Every colony became a slave colony because only compulsion could maintain the stable labor force needed to provide the capital accretion for transforming the early settlements into a viable society. Slavery was the ultimate means of compelling labor that could not be obtained by voluntary incentives. And the manpower supporting the system inevitably had to come from Africa, for no other source of exploitable labor was then available. Negroes were technically and culturally superior to the Amerindians in the English colonies and therefore better able to contribute to economic development. The amount of compulsion employed and the forms it took varied according to differences in climate, geography, and the level of economic development. But all the colonies in their early stages shared a common dependence upon the exploitation of subject people to achieve a measure of prosperity.[3]

Beginning in 1626, the Dutch West India Company made sytematic use of Nergo slaves to promote its settlements in New Netherland.[4] The economic progress of the colony had been hampered by a chronic shortage of agricultural labor. The company found that the white settlers and servants sent over from Holland at great expense "sooner or later apply themselves to trade and neglect agriculture altogether."[5] Most of these settlers came to New

1. Richard B. Morris, *Government and Labor in Early America* (New York: Octagon Books, 1965), pp. 148–54.

2. Marcus W. Jernegan, *Laboring and Dependent Classes in Colonial America* (Chicago: University of Chicago Press, 1931), pp. 45–46.

3. David Brion Davis, *The Problem of Slavery in Western Culture* (Ithaca, N.Y.: Cornell University Press, 1966, pp. 244–53.

4. E. B. O'Callaghan, ed., *Voyage of the Slavers St. John and Arms of Amsterdam* (Albany: Munsell, 1967), p. xiii; I. N. Phelps Stokes, ed., *The Iconography of Manhattan Island,* 6 vols. (New York: Dodd, 1915–28), II, 297. See John Yates and Joseph Moulton, *History of the State of New York* (New York: Goodrich, 1824–26), p. 427.

5. E. B. O'Callaghan and Berthold Fernow, eds., *Documents Relative to the*

Netherland with the expectation of making fortunes in the fur trade and returning home after a few years.[6] There was no reason for them to stay permanently, for life in prosperous Holland was far more preferable to life in the colonial wilderness. With free workers generally unobtainable, the West India Company came to rely heavily on Negro slaves to clear the forests, build roads, construct dwellings, and produce the food that made the colony viable.[7]

Black labor contributed decisively to New Netherland's economy. As new lands were brought under cultivation, many of the whites turned from the fur trade to farming with a view to settling permanently.[8] Slavery made this transition possible by providing the cheap, reliable labor that made agriculture acceptable and profitable.[9] During the 1640s free workers, when available, earned about 280 guilders annually, plus an allowance for food and lodging; slaves from the West Indies, on the other hand, could be purchased outright for about 300 guilders and those from Angola for considerably less.[10] Slaves were particularly important in the agricultural development of the Hudson Valley, where the land monopolies of the patroons discouraged free immigration. So great was the demand for labor on the large Hudson estates that one prominent planter offered to buy "any suitable blacks available."[11]

Slavery also provided the Dutch settlements with a source of labor for public projects. Negro slaves raised food for the garrison at New Amsterdam, and they also kept the military works around

Colonial History of the State of New York, 15 vols. (Albany: Weed, Parsons, 1856–87), I, 246, hereafter cited as *N.Y. Col. Docs.*

6. J. Franklin Jameson, ed., *Narratives of New Netherland, 1609–1664* (New York: Scribner's, 1909), p. 89.

7. *N.Y. Col. Docs.,* I, 246.

8. Edward C. Kirkland, *A History of American Economic Life* (New York: Appleton-Century-Crofts, 1951), pp. 11, 38–39.

9. A. J. F. Van Laer, ed., *The Van Rensselaer Bowier Manuscripts* (Albany: State University of New York, 1908), pp. 222, 261, 278; A. J. F. Van Laer, ed., *Correspondence of Jeremias Van Rensselaer* (Albany: State University of New York, 1932), pp. 167–68.

10. A. J. F. Van Laer and Jonathan Pearson, eds., *Early Records of the City and County of Albany and Colony of Rensselaerswyck,* 4 vols. (Albany: State University of New York, 1915–19), III, 122–80; Van Laer, *Correspondence of Jeremias Van Rensselaer,* p. 167.

11. Van Laer, *Van Rensselaer Bowier MSS.,* p. 642.

the town in repair.[12] In 1659 blacks helped fortify Oyster Bay in order to strengthen the Dutch West India Company's hold on Long Island.[13] Since company-owned slaves were self-sufficient, raising food for themselves on land allotted to them for that purpose, the public labor that they performed accelerated economic progress.[14] It made possible a rapid recapitalization of profits, for the taxes that would otherwise have been levied to support public works were channeled instead into the productive sector of the economy.

The company also sent slaves to the Dutch and Swedish settlements along the Delaware River. As early as 1639 blacks began to take up the labor slack that had retarded economic growth.[15] In 1664 the Delaware settlers made a contract with the company "to transport hither a lot of Negroes for agricultural purposes."[16] The demand for slaves continued to grow after the region came under English control. Black labor played a vital role in the development of New Castle, the most important settlement on the Delaware.[17] In 1678 the town magistrates urged "that liberty of trade may be granted us with the neighboring colony of Maryland for the supplying us with Negroes . . . without which we cannot subsist."[18]

Slave imports increased sharply after the region passed under the proprietorship of William Penn.[19] Penn himself preferred to buy slaves rather than contract for white servants, "for then a

12. Berthold Fernow, ed., *Minutes of the Orphanmasters Court of New Amsterdam,* 2 vols. (New York: Francis P. Harper, 1907), II, 191.

13. John Cox, ed., *Oyster Bay Town Records,* 2 vols. (New York: Tobias A. Wright, 1916–24), II, 297–98.

14. J. H. Innes, *New Amsterdam and Its People* (New York: Scribner's, 1902), p. 9.

15. John B. Linn and W. H. Egle, eds., *Pennsylvania Archives,* 2d ser., 19 vols. (Harrisburg: State Printer, 1878–96), XVI, 234; C. T. Odhner, "The Founding of New Sweden, 1637–1642," trans. by G. B. Keen in *PMHB,* III (1879), 277. See Edward R. Turner, *The Negro in Pennsylvania* (Washington, D.C.: The American Historical Association, 1911), p. 1.

16. O'Callaghan, *Voyage of the Slavers,* pp. 200–201, 223–25; *N.Y. Col. Docs.,* II, 213–14.

17. Darold D. Wax, "The Negro Slave Trade in Colonial Pennsylvania," unpublished Ph.D. dissertation (University of Washington, 1962), p. 20.

18. New Castle County Court Records, 1676–78, Liber A, p. 304, MS., coll., HSP.

19. "Articles of the Free Society of Traders," *PMHB,* V (1881), 37–50.

man has them while they live."[20] The use of slaves on the proprietor's estate at Pennsbury firmly established the system in the colony.[21] Philadelphia merchants who brought back slaves as part of their return cargoes from the West Indies provided users of labor with a steady stream of black manpower.[22] There were slaves in Philadelphia County by 1684 and in Chester County by 1687.[23] So rapid was the growth of the black working force that in 1693 the Provincial Council expressed alarm at "the tumultuous gatherings of the Negroes in the town of Philadelphia."[24]

The Dutch also brought slaves to their settlements on the west bank of the Hudson. Efforts to colonize there had made little progress, and blacks were badly needed to shore up the shaky economy.[25] When the region became part of New Jersey after the English occupation, slavery received strong support from the proprietary regime of Berkeley and Carteret. So that "the planting of the said province may be more speedily promoted," the proprietors offered sixty acres of land for every slave imported during 1664, forty-five acres for slaves imported the following year, and thirty acres for those brought in before the end of 1666.[26] A rapid increase in the slave force followed, and by the end of the century black workers were common throughout the colony. Slaves became particularly numerous around Perth Amboy, the main port of entry for northern New Jersey.[27] By 1690 most of the inhabitants of the region owned one or more Negroes.[28]

20. William Penn to James Harrison, October 25, 1685, Penn MSS., Domestic and Miscellaneous Papers, HSP.

21. William Penn's Cash Book (1699), pp. 3, 6, 9, 15, 18, MS. coll., APS, cited in Wax, "The Negro Slave Trade in Colonial Pennsylvania," pp. 21–22.

22. Albert C. Myers, ed., Narratives of Early Pennsylvania, West Jersey and Delaware, 1630–1707 (New York: Scribner's, 1912), p. 325; Turner, The Negro in Pennsylvania, p. 2.

23. Turner, The Negro in Pennsylvania, pp. 2–3.

24. Samuel Hazard, ed., Colonial Records of Pennsylvania, 16 vols. (Philadelphia: Severns, 1852), I, 381, hereafter cited as Pa. Col. Recs.

25. N.Y. Col. Docs., III, 71.

26. Aaron Leaming and Jacob Spicer, eds., The Grants, Concessions and Original Consitutions of the Province of New Jersey (Somerville, N.J.: Honeyman, 1881), pp. 20–23; Henry S. Cooley, A Study of Slavery in New Jersey (Baltimore: The Johns Hopkins Press, 1896), pp. 9–10.

27. William A. Whitehead, Contributions to the Early History of Perth Amboy and Adjoining Country (New York, 1856), p. 318.

28. James P. Snell, History of Sussex and Warren Counties, N.J. (Philadelphia: Everts & Peck, 1881), p. 76.

Chattel bondage in New England began with the enslavement of Indians captured during the bloody Pequot war of 1637.[29] Most of the male captives were transported to the West Indies and exchanged for Negro slaves. The women and girls could be kept in bondage without much risk, but captured warriors posed a threat to security.[30] In 1638 Captain William Pierce returned to Boston with a cargo of blacks who had been purchased with the Pequot captives.[31] Such exchanges became routine during subsequent Indian wars, for the danger of keeping revengeful warriors in the colony far outweighed the value of their labor.[32] So marked was the preference for black workers that the New England Confederation agreed in 1646 that Indians enslaved as spoils of war should automatically "be shipped out and exchanged for Negroes."[33]

The use of black labor soon became general throughout New England. Connecticut had slaves as early as 1639, and by 1645 the presence of blacks was officially noted in New Hampshire.[34] Some New Englanders, like Emanuel Dowling of Massachusetts, believed that the prosperity of the region required "a stock of slaves sufficient to do all our business."[35] The largest slave concentrations were in the agricultural and commercial counties: Rock-

29. Alden T. Vaughan, *New England Frontier: Puritans and Indians, 1620–1675* (Boston: Little, Brown, 1965), pp. 150–51.

30. William Bradford, "History of Plymouth Plantation," in MHS *Colls.*, 4th ser., III (1856), 358–60.

31. John Winthrop, *History of New England, 1630–1649*, James K. Hosmer, ed., 2 vols. (New York: Scribner's, 1908), I, 148, 233–34. There is some evidence that blacks had reached Massachusetts before Pierce's voyage. See Thomas Hutchinson, *The History of the Colony and the Province of the Massachusetts Bay*, Lawrence S. Mayo, ed., 3 vols. (Cambridge, Mass.: Harvard University Press, 1936), I, 374, and John G. Palfrey, *History of New England during the Stuart Dynasty*, 3 vols. (Boston: Little, Brown, 1859–64), II, 30n. See Lorenzo J. Greene, *The Negro in Colonial New England, 1620–1776* (New York: Columbit University Press, 1942), pp. 15–17.

32. Bernard Steiner, *History of Slavery in Connecticut* (Baltimore: The Johns Hopkins Press, 1893), p. 11.

33. Nathaniel B. Shurtleff and David Pulsifer, eds., *Records of the Colony of New Plymouth*, 12 vols. (Boston: White, 1855–61), IX, 71, hereafter cited as *Ply. Col. Recs.*

34. Steiner, *History of Slavery in Connecticut*, p. 23n; Nathaniel B. Shurtleff, ed., *Records of the Governor and Company of the Massachusetts Bay in New England, 1628–1674*, 5 vols. (Boston: White, 1853–54), II, 136, hereafter cited as *Mass. Bay Recs.*

35. "Winthrop Papers," MHS *Colls.*, 4th ser., VI (1863), 65.

ingham in New Hampshire; Essex, Suffolk, Bristol, and Plymouth in Massachusetts; New London, Hartford, and Fairfield in Connecticut; and Newport and Washington in Rhode Island.[36] In the coastal districts and towns, where most of the region's wealth was centered, blacks played an important role in industry and shipbuilding.[37]

Slavery was particularly suitable to conditions in Rhode Island's Narragansett region. Large-scale agriculture and proximity to a slave-trading center like Newport resulted in a black working force that varied from a third to a half of the total population.[38] There was a heavy demand for slaves on the larger estates, and one planter in need of labor imported twenty-eight in a single shipment.[39] Robert Hazard, perhaps the greatest landowner in the colony, employed twelve black women whose specialized duty was "to make one to two dozen cheeses every day."[40] No upper-class household was considered complete without a staff of Negro retainers and domestic servants.[41] By the mid-eighteenth century the district had the largest proportion of slaves to free inhabitants to be found anywhere in the North.[42]

Dependence on black labor drew the North into the overseas slave trade. During the New Netherland period efforts were made by the Dutch West India Company to form close links between the colony and the Dutch slave stations in Angola. The directors believed that direct participation in the slave traffic would increase the market for slaves and speed colonial development. In 1648 the company relaxed its trading monopoly and allowed New Netherlanders to send farm produce to Angola in order "to convey Negroes back home to be employed in the cultivation of their lands."[43] All duties on produce sent to Brazil were also remitted

36. Greene, *The Negro in Colonial New England*, pp. 81–82, 320.
37. Leonard P. Stavisky, "Negro Craftsmanship in Early America," *AHR*, LIV (1949), 319.
38. Kirkland, *History of American Economic Life*, pp. 60–61.
39. William D. Miller, *The Narragansett Planters* (Worcester, Mass.: American Antiquarian Society, 1934), p. 23.
40. William Johnston, *Slavery in Rhode Island, 1755–1776* (Providence: Rhode Island Historical Society, 1894), p. 29.
41. Thomas W. Bicknell, *History of Rhode Island and Providence Plantations*, 3 vols. (New York: American Historical Society, 1920), II, 503.
42. See Appendix, pp. 202–203.
43. E. B. O'Callaghan, ed., *Calendar of Historical Manuscripts in the Office of*

in order to encourage the importation of blacks who would promote agriculture and thereby increase the demand for slaves at
the company's stations in Angola.[44]

What ultimately defeated this trading policy was that the
slaves most in demand came not from Angola but from Curaçao.
Blacks brought directly from Africa were often dangerous and
difficult to control—"proud and treacherous," as one New Nether-
lander described them.[45] Those from Curaçao, on the other hand,
had become accustomed to slave routines on the island's plantations. Since the demand for such slaves far exceeded the supply,
New Netherland had to compete with other Dutch colonies for
its share of those available for export.[46] Repeated requests for special consideration were made on the grounds that New Netherland's shortage of workers was critical. So scarce was every sort
of labor that a tariff was imposed to prevent the diversion of
slaves to other colonies.[47] The Curaçao directors finally granted
the requested preference in 1660, on condition that any slaves
sent from the island "be employed in cultivating the land."[48]

The New Netherland slave traffic brought the West India Company only marginal trading profits. The markup on slaves was
higher in the Southern colonies and in the West Indies, so blacks
sent to New Netherland sold at somewhat lower prices.[49] The discount averaged about 10 percent—the amount of the slave duty
needed to prevent reshipment to other colonies.[50] This not only
reduced the size of the buyer's investment but indirectly subsidized the use of slaves throughout the colony. The company
went even further, allowing slaveowners to exchange unsatisfac-
tory Negroes for company slaves free of charge.[51] By keeping

the Secretary of State, 2 vols. (Albany: Weed, Parsons, 1866), I, 272; O'Callaghan,
Voyage of the Slavers, pp. 101–102.

44. N.Y. Col. Docs., I, 246.

45. Van Laer, Correspondence of Jeremias Van Rennselaer, p. 167.

46. O'Callaghan, Voyage of the Slavers, pp. 167–69.

47. E. B. O'Callaghan, ed., Laws and Ordinances of New Netherland (Albany:
Weed, Parsons, 1868), p. 191.

48. O'Callaghan, Voyage of the Slavers, pp. 167–69. See David T. Valentine,
comp., Manual of the Corporation of the City of New York, 28 vols. (New York,
1842–70), (1863), pp. 591–93.

49. Federal Writers Project, Maritime History of New York (Philadelphia:
Doubleday, Doran, 1937), p. 27.

50. O'Callaghan, Laws and Ordinances of New Netherland, p. 191.

51. Van Laer, Correspondence of Jeremias Van Rennselaer, p. 255.

slave costs down, the company tried to make slavery an economic and efficient system of labor. The policy, according to Director General Stuyvesant, was not to make a profit, but "to promote and advance the population and agriculture of the province."[52]

New England's participation in the slave trade gave the region access to a continuous supply of black labor. Boston merchants entered the African trade as early as 1644, and by 1676 they were bringing back cargoes from as far away as East Africa and Madagascar.[53] Most of these slaves went to the West Indies, where the traders usually took on experienced blacks for the return voyage home.[54] Except for women and children who could be used for household service, slaves brought directly from Africa generally did not fit into the Puritan scheme of things.[55] The New England market was highly selective, and blacks who seemed dangerous or likely to cause trouble were quickly sent out of the region.[56]

The slave traffic quickly became one of the cornerstones of New England's commercial prosperity. It was the linchpin of the triangular trade linking New England, Africa, and the West Indies in a bond of economic interdependence. Sugar, molasses, and rum from the islands were exchanged for the farm produce, lumber, and manufactured goods of New England; Africa, in return for rum from New England, furnished the slaves needed by the West Indian planters.[57] Since it was rum that held this network together, a great distilling industry sprang up in New England to keep the trade going. The trade not only yielded enormous commercial profits, but it provided New England's entrepreneurs with an almost limitless supply of labor for general economic development.[58]

52. O'Callaghan, *Voyage of the Slavers*, p. 202.
53. Greene, *The Negro in Colonial New England*, pp. 20–22.
54. J. Hammond Trumbull and Charles J. Hoadly, eds., *The Public Records of the Colony of Connecticut, 1636–1776*, 15 vols. (Hartford: Lockwood & Brainard, 1850–90), III, 298; XV, 557n. Hereafter cited as *Conn. Col. Recs.*
55. Greene, *The Negro in Colonial New England*, pp. 36–37.
56. Arthur P. Newton, *The Colonising Activities of the English Puritans: The Last Phase of the Elizabethan Struggle with Spain* (New Haven: Yale University Press, 1914), p. 261.
57. Greene, *The Negro in Colonial New England*, p. 317.
58. George F. Dow, *Slave Ships and Slaving* (Salem, Mass.: Marine Research Society, 1927), p. 268.

Although Massachusetts led the rest of New England into the slave trade, by the eighteenth century Rhode Island had become the most important slave-trading colony. In the period 1732–64 Rhode Island sent eighteen ships and 1,800 hogsheads of rum to Africa each year, earning cash balances of £40,000 annually.[59] Newport became the leading slave port, but Bristol and Providence also played important roles in the traffic. The slave trade eclipsed every other branch of commerce, sometimes to the consternation of other traders. When Captain Isaac Freeman tried to buy a cargo of molasses in 1752, his agent in Newport informed him that "there are so many vessels lading for Guinea we can't get one hogshead of rum for the cash."[60] Rhode Island's heavy traffic in Negroes, together with that of Massachusetts, made New England the leading slave-trading region in America.[61]

The heavy profits of the slave trade stimulated the growth of other industries.[62] Shipbuilding, the distilleries, the molasses trade, agricultural exports to the West Indies, and large numbers of artisans, sailors, and farmers were all dependent upon the traffic in Negroes.[63] It became the hub of New England's economy. By 1763 the Massachusetts slave trade employed about five thousand sailors in addition to the numerous coopers, tanners, and sailmakers who serviced the ships.[64] About two-thirds of Rhode Island's merchant fleet and about as many of her sailors were engaged in the traffic. Moreover, there were at least thirty distilleries in which hundreds of Rhode Islanders earned their livelihood producing rum for the trade.[65] Without the trade, these industries would have collapsed, the capital invested in them would have been wiped out, and large numbers of artisans, farmers, distillery workers, and sailors thrown out of work.

59. John R. Bartlett, ed., *Records of the Colony of Rhode Island and Providence Plantations in New England, 1636–1792,* 10 vols. (Providence: Greene, 1856–65), I, 243, hereafter cited as *R. I. Col. Recs.*

60. George C. Mason, "The African Slave Trade in Colonial Times," *Potter's American Monthly,* I (1872), 316.

61. Elizabeth Donnan, ed., *Documents Illustrative of the History of the Slave Trade to America,* 3 vols. (Washington, D.C.: Carnegie Institute, 1930–35), II, 405.

62. *Ibid.,* p. xiii.

63. Greene, *The Negro in Colonial New England,* pp. 68–69.

64. "Fitch Papers," CHS *Colls.,* XVIII (1920), 262–73.

65. *R.I. Col. Recs.,* VI, 378–83.

The British government gave strong official backing to the slave trade. Besides supporting a wide network of commercial interests, the traffic subserved the mercantilist policy of promoting the use of slaves in colonial agriculture.[66] Between 1729 and 1750 Parliament appropriated more than £90,000 for the maintenance of slave stations on the African coast.[67] Moreover, public officials in the colonies were instructed to assist traders in marketing their slaves.[68] When Lord Cornbury came to New York as governor in 1702, he brought special instructions to encourage slave imports by every means at his command.[69] In 1709 the Board of Trade instructed Governor Hunter to see to it that New Yorkers had a steady supply of Negroes at reasonable prices.[70] Such instructions were generally carried out, for the traffic in slaves not only accorded with official policy but yielded handsome profits as well. Some governors, like Belcher of Massachusetts and Wanton of Rhode Island, not only fostered the trade but also participated in it on their own account.[71]

Official policy toward slavery was most clearly revealed in the measures adopted for New Jersey and New York after the region fell to the English. The Articles of Capitulation, transferring sovereignty from the Dutch, specifically confirmed all slave titles, and a statute promulgated the following year for the first time recognized slavery as a legal institution.[72] Moreover, by restricting indentured servitude to those "who willingly sell themselves into bondage," the statute abolished the loose apprentice system

66. Malachy Postlethwayt, *The African Trade the Great Pillar and Support of the British Plantation Trade in America* (London: Robinson, 1745), *passim.* See Klaus E. Knorr, *British Colonial Theories* (Toronto: University of Toronto Press, 1944), pp. 41–48, 68–81; Fred J. Hinkhouse, *The Preliminaries of the American Revolution as Seen in the English Press, 1763–1775* (New York: Columbia University Press, 1926), pp. 107–108.

67. John R. Spears, *The American Slave Trade* (New York: Scribner's, 1901), pp. 90–91.

68. Albert Giesecke, *American Commercial Legislation before 1789* (Philadelphia: University of Pennsylvania Press, 1910), p. 34n.

69. John C. Hurd, *The Law of Freedom and Bondage in the United States,* 2 vols. (Boston: Little, Brown, 1858–62), I, 280.

70. *N.Y. Col. Docs.,* V, 136.

71. Donnan, *Slave Trade Documents,* III, 36–38; Gertrude Kimball, ed., *Correspondence of the Colonial Governors of Rhode Island, 1723–1775,* 2 vols. (Boston: Houghton, Mifflin, 1902–1903), I, xxxviii–ix.

72. *N.Y. Col. Docs.,* II, 250–53.

whereby Dutch servants had been bound for indefinite terms.[73] Once indentures were limited to fixed periods, apprentices and servants became more expensive and difficult to retain. Finally, in 1649 a law preventing illegal enslavement of Indians completed the process of restricting slavery to bondsmen of African origin.[74]

These measures resulted in a considerable increase in New York's slave force. During the first quarter of the eighteenth century, 1,570 slave imports were recorded from the West Indies and 802 from Africa.[75] These estimates, however, fall far short of the numbers actually imported, for the port records do not count the slaves smuggled into the colony by illegal traders. In 1715, for example, customs recorded only thirty-eight slaves from Africa, though at least forty more were brought in illegally by one trader.[76] No imports at all were recorded from Africa in 1726, though one merchant smuggled in at least 150 slaves on a single voyage.[77] Whether brought in legally or by smuggling, the slave population grew at a rapid rate. From a total of about two thousand slaves in 1698, it grew to over nine thousand adult blacks by 1746—the largest slave force of any colony north of Maryland.[78]

The slave trade contributed vitally to the commercial development of the Middle colonies.[79] The demand for blacks, which was estimated in 1709 to be one thousand annually for New York and North Carolina, brought enormous profits to the business community.[80] Merchants, traders, factors, and commercial agents competed for a share of the trade, and their efforts were generally rewarded. The great New York City merchants imported whole

73. *Colonial Laws of New York from 1664 to the Revolution,* 5 vols. (Albany: Lyon, 1894), I, 18, hereafter cited as *N.Y. Col. Laws.*

74. Valentine, *Manual* (1870), pp. 764–65.

75. Daniel Parish, Transcripts of Material on Slavery in the Public Records Office in London (1690–1750), p. 33, MS. Coll., NYHS. Hereafter cited as Parish's Transcripts.

76. W. Noel Sainsbury, *et al.,* eds., *Calendar of State Papers: Colonial Series, American and West Indies,* 42 vols. (London: H.M.S.O. 1860–1953), XXVIII (1714–15), 290–91, hereafter cited as *Cal. State Papers, Col.*

77. Parish's Transcripts (1720–38), p. 23.

78. Evarts B. Greene and Virginia D. Harrington, *American Population before the Federal Census of 1790* (New York: Columbia University Press, 1932), pp. 92, 95–102; E. B. O'Callaghan, ed., *Documentary History of the State of New York,* 4 vols. (Albany, 1849–51), I, 482.

79. Spears, *The American Slave Trade,* pp. 90–91.

80. *Cal. State Papers, Col.,* XXIV (1708–1709), 209–13.

cargoes, sometimes directly from Africa, and the smaller traders specialized in experienced slaves purchased on consignment.[81] The retail markup was so high—about 100 percent of cost—that anyone with enough capital for even small consignments of slaves could set up a lucrative business.[82] There were risks, of course, but profit margins were wide enough to make up for the losses that occasionally occurred.

New Jersey's slave traders received strong official support from the time the colony became a royal province. In 1702 Governor Cornbury brought instructions from England to have the settlers provided with "a constant and sufficient supply of merchantable Negroes at moderate prices." He was ordered to assist traders in the marketing of slaves and "to take especial care that payment be duly made."[83] These instructions became settled policy, and the slave traffic became one of the preferred branches of New Jersey's commerce. In rejecting a proposed slave tariff in 1744, the Provincial Council declared that nothing would be permitted to interfere with the importation of Negroes. The council observed that slaves had become essential to the colonial economy, since most entrepreneurs could not afford to pay the high wages commanded by free workers.[84] This policy of duty-free importation not only guaranteed an ample supply of black labor, but it also made New Jersey a haven for smugglers running slaves into neighboring colonies where tariffs were in effect.[85]

Pennsylvania's slave trade owed more to profits than to official encouragement. The traffic grew as the colony's commerce expanded, for traders regarded black labor as just another commodity to be bought and sold like ordinary merchandise. Philadelphia's merchant ships often carried slaves along with other

81. *New York Gazette*, May 17, 1731. *New York Weekly Journal*, February 26, March 12, 19, 1738/39. *New York Weekly Post-Boy*, July 3, 31, August 7, 21, 1749. *New York Mercury*, July 14, 28, 1760.

82. *New York Mercury*, March 30, May 11, 1761; January 10, 31, March 7, June 13, August 25, October 17, 1762; September 10, 1764.

83. Leaming and Spicer, *N.J. Grants, Concessions, Constitutions*, pp. 640, 642. See Cooley, *Study of Slavery in New Jersey*, p. 12.

84. *Documents Relating to the Colonial, Revolutionary, and Post-Revolutionary History of the State of New Jersey*, 42 vols. (Newark: New Jersey Historical Society, 1900–49), VI, 219, 232; XV, 351, 384–85. Hereafter cited as *N.J. Archives* (binder's title).

85. Cooley, *Study of Slavery in New Jersey*, p. 16.

cargo, a circumstance that diffused the traffic among the business class and diluted the risks of slave-trading. The Philadelphia ship *Constant Alice,* which regularly traded with Barbados, usually brought back slave cargoes valued at about one-half its total freight. Moreover, the trade was easy to enter, for ships engaged in general commerce could be adapted to slave-trading with little expense. Since the slaves were generally shipped in small lots, there was almost no need for special equipment to take on slaves for the return voyage home.[86]

The Pennsylvania slave trade increased sharply during the 1730s. Slave imports had previously been limited mainly to small consignments from the West Indies and South Carolina.[87] But by 1730 the demand for labor had become so pressing that larger cargoes could be brought in without much economic risk to the importer. Most of the slaves were still imported from the West Indies, though increasing numbers were shipped directly from Africa. The demand for slaves was particularly heavy during the French and Indian War, which drew hundreds of indentured servants into the armed forces and further depleted the labor supply.[88] Slaves of all types commanded a ready market during the war. Besides agriculture, which consumed the most labor, they were also used to manufacture iron, for commerce, and in various phases of the shipbuilding industry.[89] Though the demand fell off slightly with the return of peace, slaves continued to be an important item of commerce for the rest of the colonial era.[90]

The slave trade provided Northern entrepreneurs with a steady stream of black labor. During the first half of the eighteenth century the slave force in many areas of New England increased much more rapidly than the free population. Though the ratio of slaves to whites varied from place to place, between 1700 and

86. Wax, "The Negro Slave Trade in Colonial Pennsylvania," pp. 23–24, 81, 90–91.

87. Isaac Norris Letter Book (1702–1704), *passim,* MS. coll., HSP; Jonathan Dickinson Letter Book (1715–1721), *passim,* MS. coll., LCP.

88. Darold D. Wax, "Negro Imports into Pennsylvania, 1720–1766," *Pennsylvania History,* XXXII 1965), 256.

89. Darold D. Wax, "The Demand for Slave Labor in Colonial Pennsylvania," *Pennsylvania History,* XXXIV (1967), 334–35.

90. Wax, "Negro Imports into Pennsylvania," *Pennsylvania History,* XXXII, 255–56.

1715 the proportion of slaves in the general population more than doubled.[91] Even in Massachusetts and New Hampshire, where there were proportionally fewer blacks to whites, every census up to the Revolution showed an increase in the black population. Slaves constituted 5.9 percent of the Rhode Island population in 1708, 9.3 percent in 1749, and 11.5 percent in 1755. During the period 1756–74 the proportion of slaves to free inhabitants in Connecticut increased by over 40 percent.[92] By the end of the colonial era Connecticut's slave population was greater than that of any other New England colony.[93]

In the Middle colonies the black population also grew rapidly. Between 1721 and 1754 the number of slaves in Pennsylvania increased from five thousand to about eleven thousand.[94] Although population data for Pennsylvania are generally imprecise, one source estimates that by 1766 there were about thirty thousand in the colony.[95] In New Jersey the slave population grew from 2,581 in 1726 to nearly 4,000 in 1738. By 1745 there were 4,606 Negroes to 56,797 whites, a ratio that held for the rest of the colonial era.[96] But by far the greatest increase occurred in New York. During the period 1732–54 black bondsmen accounted for more than 35 percent of the total immigration that passed through the port of New York.[97] Since large numbers also came in illegally and unrecorded, the ratio of slaves to whites was actually greater.

91. Greene and Harrington, *American Population before the Federal Census of 1790*, pp. 4, 10; Greene, *The Negro in Colonial New England*, p. 73.

92. See Appendix, pp. 199–200, 202–205.

93. Charles M. Andrews, *Connecticut's Place in Colonial History* (New Haven: Yale University Press, 1924), p. 9; Greene, *The Negro in Colonial New England*, pp. 74–75, 89–90.

94. *N.Y. Col. Docs.*, V, 604; Greene and Harrington, *American Population before the Federal Census of 1790*, pp. 114–15.

95. Population data for colonial Pennsylvania vary so widely that even official reports are not very reliable. Contemporary estimates put the black population as high as a hundred thousand one year, and as low as two thousand the next. J. F. D. Smyth, *Tour in the United States of America*, 2 vols. (London: Robinson, 1784), II, 309; Samuel Hazard, ed., *Pennsylvania Archives*, 1st ser., 12 vols. (Philadelphia: Severns, 1852–56), IV, 597; Greene and Harrington, *American Population before the Federal Census of 1790*, pp. 113–16. See U.S. Bureau of the Census, *Historical Statistics of the United States, Colonial Times to 1957* (Washington, D.C.: GPO, 1960), p. 756.

96. Greene and Harrington, *American Population before the Federal Census of 1790*, pp. 106–11.

97. Morris, *Government and Labor in Early America*, p. 315n.

By 1756 New York had 13,000 adult Negroes, giving it the largest slave force of any Northern colony.[98]

The number of slaves working in any locality was determined primarily by economic conditions. Rhode Island, for example, whose population was less than one-third that of Connecticut, had proportionally almost twice as many slaves. The great commercial centers of Newport, Providence, and Bristol, together with the large-scale agriculture of the Narragansett region, resulted in a heavier demand for slave labor than anywhere else in New England.[99] In New Hampshire, most of the slaves were concentrated in Rockingham County, mainly around the commercial center of Portsmouth. In 1767 Portsmouth had about one-third of all the slaves in the colony.[100] Although slaves were more evenly distributed in Massachusetts, they tended to be concentrated in the commercial and industrial counties of Suffolk, Essex, and Plymouth. Much of the colony's wealth centered in these districts, and the demand for labor was accordingly greater.[101] There was a similar pattern in Connecticut, where slaves were heavily concentrated in the commercial counties of New London, New Haven, and Fairfield. By 1774 New London had become the largest slaveholding county, with nearly twice the slave population of any other county.[102]

Population patterns were similar in the Middle colonies. Most of Pennsylvania's Negroes were located in the commercial counties, mainly in Philadelphia and the surrounding region. In 1751 Philadelphia's 6,000 blacks accounted for about one-half of all the slaves in the colony.[103] In New Jersey, a 1745 census showed that 74 percent of the slaves were concentrated in the five eastern counties, particularly around Perth Amboy, though the six western counties had a larger population.[104] New York's slave force

98. Greene and Harrington, *American Population before the Federal Census of 1790*, p. 101.
99. Greene, *The Negro in Colonial New England*, pp. 74–75.
100. Greene and Harrington, *American Population before the Federal Census of 1790*, pp. 70–85.
101. Greene, *The Negro in Colonial New England*, pp. 81–82.
102. *Conn. Col. Recs.*, XIV, 483–92; Greene and Harrington, *American Population before the Federal Census of 1790*, pp. 58–60. See Greene, *The Negro in Colonial New England*, pp. 89–93.
103. Turner, *The Negro in Pennsylvania*, pp. 11–12.
104. Whitehead, *Contributions to the Early History of Perth Amboy*, p. 318;

was much more evenly distributed, though the heaviest concentrations of blacks were in the southern counties around New York City. In 1756 slaves constituted about 25 percent of the population of Kings, Queens, Richmond, New York, and Westchester, while the proportion of slaves for the rest of the colony was only about 14 percent.[105] These counties remained the principal stronghold of slavery for the rest of the colonial era.[106]

The slave force everywhere made a vital contribution to the Northern economy. Whether at work in the shipyards and distilleries of Massachusetts, or in the manufactories and farms of Pennsylvania, black bondsmen played an important role in determining the rate of economic growth. Stock farming, dairying, lumbering, and other enterprises requiring heavy labor could not have been carried on extensively without them. Reporting to England in 1699 on the production of strategically important naval stores, New York's Governor Bellomont informed the Board of Trade that there were "no other servants in this country but Negroes" available to do the work.[107] To claim that the colonies would not have survived without slaves would be a distortion, but there can be no doubt that development was significantly speeded by their labor. They provided the basic working force that transformed shaky outposts of empire into areas of permanent settlement.

Cooley, *Study of Slavery in New Jersey*, pp. 30–31; Greene and Harrington, *American Population before the Federal Census of 1790*, p. 111.

105. See Appendix, p. 209.

106. Greene and Harrington, *American Population before the Federal Census of 1790*, pp. 90–115.

107. *Cal. State Papers, Col.*, XVII (1699), 176.

2

The Business of Slavery

Slavery became so important to the North that no stigma attached to trading in Negroes. The traffic was as honorable an enterprise as farming, manufacturing, or ordinary commerce. Leading slave importers like Gabriel Ludlow, Philip Livingston, and Nicholas De Ronde of New York and Isaac Norris and Jonathan Dickinson of Philadelphia enjoyed unimpeachable social standing.[1] The highest public offices were frequently held by slave traders. Robert Morris, William Plumsted, and Thomas Willing were elected to the Pennsylvania Assembly while actively involved in the traffic.[2] Six slave merchants served as mayor and fifteen as members of the Common Council of Philadelphia.[3] Jonathan Belcher of Massachusetts and four members of the Wanton family of Rhode Island held governorships, and William Robinson and William Ellery of Rhode Island served as lieutenant governors. John Saffin, John Coleman, and John Campbell of Massa-

1. Book of Trade of the Sloop Rhode Island, 1748–49, MS. coll., NYHS; Isaac Norris to Jonathan Dickinson, November 12, 1703, Norris Letter Book, 1702–1704, MS. coll., HSP.
2. Carl and Jessica Bridenbaugh, *Rebels and Gentlemen: Philadelphia in the Age of Franklin* (New York: Reynal & Hitchcock, 1942), pp. 185–86; Theodore Thayer, "The Quaker Party of Pennsylvania, 1755–1765," *PMHB*, LXXI (1947), 20–21.
3. John B. Linn and W. H. Egle, eds., *Pennsylvania Archives*, 2d ser., 19 vols. (Harrisburg: State Printer, 1878–96), IX, 621–800; Edward P. Allinson and Boise Penrose, *Philadelphia, 1681–1887: A History of Municipal Development* (Philadelphia: Allen, Lane & Scott, 1887), pp. 11–18. See Darold D. Wax, "The Negro Slave Trade in Colonial Pennsylvania," unpublished Ph.D. dissertation. (University of Washington, 1962), pp. 75–77.

chusetts became judges, and Caleb Gardner, Peleg Clarke, and Moses Brown of Rhode Island served in the assembly.[4] Ezra Stiles imported slaves while president of Yale, and two prominent slave traders, William Pepperell and Charles Hobby of Massachusetts, were among the few Americans raised to knighthood by England.[5]

That men of such rank and social standing could be slave traders legitimated the traffic for the rest of the community. Besides the great merchants who did the importing, there was an extensive network of factors, agents, insurers, lawyers, clerks, and scriveners who handled the paper work of the trade.[6] Many of the vendue houses drew a considerable part of their income from slave transactions. Even Quakers had no apparent qualms about selling slaves openly in the public marketplaces of Philadelphia.[7] In New York City slave auctions were held weekly, sometimes daily, at the Merchant's Coffee House, the Fly Market, and Proctor's Vendue House. Virtually all the commission houses were involved in the trade, and some, like the Meal Market, were almost exclusively places for the sale or hire of slaves.[8]

Anyone on the lookout for quick profits might take a hand in the trade. Ship's officers and even ordinary seamen engaged in slave-trading on their own account during voyages to Africa.[9] The

4. Lorenzo J. Greene, *The Negro in Colonial New England, 1620–1776* (New York: Columbia University Press, 1942), pp. 57–58.

5. Ezra Stiles, *Literary Diary*, F. B. Dexter, ed., 3 vols. (New York: Scribner's, 1901), I, 521n; Frederick C. Norton, "Negro Slavery in Connecticut," *Connecticut Magazine*, V (1899), 321; CSM *Transactions*, XIX (1918), 151–52; Usher Parsons, *The Life of Sir William Pepperell* (Boston: Little, Brown, 1855), p. 27; Greene, *The Negro in Colonial New England*, p. 59.

6. *New York Weekly Post-Boy*, October 7, 1748; January 16, February 20, March 6, 13, May 1, 1749; June 8, 1752; December 10, 1753; May 20, 1754; March 31, May 19, 1755; September 30, 1756; July 13, 1772.

7. Minutes of the Philadelphia Monthly Meeting (1682–1714), p. 115, MS. coll., Friends Historical Library of Swarthmore College.

8. *New York Weekly Journal*, April 16, May 14, 1739. *New York Weekly Post-Boy*, July 11, 1748; September 25, 1749; January 8, 1749/50; May 6, 1751; March 20, 1758; March 31, 1760; April 15, 1762; October 3, 1765. *New York Mercury*, March 22, August 4, 7, 1756; October 30, 1757; March 20, 27, May 22, 1758; July 26, October 11, 1762; January 24, 1763; August 8, 1763; March 12, April 30, November 19, 1764; October 7, 28, 1765. *New York Weekly Mercury*, February 24, July 6, September 7, 1772; July 23, 1775.

9. "Commerce of Rhode Island, 1726–1800," in MHS Colls., 7th ser., IX (1914), 64, 96–97. See Richard B. Morris, ed., *Select Cases of the Mayor's Court of New York City, 1674–1784* (Washington, D.C.: The American Historical Association, 1935), pp. 701–704.

trade was so lucrative that disreputable individuals were naturally attracted. Captain William Kidd, for example, carried slaves to New York when not preoccupied with shadier maritime adventures.[10] Nor were buyers in the colonies averse to dealing with the criminal element in order to obtain slaves at bargain prices. In 1698 a pirate vessel delivered slaves to the Hudson Valley estate of Frederick Philipse.[11] Such transactions were not uncommon, for slave ships were frequently seized by pirates and privateers.[12] Many of the slaves brought to Pennsylvania in the early eighteenth century were sold as prize goods or outright plunder.[13]

Buyers of slaves had a strong preference for bondsmen from the West Indies. During the first half of the eighteenth century thousands of blacks were brought to New York and New Jersey from Barbados and Jamaica.[14] Pennsylvania regularly imported slaves from Antigua, Barbados, St. Christopher, and Jamaica in exchange for agricultural produce.[15] The New England colonies sent large quantities of food, lumber, and manufactured goods to the islands and brought back West Indian slaves on the return voyage.[16] These slaves were familiar with Western customs and habits of work, qualities highly prized in a region where masters and slaves worked and lived in close proximity. Moreover, they were better able to endure Northern winters than those brought directly from Africa. One Philadelphia slave trader reported that during the cold season the Africans became "so chilly they can

10. W. Noel Sainsbury, et al., Calendar of State Papers: Colonial Series, America and West Indies, 42 vols. (London: H.M.S.O., 1860–1953), XVII (1699), 447–48, hereafter cited as Cal. State Papers, Col.

11. J. Thomas Scharf, History of Westchester County, 2 vols. (Philadelphia: Preston, 1886), I, 30.

12. E. B. O'Callaghan and Berthold Fernow, eds., Documents Relative to the Colonial History of the State of New York, 15 vols. (Albany: Weed, Parsons, 1856–87), II, 23–32, hereafter cited as N.Y. Col. Docs.

13. Board of Trade, Proprieties, 1697–1776, III, 285–86; IV, 369; V, 408; MS. coll., HSP. See Edward R. Turner, The Negro in Pennsylvania (Washington, D.C.: The American Historical Association, 1911), p. 10n.

14. Daniel Parish, Transcripts of Material on Slavery in the Public Records Office in London (1690–1750), p. 30, MS. coll., NYHS, hereafter cited as Parish's Transcripts.

15. Turner, The Negro in Pennsylvania, pp. 9–10.

16. William Johnston, Slavery in Rhode Island, 1755–1776 (Providence: Rhode Island Historical Society, 1894), p. 18; Justin Winsor, ed., The Memorial History of Boston, 3 vols. (Boston: Osgood, 1880–81), II, 262–63; Parsons, The Life of Sir William Pepperell, p. 28; Greene, The Negro in Colonial New England, p. 36.

hardly stir from the fire."[17] Peter Kalm found that Africans suffered miserably during the Pennsylvania winter, and that their "toes and fingers . . . are frequently frozen."[18] So strong was the preference for West Indians that merchants made a special point of advertising that their slaves had been "seasoned" in the islands and hence more accustomed to Northern conditions of life and labor.[19]

Prior to 1750 relatively few slaves were imported directly from Africa. The occasional cargoes brought over consisted mainly of children under the age of thirteen.[20] Such slaves were generally more assimilable than their older and more turbulent countrymen. The market for adults was so limited that Governor Cornbury of New York advised traders to ship their African slaves directly to the Southern colonies.[21] Indeed, for many years the traffic in Africans was little more than a sideline for New Yorkers engaged in the gold and ivory trade.[22] Most of Pennsylvania's slave trade was confined to the West Indies and to the plantation colonies of the South.[23] During the period 1720–50 only one cargo of slaves from Africa was advertised for sale.[24] Though more were doubtless imported privately or on consignment, it seems clear that such imports were an insignificant part of the total trade.

New England imported somewhat larger numbers of Africans because of its involvement in the triangular trade. Ships carrying slaves from Africa to the West Indies frequently had blacks left over who were not up to the standards of the islands. These unwanted slaves were brought back to New England on the return

17. Isaac Norris Letter Book, 1702–1704, p. 109, MS. coll., HSP. See Turner, *The Negro in Pennsylvania*, p. 10.

18. Peter Kalm, *Travels into North America*, John R. Forster, trans., 3 vols. (London: Eyres, 1770–71), I, 392.

19. *American Weekly Mercury* (Philadelphia), March 16, April 6, July 20, 1727; May 1, June 26, July 24, 1729; June 11, July 16, 1730. *New England Weekly Journal*, April 3, May 1, 8, June 12, 1727; August 19, 26, 1728. *Boston Gazette*, March 13, 1753; January 15, 1754.

20. Book of Trade of the Sloop Rhode Island, 1748–49, *passim*, MS. coll., NYHS.

21. *N.Y. Col. Docs.*, V, 57.

22. Book of Trade of the Sloop Rhode Island, *passim*.

23. Darold D. Wax, "Negro Imports into Pennsylvania, 1720–1766," *Pennsylvania History*, XXXII (1965), 255–56, 260–87.

24. *Pennsylvania Gazette*, June 25, 1747.

voyage and sold for whatever they would bring.[25] Thus many of the slaves technically imported from the West Indies were actually Africans unfit for the heavy labor demanded on the West Indian plantations. Writing to England in 1708, Governor Dudley of Massachusetts described such West Indian rejects as "usually the worst servants" in the province.[26] But because they sold for as little as £15 to £25 each, even these "worst servants" found a market among buyers not requiring high-quality workers.[27]

The revocation of the Assiento in 1750 brought many African slaves into the Northern market.[28] With the Spanish colonies closed to English traders, a flood of low-priced Africans hit the English colonies. So many were shipped to New York between 1750 and 1756 that the wholesale price declined by about 50 percent.[29] This decline resulted in the sort of low-price market that had long existed for African slaves in New England. Many employers who would otherwise have purchased West Indian slaves now bought Africans instead at bargain prices. The leading slave ports of the Middle colonies—Philadelphia, New York, and Perth Amboy—for the first time developed a heavy traffic in African slaves.[30]

As the market for Africans grew, traders competed intensely for a share of it. Prominent Philadelphia merchants like Robert Morris, Thomas Willing, and Samuel McCall sent their ships to Africa for cargoes of slaves.[31] Sometimes as many as a hundred

25. *The Letter Book of James Browne of Providence, Merchant, 1735–1738* (Providence: Rhode Island Historical Society, 1929), p. xi. See Greene, *The Negro in Colonial New England*, pp. 34–35.
26. *Cal. State Papers, Col.*, XXIV (1708–1709), 110.
27. Greene, *The Negro in Colonial New England*, p. 35.
28. Clarence E. Haring, *The Spanish Empire in America* (New York: Oxford University Press, 1947), p. 220.
29. *New York Weekly Post-Boy*, July 14, 1755; December 25, 1756.
30. *Pennsylvania Gazette*, May 24, June 21, 1759; August 14, 1760; August 6, October 1, 1761; May 6, 1762. *Pennsylvania Journal*, May 27, 1762; September 20, 1764; August 21, 1766. *New York Mercury*, October 14, 1754; August 18, 1757; July 17, 1758; July 9, 1759; June 6, 30, August 18, 1760; June 29, 1761; October 11, November 15, 1762; June 27, July 11, 1763. *New York Weekly Post-Boy*, August 19, 1751; June 1, 1752; May 13, September 16, 1754; July 25, 1757; July 17, 1758; August 6, 1759; June 24, 30, August 21, 1760; October 1, 1761; June 27, 1765; July 23, 1770. See Ira K. Morris, *Memorial History of Staten Island*, 2 vols. (New York: The Winthrop Press, 1900), II, 37.
31. Wax, "Negro Imports into Pennsylvania," *Pennsylvania History*, XXXII, 256.

blacks or more were brought back on a single voyage.[32] In New York the competition became so intense that many traders tried to reduce their overhead by selling slaves at dockside. For over a decade the principal wharves of the city became markets for the sale of African slaves.[33] Only those who could not be sold on the docks were passed along to middlemen and commission merchants.[34] Even at bargain prices, however, the market could not absorb the increased influx of slaves. Hundreds of unsold blacks were sent to Perth Amboy and quartered in makeshift barracks where buyers could have them at distress prices.[35]

This traffic lasted for about twenty years and then entered a period of sharp and continuous decline. By 1770 the slave raids had depopulated whole regions in West Africa, and the supply of slaves was so reduced that even the demand for replacements could not be met.[36] Although scarcity drove prices upward, traders nevertheless suffered because shipping quotas often could not be filled.[37] The cost of slaves at some of the African stations increased by more than 100 percent, reaching levels much too high for the Northern market.[38] By 1764 Thomas Riche, one of Philadelphia's leading traders, noted that "the time is over for the sale of Negroes here."[39] No cargoes from Africa were brought to Pennsylvania after 1766, and by the end of the decade the trade had virtually ended for the rest of the North as well.[40]

32. Riche to Van Zandt, July 30, 1761. Riche to Tucker, August 16, 1762, Thomas Riche Letter Book, 1750–1764, MS. coll., HSP. See *Pennsylvania Gazette*, May 24, June 21, 1759; August 6, 1761; May 6, 1762; July 25, 1765. *Pennsylvania Journal*, May 27, 1762; August 21, 1766.

33. *New York Weekly Post-Boy*, July 31, 1749; June 22, 1772. *New York Mercury*, June 16, 30, 1760. *New York Weekly Mercury*, July 23, 1770.

34. *New York Mercury*, August 19, 1751; August 18, 1757; July 17, 1758; August 18, 1760. *New York Weekly Post-Boy*, August 6, 1759; June 30, 1760; June 27, 1765.

35. Morris, *Memorial History of Staten Island*, II, 37.

36. W. E. B. Du Bois, *The Negro* (New York: Holt, 1915), p. 155; Carter G. Woodson, *The Negro in Our History* (Washington, D.C.: The Association for the Study of Negro Life and History, 1936), p. 69.

37. Miscellaneous Slavery Manuscripts, Box II, R–S, p. 9, MS. coll., NYHS.

38. *Ibid.*, Box I, D, pp. 16, 24; Box II, G, p. 12.

39. Thomas Riche to Gampirk and Heyman, April 23, 1764, Thomas Riche Letter Book, 1764–71, MS. coll., HSP. See Wax, "Negro Imports into Pennsylvania," *Pennsylvania History*, XXXII, 255.

40. Johnston, *Slavery in Rhode Island*, pp. 15–17; Wax, "Negro Imports into Pennsylvania," *Pennsylvania History*, XXXII, 255, 287.

The scarcity of slaves in Africa adversely affected slave imports from the West Indies. The island plantation system took such a heavy toll that new supplies of black labor were continually needed.[41] Thus the shortage of African manpower not only raised the cost of replacements but threatened the plantation system itself. One slave trader, Captain David Lindsay of Rhode Island, reported that "the trade is so dull it is actually enough to make a man crazy."[42] With the African labor reserve fast disappearing, West Indian planters became acutely aware of the need to conserve their own working force. The result was that fewer slaves were exported and then only at prices far too high for the Northern market. By 1770 the slave trade between the North and the West Indies had virtually come to a halt.[43]

But the decline of the overseas trade did not affect the internal traffic carried on in every colony. Indeed, from the standpoint of total sales the domestic trade was much more important, for slave-owners were continually increasing or reducing their labor force. These transactions provided the colonial newspapers with much of their income, for users of labor were bombarded with advertisements of slaves for sale or hire.[44] In order to promote the trade, the newspapers often provided buyers and sellers with special services free of charge. Some served as agents of one party or the other, and some compiled lists of slaves being offered for sale. So close was the involvement of the colonial press that instructions directing potential buyers to "enquire of the printer

41. Frank W. Pitman, "Slavery on British West India Plantations in the Eighteenth Century," *JNH*, XI (1926), 610–17; Thomas R. R. Cobb, *An Inquiry into the Law of Slavery in the United States of America* (Philadelphia: Johnson, 1858), pp. clvii–ix.

42. George C. Mason, "The African Slave Trade in Colonial Times," *Potter's American Monthly*, I (1872), 338.

43. *Boston News Letter*, 1770–76; *Massachusetts Spy*, 1770–75; *Pennsylvania Chronicle*, 1770–74; *Pennsylvania Gazette*, 1770–75; *Pennsylvania Journal*, 1770–75; *New York Weekly Mercury*, 1770–75; Rivington's *Royal Gazette* (New York), 1773–75.

44. *Boston News Letter*, 1704–76; *New England Weekly Journal*, 1727–41; *Massachusetts Spy*, 1770–75; *Weekly Rehearsal*, Boston, 1731–35; *New London Summary*, 1758–63; *American Weekly Mercury*, Philadelphia, 1719–46; *Pennsylvania Gazette*, 1728–70; *Pennsylvania Journal*, 1742–70; *Pennsylvania Chronicle*, 1767–74; *New York Gazette*, 1726–34; *New York Weekly Journal*, 1733–51; Weyman's *New York Gazette*, 1759–67; *New York Weekly Post-Boy*, 1743–73; *New York Mercury*, 1752–68; *New York Weekly Mercury*, 1768–75.

hereof" appear in most of the slave advertisements.[45]

Sales were also arranged by retail merchants who acted as slave agents as an adjunct to their regular business.[46] The Philadelphia firm of Willing and Morris sold Negroes "at their store in Front-Street," while Hugh Hall of Boston sold them at his warehouse along with rum, sugar, and "sundry European goods."[47] Tavernkeepers like Josiah Franklin and William Nichols of Boston made their premises available for the auction of Negroes.[48] Obadiah Wells of New York City became involved in the trade by allowing buyers and sellers in the neighborhood to use his drygoods store. His interest in the trade grew steadily, eclipsing his other activities, and eventually extended throughout the province.[49] Wells and other retail merchants played an important role in bringing buyers and sellers together.[50] They facilitated slave transactions and thus helped to channel labor into productive uses. Without them, neither the trade nor slavery itself would have functioned very efficiently.

Frequently lawyers and scriveners set up registries with detailed information on slaves being offered for sale. The most successful of these services was the one operated by John C. Knapp in New York City. Deported from England for fraud, Knapp was described by the London Daily Advertiser, May 19, 1763, as "the

45. *Pennsylvania Gazette*, August 31, September 7, 1774. *New York Weekly Post-Boy*, May 27, 1751. *New York Mercury*, August 6, 1764.

46. *New England Weekly Journal*, June 12, 1727; October 17, 24, 31, 1738. *New Hampshire Gazette and Historical Chronicle*, April 3, 1767. *New York Weekly Post-Boy*, October 7, 1748; May 1, 1749; June 8, 1752. *New York Mercury*, September 18, 1758; October 22, 1759; October 11, 1762. *Pennsylvania Gazette*, May 18, 1738; September 10, 1741; May 24, June 21, 1759.

47. *Pennsylvania Gazette*, July 12, 1759. *New England Weekly Journal*, September 2, 9, 16, 1728.

48. *Boston News Letter*, August 3, 1713. *New England Weekly Journal*, October 17, 1738. See Greene, *The Negro in Colonial New England*, p. 42.

49. *New York Weekly Post-Boy*, October 17, 1748; January 16, February 20, March 6, 13, 1748/49; March 12, 1749/50; April 19, 1756. *New York Mercury*, April 19, 1756.

50. *New England Weekly Journal*, September 30, October 7, 1728; May 19, June 31, August 4, 11, September 1, October 27, November 3, 10, 1729; June 8, 15, 22, 29, July 6, August 24, 1730; May 10, October 11, 1731; January 24, 31, February 7, April 3, August 14, 21, 28, September 4, 11, 1732. *Pennsylvania Gazette*, May 18, 1738; September 10, 1741; May 24, June 21, July 12, 1759. *New York Weekly Post-Boy*, May 20, 1754; March 31, May 19, 1755; September 30, 1756; July 13, 1772. *New York Mercury*, December 19, 1763. *New York Weekly Mercury*, June 11, 1770; November 4, 1771.

most notorious cheat and sharper on record." In New York, he became a controversial figure who sold legal advice, stirred up litigation, and took a hand in just about anything that offered easy profits. His registry listed slaves according to age, sex, and occupation for a fee of two shillings paid by the seller.[51] Regularly using the newspapers to advertise his service, Knapp gained wide repute as an aggressive and effective slave broker.[52] Since the advertising alone was worth the small registration fee, the registry was used by most sellers seeking to make contact with potential buyers.

Slave sales were usually executed in about the same form as other property transactions. Bills of sale were drawn describing the slave and the conditions of sale, and the bills were then signed, witnessed, and sometimes even recorded with the town clerk.[53] Slaves were sold for cash and on credit, and when money was scarce, installment buying was common.[54] When the sale was on credit, sellers usually required "good security" so that payment would be made or the slave returned within a stipulated time.[55] In most cases sale conditions were kept flexible in order to accommodate individual needs. Advertisements frequently informed prospective buyers that "reasonable terms" might be arranged, including the barter of slaves for goods or a combination barter and cash arrangement.[56] In the May 1, 1729, edition of the *Amer-*

51. *New York Weekly Post-Boy,* July 26, 1764.
52. *New York Mercury,* June 25, July 2, 9, 1764; October 21, 1765. *New York Weekly Post-Boy,* July 18, December 20, 1764; February 21, March 7, August 1, 1765.
53. Miscellaneous Slavery Manuscripts, *passim,* MS. coll. NYHS. See Greene, *The Negro in Colonial New England,* p. 46n.
54. *American Weekly Mercury* (Philadelphia), July 24, 31, October 16, 23, 1729; September 10, 1730. See Greene, *The Negro in Colonial New England,* p. 46.
55. *New England Weekly Journal,* May 27, June 3, September 2, 9, 16, 1728; June 31, August 4, 11, October 27, November 3, 10, 1729. *Pennsylvania Chronicle,* June 11, 18, 1770.
56. *American Weekly Mercury* (Philadelphia), May 24, 31, June 7, 14, 1722; September 26, October 10, 1723; November 12, 19, 1724; August 4, December 1, 13, 20, 1726; October 5, 12, 1727; March 27, April 5, 19, October 18, November 29, December 15, 22, 1733; January 8, August 29, September 12, 1734. *New England Weekly Journal,* August 3, 11, 1730; February 15, 22, May 15, September 18, 25, 1732. *New Hampshire Gazette and Historical Chronicle,* April 3, 1767. *New Haven Gazette,* January 27, 1785. See Greene, *The Negro in Colonial New England,* pp. 46–47.

ican Weekly Mercury, George McCall of Philadelphia offered to sell "a parcel of very likely young Negroes . . . either for money, flour, bisquit, or pork." Sometimes slaves were sold to several buyers in common, an arrangement particularly convenient for small artisans who wished to share maintenance costs.[57]

Some sellers preferred the public auction as a time-saving alternative to arranging a private sale. Such transactions were always for cash, and the method was particularly useful in liquidating estates when there was need for a quick settlement.[58] The only disadvantage was the possibility that the slave might be sold for less than full value, but this was somewhat offset by the expense and inconvenience involved in finding a private buyer. Even slaveowners who preferred private sales were sometimes constrained to use the auction when buyers were not forthcoming.[59] Slave auctions were so common in New York City that they provided the vendue houses with considerable revenue.[60] In Boston slave auctions were held in warehouses, taverns, and even in the homes of merchants.[61] Slave auctions were held regularly in Philadelphia's Market House and at the London Coffee House, where prospective buyers could drink coffee as they made their bids.[62]

The most common reasons for selling a slave were lack of employment, the need to raise cash, an opportunity to make a profit,

57. "Abstracts of Wills on File in the Surrogate's Office, City of New York," in NYHS Colls., XXV–XLI (17 vols., 1892–1908), V, 134, 137–38; VI, 94–95, 435–36; VII, 28–30, 219, 445–46; IX, 35–36; X, 102–103. Hereafter cited as "N.Y. Abstracts of Wills."
58. Wax, "The Negro Slave Trade in Colonial Pennsylvania," p. 163.
59. *Pennsylvania Gazette,* March 24, 1747; September 29, 1763. *New Haven Gazette and Connecticut Magazine,* November 9, 1786.
60. *New York Weekly Journal,* April 16, May 14, 1739. *New York Weekly Post-Boy,* July 11, 1748; September 25, 1749; January 8, 1749/50; May 6, 1751; March 20, 1758; March 31, 1760; April 15, 1762. *New York Mercury,* March 22, August 4, 7, 1756; March 20, 27, May 22, 1758; January 24, 1763; March 12, April 30, 1764. *New York Weekly Mercury,* February 24, July 6, September 7, 1772; January 23, 1775.
61. *New England Weekly Journal,* September 22, 1729; April 20, 1730; April 19, September 20, 1731. See Greene, *The Negro in Colonial New England,* p. 42.
62. *Pennsylvania Gazette,* September 20, 1744; July 18, 1765. *Pennsylvania Chronicle,* March 21, 28, May 2, September 5, October 12, 17, 1768; March 13, 1769. See John F. Watson, *Annals of Philadelphia and Pennsylvania in the Olden Time,* 3 vols. (Philadelphia: Stoddart, 1879–81), II, 264; Bridenbaugh, *Rebels and Gentlemen,* p. 22; Wax, "The Negro Slave Trade in Colonial Pennsylvania," pp. 163–64.

or the need to liquidate the master's estate.[63] If a business requiring special skills was being sold, experienced slaves were sometimes included in the sale to make sure that things went smoothly for the new owner.[64] The July 1, 1734, edition of the *New England Weekly Journal* advertised a Boston bakery for sale with "two Negro men used to the business." Many masters were remarkably candid about their slaves, like the seller who advertised in the January 1, 1727/28, edition of the same paper that his Negro needed "a severe master." Another seller put prospective buyers on notice that his slave, though "a strong fellow for any work," was "given to drink."[65] Some slaves were sold for purely personal reasons. A Boston master averse to garrulity put his slave on the market because he had "too long a tongue."[66] Another owner in Philadelphia advertised in the *Pennsylvania Chronicle*, March 2, 1767, that he was selling a slave woman "for no other fault only she wants to be married, which does not suit the family she is in."

Though some sellers admitted the shortcomings of their slaves, others attempted to conceal defects in order to get higher prices.[67] Buyers were frequently misled by vague advertisements for "healthy," "likely strong," "strong," "active," "likely," and "hearty" slaves.[68] According to the *New York Weekly Journal*, December 31, 1733, some unscrupulous dealers perpetrated outright fraud by selling mortgaged slaves to unwary buyers. Others purchased sickly Negroes, masked their defects, and then resold them for

63. *New York Weekly Mercury*, September 21, 1772. *Pennsylvania Gazette*, February 19, 1754; November 12, 1767; September 22, 1768; July 29, November 2, 1769. *New England Weekly Journal*, January 8, 1727/28. "N.Y. Abstracts of Wills," IX, 103–104; XII, 182–83.

64. *New York Weekly Post-Boy*, April 1, 1762. *New York Mercury*, March 22, 1762. *New York Weekly Mercury*, November 1, 1773.

65. *New England Weekly Journal*, January 8, 1727/28.

66. *Boston Gazette*, September 4, 1767, cited in Greene, *The Negro in Colonial New England*, p. 41.

67. *New York Mercury*, December 7, 1761; June 7, 1762. *New York Weekly Mercury*, April 16, 1770; May 13, 1771; April 10, 1775; October 21, 1782.

68. *New England Weekly Journal*, May 1, 8, 15, 22, June 12, July 10, October 23, November 6, 13, 20, December 11, 18, 1727; January 1, 8, 15, 22, March 18, 25, April 1, 8, 15, 22, 29, July 15, 22, 29, September 9, 16, 23, 30, October 7, 14, 21, 28, November 4, 11, 25, December 16, 23, 30, 1728; January 6, 20, 27, February 3, 10, 17, 24, March 3, 10, 17, 30, April 7, May 12, 19, 26, 1729. *New Haven Gazette*, January 27, 1785. *New Haven Gazette and Connecticut Magazine*, April 12, 1787.

more than their actual value.[69] Older slaves were sometimes made salable by dyeing their hair with lampblack. Trickery and misrepresentation became so common in Massachusetts that the General Court considered measures to prevent "divers fraudulent sales of Negroes."[70] Nothing was done, however, so fraudulent sales remained a matter for private litigation in the civil courts.

Buyers could best protect themselves by reserving the right to cancel the sale if the slave did not measure up to the seller's representations.[71] A conditional sale also protected the buyer against loss if, during the trial period, the slave became ill, died, or ran away. His only liability was for losses attributable to his own negligence.[72] But if the sale was final, as at an auction, the buyer had no recourse against the seller.[73] Although he could bring a civil suit for deceit, the action was maintainable only if he could prove that he had relied upon the seller's misrepresentations.[74] Both misrepresentation and reliance had to be proved, and the burden of proof was squarely on the buyer. In cases of clear-cut fraud, where seemingly healthy slaves turned out to be cripples or epileptics or developed some fatal disease soon after the sale, buyers sometimes recovered damages.[75] But there was no certainty of winning even when fraud seemed obvious, for the courts made liberal use of the rule of *caveat emptor*. In one case a New York court denied recovery to the buyer of a supposedly healthy slave who died a few hours after the sale.[76] Similarly, a Connecticut court denied recovery for a slave woman subject to epileptic seizures that rendered her worthless.[77]

A master incurred no social disapproval for selling his slaves,

69. Morris, *Select Cases of the Mayor's Court*, pp. 384–87.
70. Massachusetts Archives, IX, 450, MS. coll., MSL. See Greene, *The Negro in Colonial New England*, p. 49.
71. A. J. F. Van Laer and Jonathan Pearson, eds., *Early Records of the City and County of Albany and Colony of Rensselaerswyck*, 4 vols. (Albany: State University of New York, 1915–19), III, 493. *New York Weekly Post-Boy*, October 3, 1748. *New York Weekly Mercury*, October 11, 1773; August 11, 1777.
72. *De Fonclear* v. *Shottenkirk*, 3 Johnson's Reports 170 (New York Supreme Court, 1808).
73. "Proceedings of the General Court of Assizes, 1680–1682," in NYHS *Colls.*, XLV (1912), 32.
74. Morris, *Select Cases of the Mayor's Court*, pp. 374–75.
75. Connecticut Archives, Miscellaneous, II, 135a–135d, MS. coll., CSL.
76. Morris, *Select Cases of the Mayor's Court*, pp. 368–70, 548–51.
77. Connecticut Archives, II, 50a–50d.

nor did it matter whether he sold privately to the buyer or through a slave trader. Moreover, no distinction was made between a speculative sale and one that was forced upon the owner by economic necessity. Too many members of the slaveholding class were small farmers and artisans for moral reflections to be a factor in buying and selling. Even in Pennsylvania, where many Quakers spoke out strongly against slavery, the right of an owner to dispose of his slaves was unquestioned.[78] Slaves were sold in order to settle estates, to satisfy the claims of creditors, and often just to turn a profit.[79] There was nothing invidious about making a profit; the heavy volume of slave advertisements make it clear that the moral right of an owner to sell his slaves for any reason was universally recognized.[80]

The traffic in slaves was taxed during most of the colonial period.[81] Only Connecticut and New Hampshire failed to levy tariffs, and in the case of the latter the reason given was that the traffic was so slight that "it would not be worth the public notice."[82] Elsewhere slave duties varied in purpose and amount from colony to colony. Some were designed to discourage imports and

78. Darold D. Wax, "Quaker Merchants and the Slave Trade in Colonial Pennsylvania," *PMHB*, LXXXVI (1962), 143–59.

79. Gerardus Beekman's Day Book, 1752–57, Beekman Merchantile Papers, MS. coll., NYHS; "N.Y. Abstracts of Wills," IX, 103–104, XII, 182–83. *New York Weekly Mercury*, September 21, 1772. *Boston Gazette*, May 14, 21, 1757. *New Hampshire Gazette and Historical Chronicle*, April 3, 1767.

80. *Boston News Letter*, 1704–76; *New England Weekly Journal*, 1727–41; *New London Summary*, 1758–63; *Essex Gazette*, Salem, 1768–75; *New York Gazette*, 1726–34; *New York Weekly Post-Boy*, 1743–73; *New York Mercury*, 1752–68; *American Weekly Mercury*, Philadelphia, 1719–46; *Pennsylvania Gazette*, 1728–75; *Pennsylvania Chronicle*, 1767–74.

81. *Acts and Resolves, Public and Private, of the Province of the Massachusetts Bay*, 5 vols. (Boston: Wright & Potter, 1869–86), I, 578–79; John R. Bartlett, ed., *Records of the Colony of Rhode Island and Providence Plantations in New England, 1636–1792*, 10 vols. (Providence: Greene, 1856–65), IV, 34, 225; *Colonial Laws of New York from 1664 to the Revolution*, 5 vols. (Albany: James B. Lyon, 1894), II, 722; *Documents Relating to the Colonial, Revolutionary, and Post-Revolutionary History of the State of New Jersey*, 42 vols. (Newark: New Jersey Historical Society, 1900–49), XIII, 516–20; James T. Mitchell and Henry Flanders, comps., *The Statutes at Large of Pennsylvania from 1682–1801*, 16 vols. (Harrisburg: State Printer, 1896–1911), II, 107, 285, 383; III, 117, 159, 238; IV, 42, 123. Hereafter cited as *Mass. Acts and Resolves, R.I. Col. Recs., N.Y. Col. Laws, N.J. Archives,* and *Pa. Stat. at L.*

82. Nathaniel Bouton, ed., *Provincial Papers: Documents and Records Relating to the Province of New-Hampshire from the Earliest Period of Its Settlement, 1623–1776*, 7 vols. (Concord and Nashua: Jenks, 1867–73), IV, 617. Hereafter cited as *N.H. Provincial Papers.*

others to raise revenue. Pennsylvania's tariff of 1712, for example, was a restrictive measure passed because "divers plots and insurrections" among Negroes had occurred in New York.[83] Rhode Island, on the other hand, wanted revenue, and the slave duties were allocated to public improvements. The tariff of 1717 appropriated £100 for paving the streets of Newport. One-half the duties levied in 1729 were used for street improvements in Newport, and the other half for repairing bridges on the mainland.[84]

Whether levied to reduce imports or to produce revenue, tariff rates generally favored African slaves over those from the West Indies or the South.[85] New York taxed West Indians at a rate from four to six times higher, and Rhode Island exempted African slaves completely.[86] One of the reasons for encouraging African imports was that the slaves brought from other colonies often had criminal records.[87] Since some colonies allowed the masters to export slaves guilty of capital crimes, the risk of acquiring dangerous blacks was considerable.[88] How many of these slaves were thrown on the intercolonial market cannot be estimated, but the number was large enough to require preventive measures. Pennsylvania imposed an extra duty of £5 on slaves convicted of crimes or misdemeanors, and the New York Assembly specifically warned buyers against "refuse Negroes and such malefactors as would have suffered death in the places whence they came had not the avarice of their owners saved them from the public justice."[89]

Another reason for tariff discrimination was that African commerce helped the North to maintain a favorable balance of trade. Slaves from other colonies usually had to be paid for in cash,

83. *Pa. Stat. at L.*, II, 433.
84. *R.I. Col. Recs.*, IV, 225; *Acts and Laws of His Majesty's Colony of Rhode Island and Providence Plantations in America* (Newport: James Franklin, 1730), p. 183, hereafter cited as *R.I. Acts and Laws, 1730*.
85. *Cal. State Papers, Col.*, XX (1701), 567–68; *N.Y. Col. Docs.*, V, 178, 185, 293; *Pa. Stat. at L.*, IV, 59–64, 500.
86. *N.Y. Col. Laws*, II, 722; *N.Y. Col. Docs.*, V, 178, 185, 293; *Charter and the Acts and Laws of His Majesty's Colony of Rhode Island and Providence Plantations in America* (Providence: Sidney & Burnett Rider, 1858), p. 64, hereafter cited as *R.I. Charter, Acts, and Laws*.
87. Rip Van Dam to the Lords of Trade, November 2, 1731, in *N.Y. Col. Docs.*, V, 927–28.
88. Herbert L. Osgood, *The American Colonies in the Eighteenth Century*, 4 vols. (New York: Columbia University Press, 1924), II, 413.
89. *Pa. Stat. at L.*, IV, 59–64, 500; Parish's Transcripts (1713–19), pp. 8–14.

while Africans could be purchased for rum, iron, and other goods.[90] Ships trading with Africa often brought back gold as well as slaves, thereby increasing the specie reserves.[91] Moreover, preferential treatment of the African trade tended to mitigate England's opposition to slave tariffs. Much of the African trade was controlled by English merchants whose political influence had to be reckoned with. By giving favored treatment to the interests of such merchants, colonial assemblies were able to levy tariffs that otherwise might have been disallowed by the home government.[92]

Certainly England showed vigilance in protecting the African trade. A slight increase in the African duties by New York in 1728 brought a sharp rebuke from the secretary of state. The secretary made it clear that encumbrances of the African trade would not be tolerated regardless of how much the colony needed the revenue.[93] When the same rates were reenacted four years later, the merchants of Bristol sent a petition to Parliament denouncing slave tariffs as a blow to England's commerce.[94] They raised such a storm that only the reluctance of the Privy Council to precipitate a revenue crisis for the colony saved the measure from disallowance.[95] The tariff was allowed to stand, but New York officials were warned not to extend the rates beyond the current year. The Board of Trade urged complete repeal of the African duties and the substitution of a property tax on slaves to make up the revenue loss.[96]

The home government moved vigorously when the African trade seemed to be threatened. Tariffs that interfered with the traffic were repeatedly disallowed, and colonial officials were left to their own devices to obtain revenue. Despite appeals from both

90. Max Savelle and Robert Middlekauff, A History of Colonial America (New York: Holt, Rinehart & Winston, 1964), pp. 433–34, 507.

91. Book of Trade of the Sloop Rhode Island, passim, MS. coll., NYHS; "Commerce of Rhode Island, 1726–1800," in MHS Colls., 7th ser., IX (1914), 59–60, 64.

92. John C. Hurd, The Law of Freedom and Bondage in the United States, 2 vols. (Boston: Little, Brown, 1858–62), I, 280.

93. Albert Giesecke, American Commercial Legislation before 1789 (Philadelphia: University of Pennsylvania Press, 1910), p. 32.

94. Cal. State Papers, Col., XLI (1734–35), 278–79.

95. W. L. Grant and James Munro, eds., Acts of the Privy Council: Colonial Series, 1613–1783, 6 vols. (London: Wyman, 1908–12), III, 422–23.

96. Cal. State Papers, Col., XXXIX (1732), 55.

the governor and the assembly, New Jersey could not obtain approval for a tariff for nearly fifty years.[97] But this anti-tariff policy could be circumvented by means of "temporary" duties which remained in effect until formally disallowed. By enacting sequential tariffs which took effect as soon as the preceding duties expired, a colony could keep one step ahead of the royal veto.[98] Such evasions became so commonplace that the home government finally sent instructions to the royal governors not to approve "any law imposing duties upon Negroes."[99]

The New York Assembly made frequent use of temporary tariffs to keep the home government off balance. Neither appeals nor warnings from England could dissuade the lawmakers from taxing the slave trade. Regarding the issue as a challenge to local fiscal autonomy, the assembly ignored suggestions by the Board of Trade that slave duties be shifted from importers to the buyers. In 1734 the same duties were placed on African imports that had raised a storm two years before. This open intransigence led to demands in Parliament that the Privy Council disallow the legislation. The Board of Trade, however, advised against disallowance until a substitute revenue measure could be passed. In the meantime, Governor Cosby was ordered to veto any bill extending the African duties beyond the current year.[100]

What happened next underscores the dilemma of British power in America. Probably fearing fiscal reprisals, Cosby failed to use his veto a year later when the assembly reenacted the African duties for another year. The Privy Council, however, finally took a stand. It disallowed the tariff with a warning that slave duties would no longer be tolerated.[101] But the warning had little substance, for the assembly's money power gave it a decisive advantage in revenue disputes. Slave tariffs could not be disallowed in-

97. *N.J. Archives*, IX, 345, 444, 447; XVIII, 333, 338–85. See Henry S. Cooley, *A Study of Slavery in New Jersey* (Baltimore: The Johns Hopkins Press, 1896), pp. 14–18.

98. *Mass. Acts and Resolves*, II, 981–82; *Pa. Stat. at L.*, III, 117–18, 465; Samuel Hazard, ed., *Colonial Records of Pennsylvania*, 16 vols. (Philadelphia: Severns, 1852), III, 38, 141, 171, hereafter cited as *Pa. Col. Recs.*

99. Elizabeth Donnan, ed., *Documents Illustrative of the History of the Slave Trade to America*, 3 vols. (Washington, D.C.: Carnegie Institute, 1930–35), III, 38.

100. *Cal. State Papers, Col.*, XLII (1735–36), 30–31.

101. *N.Y. Col. Docs.*, VI, 32–34, 37–38.

definitely without subjecting the colonial administration to fiscal strangulation. Three years later, when tempers had cooled, the assembly imposed somewhat lower duties on African slaves without any objection from England.[102]

Numerous rebates and exemptions cut deeply into tariff revenues. Massachusetts admitted slaves duty free on the owner's promise to re-export them within a year, and Rhode Island had a similar provision for slaves who did not remain longer than six months.[103] These exemptions often became loopholes for traders who imported slaves duty free under the pretense that their stay would be temporary. In 1752 the collector of customs for New York reported that frequent abuse of the import exemptions had seriously reduced the revenues of the port.[104] So much fraud occurred in Pennsylvania that importers claiming to be resident slaveowners had to give security that the slaves would not be sold within a year of importation.[105]

Smugglers also cut into tariff revenues. Slaves were regularly brought into Massachusetts from duty-free Connecticut and also from Rhode Island, which did not impose a tariff on slaves from Africa. The numerous coves and inlets of Long Island enabled smugglers to land Negroes before clearing the New York customs.[106] Frequently slaves were landed in New Jersey and then smuggled overland or by small boat into Pennsylvania and New York.[107] Even reputable merchants, like John Watts and Gedney Clarke of New York and John Saffin, Andrew Belcher, and James Wetcomb of Boston, smuggled slaves with complete disregard of the law.[108] The highly respected Philadelphia firm of Willing,

102. "Letter Book of John Watts, 1762–1765," in NYHS *Colls.*, LXI (1928), 355. See W. E. B. Du Bois, *The Suppression of the African Slave Trade to the United States of America, 1638–1870* (New York: Longmans, Green, 1896), p. 19.

103. *Mass. Acts and Resolves*, I, 579; *R.I. Charter, Acts and Laws*, p. 64. See also *Journals of the House of Representatives of Massachusetts, 1715–1764*, 40 vols. (Cambridge, Mass.: Massachusetts Historical Society, 1919–70), I, 48–49, 52; II, 242. *Pa. Stat. at L.*, II, 433; III, 117–21, 275–79; IV, 52–56.

104. Parish's Transcripts (1713–19), pp. 6–7.

105. *Pa. Stat. at L.*, II, 382.

106. Charles M. Andrews, *The Colonial Period of American History*, 4 vols. (New Haven: Yale University Press, 1934–38), IV, 83.

107. Parish's Transcripts (1729–60), pp. 19–20. See Cooley, *Study of Slavery in New Jersey*, pp. 15–16.

108. "Letter Book of John Watts," pp. 31–32; "John Saffin to William Weltstead, June 12, 1681," *New England Historical and Genealogical Register*, XXXI (1877), 75–76. See Donnan, *Slave Trade Documents*, III, 15–16.

Morris, and Company landed slaves in New Jersey, and then advertised them in Pennsylvania for sale on the Jersey shore.[109] Writing to the Board of Trade in 1762, New Jersey's Governor Hardy reported that it was impossible to control the "great numbers of Negroes . . . landed in this province every year in order to be run into New York and Pennsylvania."[110]

The authorities tried with mixed success to stamp out the illegal traffic. Massachusetts required purchasers to register newly imported slaves with the clerk of the town where the transaction had taken place.[111] Rhode Island made ship captains liable to imprisonment for failure to register slave cargoes; they were also required to give security that the duty would be paid before landing their slaves.[112] Slaves smuggled into Pennsylvania were subject to forfeiture, and the customs officers were empowered to enter "any house, warehouse, cellar or other place where any of the said Negroes . . . may be suspected to be concealed."[113]

Despite these measures, the smuggling of slaves continued throughout the colonial period. To have dealt effectively with the problem would have required a fundamental change in American attitudes. It would have been a reversal of character for merchants who repeatedly broke the mercantile regulations of England to submit to local laws that reduced their profits. Writing to England in 1729, New York's Governor Montgomery reported that it was virtually impossible to prevent traders from bringing in slaves "with an absolute intent to defraud the government."[114] Long, unfrequented coastlines and inadequate naval patrols facilitated the evasion of the laws. Despite the hundreds of slaves brought into New York illegally, only one ship was libeled for smuggling during the whole colonial era.[115] So slight was the chance of being caught that traders could carry on their operations with almost complete disregard for the tariff regulations.

109. *Pennsylvania Gazette,* May 7, 1761. See Wax, "The Negro Slave Trade in Colonial Pennsylvania," pp. 260–61.
110. *N.J. Archives,* IX, 345–46.
111. *Mass. Acts and Resolves,* II, 517–18, 981–82.
112. *R.I. Col. Recs.,* IV, 131–35.
113. *Pa. Stat. at L.,* II, 287, 382–85, 434.
114. *N.Y. Col. Docs.,* V, 895.
115. *Cal. State Papers, Col.,* XXVIII (1714–15), 290–91.

3

The Slave Economy

As the Northern economy became more complex, with industry and commerce playing larger roles in most of the colonies, employers were willing to pay high prices for slaves capable of productive labor. Generally the bondsmen most in demand were young adults from whom the buyer could expect many years of service. Besides having a larger proportion of their lives to live, young slaves were more active and also likelier to learn new tasks and skills. Writing to a business associate in 1715, Jonathan Dickinson reported that Pennsylvania employers were reluctant to buy any slaves "except boys or girls."[1] Many of the slave cargoes landed at Northern ports were almost exclusively blacks between the ages of fourteen and twenty.[2] Buyers naturally

1. Jonathan Dickinson to Caleb Dickinson, April 30, 1715, Jonathan Dickinson Letter Book, 1715–21, MS. coll., LCP. See Darold D. Wax, "The Demand for Slave Labor in Colonial Pennsylvania," *Pennsylvania History*, XXXIV (1967), 337.
2. *New England Weekly Journal*, June 12, 1727; March 25, April 1, June 3, September 9, 16, October 7, 1728; September 1, October 27, November 3, 10, 1729; June 12, 19, September 11, 1732; June 11, August 6, 1733; September 9, 1734. *New York Weekly Post-Boy*, July 31, 1749; May 13, 1754; July 25, 1757; August 21, 1760; June 22, 1772. *New York Mercury*, July 9, 1759; June 16, 30, August 18, 1760; January 5, September 20, November 15, 1762; June 27, July 11, 1763; June 24, 1765. *American Weekly Mercury* (Philadelphia), July 28, August 4, 1726; July 6, 13, September 7, 14, 1727; June 20, 27, 1728; April 17, 24, 1729; August 13, 20, 1730; September 9, 16, 1731; July 5, 12, 1733; August 1, 8, September 12, 19, 1734; October 12, 19, 26, 1738; January 28, February 4, 25, March 4, 1741/42. *Pennsylvania Gazette*, August 21, 28, 1732; August 7, 12, 1736; June 23, 30, 1737; May 18, 25, 1738; May 10, 17, 1739; September 4, 25, 1740; July 30, September 10, 1741; October 21, 1742; July 28, 1743; August 10, November 23, 1749; May 30, 1751; August 23, 1753; August 19, 1756; July 7, 1757.

wanted slaves who were in a good state of general health, but particularly those with an immunity to smallpox since there would be no danger that an immune slave might contract that dread disease and perhaps communicate it to his master. Sales advertisements make it clear that smallpox immunity greatly enhanced the market value of a slave.[3]

So much emphasis on youth and good health naturally undercut the market for older blacks.[4] Slaves older than forty were rarely sold but generally remained with the master for whom they had worked during their more productive years. Although an optimistic owner advertised a Negro of seventy-two for sale in the March 3, 1762, edition of the *New York Gazette*, it is unlikely that he found a buyer. Next to superannuated blacks, women with a record of fecundity were least in demand. That a slave birth technically increased the owner's capital did not offset the personal inconvenience of sharing living space with unwanted children. Anne Grant, who left a detailed account of social conditions in New York in the 1750s, reported that the high birth rate of slaves in Albany County had turned some of the households into "overstocked hives."[5] According to the *New York Weekly Mercury*, February 15, 1773, a New York slave woman had given birth to twenty-three children by the age of thirty-six. Sometimes such children were advertised "to be given away" by owners who

3. *New England Weekly Journal*, January 1, 8, 1727/28; October 27, November 3, 1729; February 23, March 30, April 6, May 4, June 1, 8, 15, 22, 29, July 6, 13, 20, 27, August 3, 11, 1730; February 1, 8, 15, 22, March 1, June 7, 14, July 26, August 2, 9, November 11, 1731; January 24, May 29, June 12, 19, August 14, 21, 28, September 4, November 27, December 4, 1732. *New York Gazette*, October 4, 1731; September 3, 24, 1733. *New York Weekly Journal*, September 23, 1734; April 28, 1735; June 19, 1738; April 16, 1739; March 31, 1740. *New York Weekly Post-Boy*, August 28, 1749; June 15, July 13, August 3, October 23, 30, November 27, 1752. *American Weekly Mercury* (Philadelphia), January 26, June 3, 10, 17, 24, July 8; October 7, 21, November 11, 1731; December 7, 1732; April 19, 26, May 10, 17, July 26, August 9, 16, 30, September 13, 1733; May 22, 29, June 5, 1735. *Pennsylvania Gazette*, January 17, 1760; September 10, 1761. *Pennsylvania Chronicle*, February 2, 9, 16, July 5, 13, 20, 27, August 3, 1767; January 4, 11, 25, February 22, March 7, 14, May 2, June 20, 1768.

4. "Letters and Papers of Cadwallader Colden, 1711–1775," in NYHS *Colls.*, L–LVI, LXVII–LXVIII (9 vols., 1917–23, 1934–35), I, 39, hereafter cited as "Colden Papers."

5. Anne Grant, *Memoirs of an American Lady*, 2 vols. (New York: Dodd, Mead, 1901), I, 266–67.

found them a costly nuisance.[6] A Boston owner was so eager to get rid of a young slave child that he ran an advertisement in the *Continental Journal*, December 21, 1780, offering to pay anyone who would take it away.

Some masters tried to get rid of their slave women at the first sign of pregnancy. One woman in Philadelphia was advertised for sale in the *Pennsylvania Gazette*, May 21, 1767, because she was "big with child," her owner noting that she was being sold "for no other fault but that she breeds fast." Another woman, "recommended for her honesty," in the February 26, 1767, edition of the same paper, was sold "on account of its not answering to have a breeding wench in the family." A Boston owner offered to sell a Negro girl "not known to have any failing but being with child, which is the only cause of her being sold."[7] Another master in New York City ran an advertisement in the *New York Weekly Post-Boy*, May 17, 1756, that his cook was being sold "because she breeds too fast for her owner to put up with such inconvenience." Sellers made a special point of stressing possible sterility, for this increased the value of most women. Hoping to attract buyers, one seller advertised that his slave woman had "been married for several years without having a child."[8] Sterility was so highly prized that women could be sold well beyond the salable age of most men. A New York City owner offered to exchange a seventeen-year-old girl with potentially many years of service for "a middle aged wench that gets no children."[9]

Since productivity largely determined the demand for slaves, men rather than women made up most of the working force. Relegated to household chores and domestic service, women did not play a significant role in the slave economy. The preference for males was reflected in the instructions carried by a slave ship bound for Africa in 1759 to "buy no girls and few women . . .

6. *New England Weekly Journal*, November 15, 22, 1731; February 25, 1733/ 34; January 4, July 19, 26, 1737; June 6, 1738. *Boston Gazette*, June 25, 1754. *Boston News Letter*, June 26, 1760.

7. *Continental Journal* (Boston), March 1, 8, 1781, cited in George H. Moore, *Notes on the History of Slavery in Massachusetts* (New York: Appleton, 1866), p. 209.

8. *New York Weekly Mercury*, April 8, 1776.

9. *New York Gazetteer*, November 16, 1784.

buy some prime boys and young men."[10] So heavy was the demand for men that a marked disproportion between the sexes developed in the North's black population. By 1755 the ratio of adult males to females in Massachusetts was nearly two to one.[11] Men were in the majority everywhere, though in some colonies the disproportion was less.[12] In New Hampshire male slaves outnumbered women by four to three, and in Connecticut the ratio was three to two.[13] A New York census taken in 1756 listed over 7,500 male slaves and fewer than 6,000 women.[14]

The average slaveowner needed only one or two men to supplement his own labor, plus a woman for domestic service. Larger holdings tended to be inconvenient, particularly for small farmers and artisans who often had to share their living space with slaves. The average holding in New England was about two slaves per family, though in eastern Connecticut and the Narragansett region of Rhode Island larger holdings were common.[15] The same pattern of small-scale slaveholding existed in the Middle colonies. In Pennsylvania masters seldom owned more than four blacks, and the average holding was no more than one or two per family.[16] A partial census taken in New York in 1755 showed that 2,456 adult slaves were divided among 1,137 different owners. The ratio of slaves to masters was 133 to 62 in Brooklyn, 88 to 37 on Staten Island, and 81 to 53 in Huntington. The average slaveowner in Rye had only two slaves, and in New Paltz no one owned

10. Elizabeth Donnan, ed., *Documents Illustrative of the History of the Slave Trade in America*, 3 vols. (Washington, D.C.: Carnegie Institute, 1930–35), III, 69.

11. "Number of Negro Slaves in the Province of the Masschusetts Bay . . . 1754," *MHS Colls.*, 2d ser., III (1846), 95–97.

12. Lorenzo J. Greene, *The Negro in Colonial New England, 1620–1776* (New York: Columbia University Press, 1942), pp. 93–96.

13. Nathaniel Bouton, ed., *Provincial Papers: Documents and Records Relating to the Province of New-Hampshire from the Earliest Period of Its Settlement, 1623–1776*, 7 vols. (Concord and Nashua: Jenks, 1867–73), VII, 168–70; J. Hammond Trumbull and Charles J. Hoadly, eds., *The Public Records of the Colony of Connecticut, 1636–1776*, 15 vols. (Hartford: Lockwood & Brainard, 1850–90), XIV, 483–92. Hereafter cited as *N.H. Provincial Papers and Conn. Col. Recs.*

14. Evarts B. Greene and Virginia D. Harrington, *American Population before the Federal Census of 1790* (New York: Columbia University Press, 1932), p. 101.

15. Greene, *The Negro in Colonial New England*, pp. 97–99.

16. Wax, "The Demand for Slave Labor," *Pennsylvania History*, XXXIV, 333–34.

more than seven. Only seven persons in the province owned ten slaves or more, while over a thousand owned fewer than five.[17]

Newspaper advertisements reveal that a large proportion of the slaves worked in various phases of agriculture.[18] Besides producing food crops and raising livestock, they also grew such staples as flax, hemp, and tobacco.[19] Since farming was on a small scale, slaves generally worked side by side with the master and shared the same living quarters.[20] Their labor followed the usual routine of duties on a Northern farm—planting, harvesting, and the care of buildings, animals, and land. Moreover, the task system was employed, so slaves were usually free to manage their own time and rate of work.[21] The system encouraged qualities of independence that distinguished Northern slaves from their plantation counterparts in the South. Frequently they were highly versatile workers, with proficiency as blacksmiths, carpenters, and shoemakers in addition to their agricultural skills.[22]

The largest slaveholders were naturally the great landowners. Godfrey Malbone, who owned thousands of acres in eastern Connecticut, was probably the largest slaveholder in New England, with a force of fifty to sixty blacks.[23] Sir William Pepperell, whose

17. W. A. Rossiter, ed., A Century of Population Growth in the United States, 1790–1900 (Washington, D.C.: G P O, 1909), pp. 180–85; Charles R. Street, ed., Huntington Town Records, 3 vols. (Huntington, N.Y.: Long Islander Print, 1887–89), III, 199; J. Thomas Scharf, History of Westchester County, 2 vols. (Philadelphia: Preston, 1886), II, 667; J. J. Clute, Annals of Staten Island (New York: Charles Vogt, 1877), p. 70; Charles W. Baird, History of Rye (New York: Anson Randolph, 1871), p. 182; Ralph Le Fevre, History of New Paltz (Albany: Fort Orange Press, 1909), pp. 456–57.

18. New England Weekly Journal, October 14, November 7, 14, 1738; January 23, 30, February 13, 20, 27, April 3, May 15, November 13, 20, 1739; April 15, 22, 29, May 6, 20, 1740. American Weekly Mercury (Philadelphia), October 26, 1721; September 3, 10, 17, October 29, November 5, 12, 1724; March 7, April 6, September 7, 14, 1727; April 25, May 2, 9, 1728; December 29, 1730; January 4, 12, 19, June 24, July 8, September 30, October 7, 1731; March 16, 30, April 13, 1732. Pennsylvania Gazette, October 26, November 2, 1738; March 22, 1747/48. Pennsylvania Chronicle, June 15, July 13, 20, August 3, 17, September 7, 14, 1767; February 22, March 7, 14, May 2, 16, 23, 30, June 20, July 18, 25, 1768; March 27, April 10, May 1, 15, 29, June 5, 12, 1769.

19. Greene, The Negro in Colonial New England, p. 103.

20. Sarah Kemble Knight, The Journal of Madam Knight (New York: Smith, 1935), p. 38; "Belknap Papers," MHS Colls., 5th ser., III (1877), 302; Wax, "The Demand for Slave Labor," Pennsylvania History, XXXIV, 333–34.

21. Greene, The Negro in Colonial New England, p. 106n.

22. Grant, Memoirs of an American Lady, I, 265–66.

23. Greene, The Negro in Colonial New England, pp. 107–108.

estates extended across New Hampshire and Massachusetts, employed numerous slaves in farming and lumbering.[24] In Rhode Island's Narragansett country William Robinson owned an estate over four miles long and two miles wide which required a force of about forty slaves. Robert Hazard of South Kingstown owned twelve thousand acres and employed twenty-four slave women on his dairy farm alone. Another Narragansett family, the Stantons, whose holdings were among the largest in the province, maintained a force of at least forty blacks.[25]

The same land-slave pattern prevailed in the Middle colonies. John Potts, the largest landholder in Douglas, Pennsylvania, owned all seven slaves listed in the county tax rolls. In Parkiomen and Shipache four of the slaveholders listed owned more than three hundred acres of land, and the fifth, who owned two hundred acres, also owned an iron mill.[26] The Morris family, with estates in both New York and New Jersey, were probably the largest slaveholders in either province. At one time the elder Lewis Morris owned sixty-six blacks. Another New York family, the Philipses, employed at least forty slaves on their Hudson Valley manor.[27] The large estate of Philip Ver Planck required a force of about eighteen blacks.[28] Sir William Johnson, whose holdings in the Mohawk Valley were among the largest in New York, purchased as many as nineteen slaves in a single transaction.[29]

Slaveholding reflected social as well as economic standing, for in colonial times servants and retainers were visible symbols of rank and distinction. The leading families of Massachusetts and Connecticut used slaves as domestic servants, and in Rhode Island no prominent household was complete without a large staff of

24. Usher Parsons, *The Life of Sir William Pepperell* (Boston: Little, Brown, 1855), pp. 27–28.

25. Greene, *The Negro in Colonial New England,* p. 106; William Johnston, *Slavery in Rhode Island, 1755–1776* (Providence: Rhode Island Historical Society, 1894), p. 29.

26. Philadelphia County Tax Record, 1767, pp. 7b–11b, 31–34, MS coll., UPL.

27. Frederick Shonnard and W. W. Spooner, *History of Westchester County* (New York: The New York History Company, 1900), pp. 153, 194.

28. "Abstracts of Wills on File in the Surrogate's Office, City of New York," in NYHS *Colls.,* XXV–XLI (17 vols., 1892–1908), VI, 459–62, hereafter cited as "N.Y. Abstracts of Wills." See Shonnard and Spooner, *History of Westchester County,* p. 153.

29. Peter Warren Papers, MS. 19, MS. coll., NYHS.

black retainers.[30] New York's rural gentry regarded the possession of black coachmen and footmen as an unmistakable sign of social standing.[31] In Boston, Philadelphia, and New York City the mercantile elite kept retinues of household slaves. Their example was followed by tradesmen and small retailers until most houses of substance had at least one or two domestics.[32] Probably the largest urban staff was kept by William Smith of New York City, who had a retinue of twelve blacks to keep his household in order.[33]

The wide diffusion of slaveholdings brought blacks into every phase of the economy. Learning virtually every trade and skill, slaves became assistants and apprentices to established craftsmen.[34] In Philadelphia, New York, and Boston, blacks worked as bakers, tailors, weavers, coopers, tanners, blacksmiths, bolters, millers, masons, goldsmiths, cabinetmakers, naval carpenters, shoemakers, brushmakers, and glaziers.[35] These industrial slaves matched the finest skills of the best white artisans. In the artistic crafts blacks also performed as ably as whites. Thomas Fleet of Boston employed three slaves in his printing shop to set type and cut wooden blocks for engravings. One of these black engravers was responsible for most of the illustrations turned out by Fleet.[36] Some slaves who served as apprentices to doctors eventually became medical practitioners on their own account.[37]

The colonial iron industry depended heavily upon black labor.

30. Greene, *The Negro in Colonial New England*, pp. 108–109.
31. Martha B. Flint, *Early Long Island* (New York: Putnam's, 1896), p. 137; Jeptha R. Simms, *History of Schoharie County and Border Wars of New York* (Albany: Munsell & Tanner, 1845), p. 83; Philip H. Smith, *General History of Dutchess County, 1609–1876* (Pawling, N.Y., 1877), p. 127.
32. Nathaniel B. Shurtleff, *A Topographical and Historical Description of Boston* (Boston: Pub. for the Common Council, 1891), pp. 46–49.
33. Charles B. Todd, *The Story of the City of New York* (New York: Putnam's, 1888), p. 244.
34. Leonard P. Stavisky, "Negro Craftsmanship in Early America," *AHR*, LIV (1949), 319.
35. Henry S. Cooley, *A Study of Slavery in New Jersey* (Baltimore: The Johns Hopkins Press, 1896), p. 55; Edgar J. McManus, *A History of Negro Slavery in New York* (Syracuse, N.Y.: Syracuse University Press, 1966), p. 47; Alfred C. Prime, *Colonial Craftsmen of Pennsylvania* (Philadelphia: Pennsylvania Museum & School of Industrial Art, 1925), p. 3; Greene, *The Negro in Colonial New England*, pp. 112–14.
36. Stavisky, "Negro Craftsmanship," *AHR*, LIV (1949), 322–23.
37. Alice M. Earle, *Customs and Fashions in Old New England* (New York: Scribner's, 1896), pp. 356–58.

In 1727 the ironmasters of Pennsylvania petitioned the assembly to reduce the import duty on slaves on the grounds that the supply of white workers was not sufficient to keep their mills working.[38] The need for forced labor increased as production grew, for the hard conditions that prevailed in the bloomeries and mills repelled free workers. Reporting on Pennsylvania's iron manufactories in 1750, Israel Acrelius noted that "the laborers are generally composed partly of Negroes (slaves), partly of servants from Germany or Ireland brought for a term of years."[39] Firms like Morriss, Shreltee, and Company and Bennett's Iron Works used slaves in every phase of production.[40] Besides performing heavy labor as hammermen, attenders, and refiners, slaves also became proficient in the iron crafts. Black ironworkers in Andover, New Jersey, produced finished goods of such high quality that their wares were accepted on the basis of the brand name alone.[41]

Slaves were also indispensable in the maritime industry upon which so much of the North's economy depended. The shipbuilding trades relied heavily on blacks as sailmakers, ropemakers, caulkers, shipwrights, and anchormakers.[42] Slaves provided manpower for the fishing and trading ships of every colony.[43] A black sailor belonging to Peter Cross of Massachusetts became so skillful at his calling that he was eventually placed in charge of a sloop. New England's whaling industry made heavy use of slaves, and in some cases half the men of a whaling crew were black.[44] Not only were Negroes common on regular fishing and trading

38. Gertrude MacKinney and C. F. Hoban, eds., *Votes and Proceedings of the House of Representatives of the Province of Pennsylvania*, 8 vols. (Harrisburg: State Printer, 1931–35), III, 1846, hereafter cited as *Votes H.R. of Pa.*
39. Israel Acrelius, *A History of New Sweden*, William M. Reynolds, trans. (Philadelphia: Historical Society of Pennsylvania, 1874), p. 168, quoted by Wax, "The Demand for Slave Labor," *Pennsylvania History*, XXXIV, 334.
40. *Pennsylvania Gazette*, July 27, 1769; April 3, 1776.
41. Stavisky, "Negro Craftsmanship," *AHR*, LIV (1949), 322.
42. *Boston News Letter*, August 4, 1718; October 10, 1751. *New England Weekly Journal*, September 6, 13, 1737. *Boston Post-Boy*, October 7, 1751; June 22, 1752. *Pennsylvania Gazette*, July 28, 1743; May 19, 1768. *New York Gazette*, March 13, 1732/33. *New York Mercury*, July 14, 1760; September 21, 1761.
43. *New York Weekly Post-Boy*, February 20, 1748/49; August 25, 1763. *New York Mercury*, February 14, 1757; September 28, 1761; August 22, 1763. *Pennsylvania Gazette*, July 28, 1743; November 7, 1745; July 3, 1746; June 23, 1748; May 19, 1768. *New England Weekly Journal*, June 12, 1732; October 11, 18, 1737.
44. Greene, *The Negro in Colonial New England*, pp. 115–17.

ships, but some served on privateers and even slave ships.[45] So great was the demand for their services that every colony had laws specifically forbidding ship officers to sign on blacks without first obtaining their master's consent.[46]

The versatility of slave labor brought blacks into competition with white workers. As early as 1660, a Boston town meeting tried to protect white mechanics by forbidding the use of slaves in the skilled crafts.[47] In 1686 workers in the market houses of New York City complained that the employment of blacks had caused "discouragement and loss to the sworn porters." To protect the whites, an ordinance was passed providing that "no slave be suffered to work . . . as a porter about any goods either imported or exported from or into this city."[48] These measures brought almost no relief, for slaves continued to be used for whatever work suited their masters.[49] By 1691 New York's free porters complained that slave competition had "so impoverished them that they could not by their labors get a competency for the maintenance of themselves and families."[50]

Slaves trained in the industrial arts were particularly ruinous competitors. In 1707 Philadelphia's white artisans petitioned the

45. Howard Chapin, *Rhode Island in the Colonial Wars: A List of Rhode Island Soldiers and Sailors in the Old French and Indian War, 1755–1762* (Providence: Rhode Island Historical Society, 1918), pp. 23, 29; Donnan, *Slave Trade Documents*, II, 374–75.

46. William H. Whitmore, ed., *The Colonial Laws of Massachusetts* [1672–1686] (Boston: Rockwell & Churchill, 1890), p. 281; John R. Bartlett, ed., *Records of the Colony of Rhode Island and Providence Plantations in New England, 1636–1792*, 10 vols. (Providence: Greene, 1856–65), VI, 64–65; *Conn. Col. Recs.*, IV, 40; *Colonial Laws of New York from 1664 to the Revolution*, 5 vols. (Albany: James B. Lyon Co., 1894), I, 520–21; James T. Mitchell and Henry Flanders, comps., *The Statutes at Large of Pennsylvania from 1682–1801*, 16 vols. (Harrisburg: State Printer, 1896–1911), IV, 64; Aaron Leaming and Jacob Spicer, eds., *The Grants, Concessions and Original Constitutions of the Province of New Jersey* (Somerville, N.J.: Honeyman, 1881), p. 109. Hereafter cited as *Mass. Col. Laws* [1672–1686], *R.I. Col. Recs.*, *N.Y. Col. Laws*, and *Pa. Stat. at L.*

47. *A Report of the Record Commissioners of the City of Boston*, 39 vols. (Boston: Rockwell & Churchill, 1881–1909), VII, 5, hereafter cited as *Registry Dept. Recs. of Boston* (binder's title).

48. *Minutes of the Common Council of the City of New York, 1675–1776*, 8 vols. (New York: Dodd, Mead, 1905), I, 179, hereafter cited as *N.Y. City Council Min.*

49. Greene, *The Negro in Colonial New England*, pp. 112–13; Marcus W. Jernegan, *Laboring and Dependent Classes in Colonial America* (Chicago: University of Chicago Press, 1931), pp. 20–23.

50. *N.Y. City Council Min.*, I, 22.

assembly against "the want of employment and lowness of wages occasioned by the number of *Negroes* . . . who being hired out to work by the day, take away the employment of the petitioners."[51] Again, in 1737, they protested the assembly's failure to pass laws protecting them against black competitors.[52] The rising tide of slave competition brought a protest from New York's coopers in 1737 against the "great numbers of Negroes" entering their trade.[53] They petitioned the assembly for protection against "the pernicious custom of breeding slaves to trades whereby the honest and industrious tradesmen are reduced to poverty for want of employ." In support of the petition Lieutenant Governor Clarke denounced slave competition for having "forced many to leave us to seek their living in other countries."[54] No protective legislation was enacted, however, for the wide diffusion of slave property made such restrictions politically inexpedient.

Since large numbers of slaves were generally available for hire, non-slaveholders could draw upon the slave force to meet their labor needs.[55] Some masters made a business of hiring slaves out, and others, without enough work of their own, did so to obtain some return on their investment.[56] Newspaper notices of slaves being sought or offered for hire attest to the prevalence of the practice.[57] Sometimes slaves were rented along with a business so

51. *Votes H.R. of Pa.*, I, 670.

52. John F. Watson, *Annals of Philadelphia and Pennsylvania in the Olden Times*, 2 vols. (Philadelphia: the Author, 1844), I, 98; W. E. B. Du Bois, *The Philadelphia Negro* (Philadelphia: University of Pennsylvania Press, 1899), pp. 14–15.

53. Daniel Parish, Transcripts of Material on Slavery in the Public Records Office in London (1688–1760), p. 1, MS. coll., NYHS, hereafter cited as Parish's Transcripts.

54. Charles Z. Lincoln, ed., *Messages from the Governors*, 11 vols. (Albany: James B. Lyon, 1909), I, 260.

55. Abraham Evertse Wendell's Day Book (1760–93), April 19, 1762; July 9, 1767; April 7, 1768; September 2, 1771; August 28, September 19, 1772; September 8, 1773; MS. coll., NYHS.

56. Greene, *The Negro in Colonial New England*, pp. 120–21.

57. *New England Weekly Journal*, October 6, 1741. *Boston Gazette*, January 22, February 26, 1754. *New York Weekly Post-Boy*, March 27, September 4, 1749; February 12, 1749/50; September 9, 16, 1751; April 12, 1764; February 28, 1774; March 6, November 6, 1775. *New York Mercury*, June 2, 1760. *New York Weekly Mercury*, September 14, 1778. *American Weekly Mercury* (Philadelphia), August 10, 1727; June 18, 25, July 2, 1730; January 14, 28, February 4, 18, 1734/35. *Pennsylvania Gazette*, July 16, 1752; April 24, 1760. *Pennsylvania Chronicle*, June 27, July 4, 11, August 1, 8, 15, 22, 1768; May 15, November 6, 13, 1769; December 24, 1770; October 31, November 7, 14, 21, 28, December 5, 1772.

that the tenants could take over with no interruption of production.[58] Slave-hiring was particularly common among craftsmen and artisans who needed labor but who did not want the responsibilities of outright ownership.[59] Iron manufacturers also used hired slaves when other labor was scarce or production was unusually heavy.[60] One Pennsylvania employer advertised for two months trying to hire a slave "that fully understands managing a bloomery."[61] Though less common outside the towns, many farmers also found it convenient to rent slaves in order to meet seasonal labor needs.[62]

Slave-hiring combined the economic flexibility of wage labor with the compulsory advantages of slavery. The system enabled employers to increase or reduce their labor force without paying the higher wages demanded by free workers and without tying up substantial capital in the purchase of slaves. That the wage savings alone could be considerable is revealed in the bitter resistance of the white mechanics to slave competition. Black workers could be hired from their masters with all the flexibility of free labor whether the period of service was for days, months, or even years. When the hiring was for longer than a week, a formal contract was usually signed specifying the period of service, the work to be performed, the wages to be paid, and the hirer's responsibility for the slave.[63] Long-term hirers usually provided the slave with room and board, while the owner was responsible for his clothing.[64] To allow the hirer to deduct the cost of clothing from the wages only invited dispute. One master who made such an agreement discovered to his chagrin that the alleged cost of the clothing exceeded the slave's annual wages.[65]

58. *New England Weekly Journal,* July 1, 8, 1734. See Cooley, *Study of Slavery in New Jersey,* p. 56.
59. *New York Weekly Post-Boy,* September 4, 1749; February 12, 1749/50; September 9, 1751; April 12, 1764; February 28, 1774.
60. *Pennsylvania Gazette,* July 27, 1769; April 3, 1776.
61. *Pennsylvania Chronicle,* June 27, July 4, 11, August 1, 8, 15, 22, 1768.
62. Abraham Evertse Wendell's Day Book (1760–93), April 19, 1762; July 9, 1767; April 19, 1769; September 2, 1771; MS. coll., NYHS.
63. Massachusetts Archives, IX, 149, MS. coll., MSL.
64. A. J. F. Van Laer and Jonathan Pearson, eds., *Early Records of the City and County of Albany and Colony of Rensselaerswyck,* 4 vols. (Albany: State University of New York, 1915–19), III, 456.
65. "Papers of the Lloyd Family of the Manor of Queens Village," in NYHS *Colls.,* LIX–LX (2 vols., 1926–27), I, 261, 277; hereafter cited as "Lloyd Papers."

The hiring system owed its success to the ability of slaves to compete effectively with all types of free labor. Slaves became so skillful and versatile that employers found it profitable to rent their services rather than bid for the labor of free workers who were both difficult to obtain and expensive to retain. Moreover, the services of slaves were easily available, for owners who did not have enough work for their bondsmen often preferred to hire them out instead of selling thm. Even when slaves were rented for long or indefinite periods, some masters preferred to retain ownership. Samuel Lynde of Boston kept title to the slave he signed aboard of privateer in 1702 until "the said brigantine's return to her commission port."[66] Slaves belonging to estates undergoing probate were often hired out to provide income for the heirs and to free the executors and administrators of the burden of supervision.[67]

Slaveholders who hired out their bondsmen for long-term service ran obvious risks. If the hirer failed to provide adequate food and shelter, or if he overworked the slave and used him for dangerous tasks, the owner might suffer a loss of capital. If the slave rebelled against the conditions of his employment by running away, the hirer had no obligation to reimburse the owner.[68] Moreover, hiring had a corrosive effect on discipline, for it underscored for the slave that he was working for the benefit of another. As slaves served under successive hirers, bonds of personal loyalty tended to weaken and discipline became more difficult to maintain. Even seemingly docile slaves turned sullen and defiant after a term of service with another master.[69]

Another problem was the possibility of collusion between slaves and employers. Once slave-hiring became commonplace, it was relatively easy for slaves to sell their services to anyone who needed cheap labor. Many employers found it profitable to hire slaves directly at bargain rates without dealing with their masters. Slaves were so eager to work for their own benefit that many neglected their regular duties; some even ran away in order

66. Massachusetts Archives, IX, 149, cited in Greene, *The Negro in Colonial New England*, p. 121.
67. "N.Y. Abstracts of Wills," X, 63–64, 271–72.
68. *New York Mercury*, April 12, 1756.
69. "Lloyd Papers," I, 256.

to work for themselves on a full-time basis. Clandestine hiring caused slaveholders such heavy losses that every colony had stringent laws against such practices.[70] In 1711 New York City's Common Council tried to bring the problem under control by restricting slave-hiring to a single market house "whereby all persons may know where to hire slaves . . . and also masters discover when their slaves are so hired."[71] The need to reenact the ordinance in 1731, and again in 1738, attests to the difficulty of preventing hiring abuses.[72]

Hired slaves played such an important role in the working force that some employers would have been hard-pressed without them. Small farmers and artisans who were unable to use slaves economically on a full-time basis found the hiring system particularly suitable for their seasonal needs. Jonathan Dickinson of Philadelphia observed that so many masters made their slaves available for hire that the "tradesmen cannot fail of constant employment."[73] There was a heavy demand for household slaves by persons who preferred to hire rather than purchase their domestic retainers. Cooks, coachmen, gardeners, and laundresses passed from employer to employer as easily and certainly less expensively than free workers.[74] There was virtually no labor need that hired bondsmen did not fill. The system worked so well that even owners who had hired out their own slaves could usually hire replacements if the need unexpectedly arose.[75]

Many owners found it convenient to permit bondsmen to find

70. *Mass. Col. Laws* [1672–86], p. 281; *Conn. Col. Recs.*, IV, 40; *R.I. Col. Recs.*, VI, 64–65; *N.Y. Col. Laws*, I, 520–21; Leaming and Spicer, *N.J. Grants, Concessions and Constitutions*, p. 109. *Charter to William Penn and Laws of the Province of Pennsylvania Passed 1682–1700* (Harrisburg: Hart, 1879), pp. 151–53, 211–13; hereafter cited as *Pa. Charter and Laws, 1682–1700*.

71. *N.Y. City Council Min.*, II, 458.

72. *Ibid.*, IV, 85. See I. N. Phelps Stokes, ed., *The Iconography of Manhattan Island*, 6 vols. (New York: Dodd, 1915–28), IV, 525.

73. Jonathan Dickinson to Charles Hill, July 14, 1715, Dickinson Letter Book, 1715–21, MS. coll., LCP.

74. *American Weekly Mercury* (Philadelphia), June 18, 25, 1730. *Pennsylvania Chronicle*, November 27, December 4, 11, 1769; October 31, November 7, 14, 21, 28, December 5, 1772. *New York Weekly Post-Boy*, October 17, 1748; February 12, March 27, September 4, 1749; February 12, 1749/50; September 9, 16, 1751; April 27, 1752; April 12, 1764; February 28, 1774; March 6, November 6, 1775. *New York Mercury*, June 2, 1760. *New England Weekly Journal*, October 6, 1741. *Boston Gazette*, January 22, February 26, 1754.

75. Elizabeth Schuyler's Account Book, 1737–69, p. 86, MS. coll., NYHS.

their own employment in return for a fixed sum and to allow the slaves to retain all that they earned over that amount. Under such an arrangement the slave would deal directly with the employer, bargain for himself over working conditions, and turn over to his master the agreed sum. This was the extent of his obligation, and he was otherwise free to change his job and move about without interference. Slaves made the most of such opportunities to raise their standard of living, and some even aroused the envy of whites by their apparent affluence.[76] Frequently an owner did not know what his slaves were doing, nor did he care so long as his remittance was forthcoming. Sometimes the arrangement provided for eventual freedom if the payments were faithfully made for a certain period.[77] One resident of New York City agreed to emancipate his slave "if he can pay . . . the sum of £4 per year for eighteen years."[78]

The type of work for which a slave was hired usually determined his pay rate. A slave who earned eight shillings a day for plowing might be worth only half as much when he was hired out to cut wood.[79] Particularly dangerous work of course was the most highly compensated. A slave hired out as a cook on a Massachusetts privateer in 1702 was to be paid "one full and whole share of all prizes . . . as much as any able sailor on board."[80] Generally slaves hired out by the day earned more than those employed at monthly or yearly rates. But the net return was not necessarily greater, because per diem slaves usually lived at home with their owners who supported them out of earnings. Moreover, the owners had to allow for more frequent periods of idleness when there would be no income at all. Per diem slaves had to earn at least double their monthly rates in order to offset these disadvantages.[81]

The hiring rates provided owners with an excellent return on their investment. Though wages fluctuated with changing eco-

76. *New York Weekly Mercury*, November 13, 1775.
77. "N.Y. Abstracts of Wills," V, 74, 149–50; X, 67; XII, 374; XIV, 202–207; XV, 77–78.
78. *Ibid.*, X, 63–64.
79. Abraham Evertse Wendell's Account Book (1760–93), August 1, 1763; August 1, 1764, June 3, 1765; Wendell's Day Book, May 13, 1763. MS. coll., NYHS.
80. Massachusetts Archives, IX, 149, MS. coll., MSL.
81. John Norris's Memorandum, October 7, 1707, John A. McAllister MS. coll., HSP.

nomic conditions, slaves generally returned from 10 to 30 percent yearly on invested capital. In 1695 blacks valued at £40 earned about £5 per year plus maintenance, or a net return of about 12 percent.[82] The earning power of bondsmen increased considerably in the eighteenth century, for the long-range tendency of colonial wages was upward. Slaves appraised at £70 in 1725 earned £20 per year, a net return to the owner of 29 percent. The return was even higher for slaves hired out at monthly or weekly rates. Negroes valued at £50 in 1740 earned about 30 shillings per month, a return of 36 percent yearly on the owner's investment.[83] When wages spiraled upward during the American Revolution, slaves could be hired out at yearly rates of 40 to 60 percent of their market value.[84] Although these rates were abnormally high, the wage scales prevailing before the war indicate that slave property was a consistently profitable form of investment.

Slave profits were enhanced by a favorable tax structure. Although tariffs were levied on imports, legal loopholes and smuggling weakened their impact. New Hampshire and Connecticut had no duties at all, and New Jersey, except for the period 1714–21, did not have a tariff until 1767. These colonies provided smugglers with bases from which slaves could be sold duty-free into neighboring provinces. Even when tariff laws were rigidly drawn and strictly enforced, the rates were usually too low to affect profits. With the price of slaves about £5 or £6 in Africa, and between £40 and £60 at Northern ports of entry, tariffs averaging £3 to £5 could easily be absorbed by the shipper.[85] Higher rates that might have had an adverse effect, like the £20

82. Jacobus Van Cortlandt's Letter Book, p. 61, MS. coll., NYHS.

83. Robert Ellis to Lawrence Williams, February 14, 1739/40, Ellis to Leyborne, Roffey, and Rockliff, February 23, 1739/40, Ellis's Letter Book (1736–48), John Norris' Memorandum, October 7, 1707, MS. coll., HSP; Parish's Transcripts (1720–38), p. 25; "Lloyd Papers," I, 307.

84. New York Weekly Mercury, July 10, 1780; April 21, 1783.

85. Acts and Resolves, Public and Private, of the Province of the Massachusetts Bay, 5 vols. (Boston: Wright & Potter, 1869–86), I, 578–79; II, 517–18, 981–82. Charter and the Acts and Laws of His Majesty's Colony of Rhode Island and Providence Plantations in America (Providence: Sidney & Burnett Rider, 1858), pp. 64–65; R.I. Col. Recs., IV, 131–35; E. B. O'Callaghan and Berthold Fernow, eds., Documents Relative to the Colonial History of the State of New York, 15 vols. (Albany: Weed, Parsons, 1856–87), V, 178, 185, 293; Samuel Hazard, ed., Colonial Records of Pennsylvania, 16 vols. (Philadelphia: Severns, 1852), III, 171, 247–48, 250. Hereafter cited as Mass. Acts and Resolves, R.I. Charter, Acts, and Laws, N.Y. Col. Docs., and Pa. Col. Recs.

duty imposed by Pennsylvania in 1712, were invariably disallowed by England.[86]

Property taxes on slaves were equally light. Most of New England's slaves were consistently assessed at only a fraction of their real value. Massachusetts taxed all slaves older than fourteen at one penny per £1, with men assessed at £20 and women at £15.[87] In New Hampshire an assessment of £20 was placed on every male slave regardless of skill or earning power.[88] These statutory valuations favored the master class, for they usually taxed slaves at less than one-half their real market value. Such rates had only a negligible effect on prices and profits. One critic of the fixed valuation system pointed out that a person "able to purchase a slave comes off in the rates cheaper than his poorer neighbor that has an apprentice."[89]

The Middle colonies taxed slaves as polls rather than as property, with levies so low that the revenue raised was negligible. Despite the urging of the governors, assemblies refused to subject slave property to regular taxation.[90] The only levies placed on slaves were temporary measures passed during wartime or for some other public emergency.[91] In 1709, during Queen Anne's War, when even fireplaces and stoves were taxed, New York imposed a levy of two shillings on every slave. A severe depression in 1734 resulted in a temporary tax of one shilling on slaves between the ages of fourteen and fifty.[92] This was about one-tenth of one percent of an adult slave's market value. Otherwise, except for small levies imposed by the towns and counties, slave property in New York escaped the tax rolls completely.[93]

Although highly profitable for most, some employers found slavery too inflexible for changing labor needs. The considerable amounts of capital that had to be tied up in slaves increased busi-

86. *Pa. Stat. at L.*, II, 433.
87. *Mass. Acts and Resolves*, I, 615.
88. *N.H. Provincial Papers*, IV, 304–305.
89. Andrew M. Davis, ed., *Colonial Currency Reprints, 1682–1751*, 4 vols. (Boston: Prince Society, 1910–11), I, 343.
90. Parish's Transcripts (1729–60), pp. 10, 13. See William Smith, *History of the Late Province of New York*, 2 vols. (New York: New-York Historical Society, 1829), II, 11–12.
91. Parish's Transcripts (1695–1713), p. 5.
92. *N.Y. Col. Laws*, I, 682–83; II, 877–80.
93. Baird, *History of Rye*, pp. 182, 393.

ness costs and made it difficult for small entrepreneurs to expand.
Not only were slaves at least twice as costly as indentured servants, but it was not always possible to hire them out during periods of unemployment to offset the cost of their maintenance.[94]
There was also the chance that all or a substantial part of the investment would be lost if the slave became ill or ran away. Employers with seasonal or irregular labor needs often found it pru-
dent to buy slaves in common in order to limit maintenance costs
and reduce the risk to capital.[95]

Every slaveholder had to be prepared for unusual expenses
that could cut deeply into profits. Blacks imported from the trop-
ics were particularly prone to respiratory diseases and other ailments during their period of adjustment to the Northern environment. Disease was so common during the cold season that buyers
hesitated to purchase slaves as winter approached.[96] In purchasing a slave in November of 1714, James Logan of Philadelphia
paid only half the price, agreeing to pay the rest "if he lives to
the spring."[97] Slaves suffering from winter maladies had to be
given medical care, which even in colonial times could be costly.
Medical services for three slaves and a servant during the winter
of 1675–76 cost Benjamin Gibbs of Massachusetts more than £6.[98]
Sometimes medical expenses completely canceled the return on a
slave, leaving the owner with a net loss.[99] One master in Massachusetts found that the cost of medical care for a slave who had
been hired out exceeded four years' wages.[100]

Maintenance costs weighed most heavily on small farmers who
had to support slaves during the long winter season without any

94. Darold D. Wax, "The Negro Slave Trade in Colonial Pennsylvania," unpublished Ph.D. dissertation (University of Washington, 1962), p. 158; Cheesman
A. Herrick, White Servitude in Pennsylvania: Indentured and Redemption Labor
in Colony and Commonwealth (Philadelphia: McVey, 1926), p. 203.

95. Miscellaneous Slavery Manuscripts, Box I, Bill of Sale, March 16, 1771,
NYHS. Philadelphia Tax Record, 1767, p. 181, MS. coll. UPL. "N.Y. Abstracts of
Wills," V, 134; VI, 94–95; VII, 28–30; XI, 135; XIII, 111–12.

96. Wax, "The Negro Slave Trade in Colonial Pennsylvania," p. 94.

97. James Logan's Account Book (1712–19), p. 91, MS. coll., HSP.

98. Samuel E. Morison, ed., "Records of the Suffolk County Court, 1671–1680,"
in CSM Colls., XXIX–XXX (2 vols., 1933), II, 648–49.

99. Wendell's Day Book (1754–60), p. 30, MS. coll., NYHS. "Lloyd Papers,"
I, 309–10, 341; II, 719.

100. George F. Dow, ed., Records and Files of the Quarterly Courts of Essex
County, Massachusetts, 8 vols. (Salem, Mass.: Essex Institute, 1911–21), VII,
394–95.

income to offset expenses.[101] Unless the slaves could be hired out to cut lumber or be kept busy caring for livestock, the owner faced a serious financial drain during the winter layoff. One New York slaveholder who raised hogs and corn found that by the time spring arrived he "had nothing left but the Negroes."[102] Another slaveholder in Pennsylvania reported in 1698 that his bondsmen had been "a great charge unto me this winter, being not able to earn their bread."[103] Only the larger estates escaped the seasonal slump, for winter employment in lumbering and dairying kept slaves productive. In the Hudson Valley, eastern Connecticut, and the Narragansett region of Rhode Island where large-scale agriculture, cattle raising, and dairy farming were carried on, slaves were self-supporting on a year-round basis.[104]

Slaveholders were also burdened with capital costs in the form of insurance, interest, and depreciation. When slaves were hired out for long periods, particularly where the work was dangerous, prudence dictated that the owner insure himself against loss.[105] Although an owner could take his chances and forego insurance in order to keep expenses down, interest and depreciation costs could not be avoided. Since interest rates on prime investments were between 7 and 9 percent, the return on slave property had to be discounted accordingly. Moreover, the market value of slaves declined with age, so there was a continual erosion of capital. In New York, a thirty-year-old slave purchased for £70 in 1754 brought only £50 when sold twelve years later.[106] Thus, despite a rising price level during these years, the owner's investment depreciated at the rate of about 2.5 percent each year. Counting interest as well as depreciation, the cost to capital averaged about 10 percent annually.

101. "Colden Papers," II, 30–34.
102. Ira K. Morris, *Memorial History of Staten Island*, 2 vols. (New York: The Winthrop Press, 1900), II, 36.
103. Jonathan Dickinson to Caleb Dickinson, April 25, 1698, Jonathan Dickinson's Letter Book (1698–1701), MS. coll., HSP.
104. Grant, *Memoirs of an American Lady*, I, 265–66, 272; William D. Miller, *The Narragansett Planters* (Worcester, Mass.: American Antiquarian Society, 1934), pp. 24–25; Edward Channing, *The Narragansett Planters* (Baltimore: The Johns Hopkins Press, 1886), pp. 5–10; Greene, *The Negro in Colonial New England*, pp. 104–105.
105. Wax, "The Demand for Slave Labor," *Pennsylvania History*, XXXIV, 334.
106. Street, *Huntington Town Records*, II, 418–20.

Despite high maintenance and capital costs, there was really no alternative to the slave system. Slaves were in fact the only workers available in sufficient numbers, and employers had to work within the system, adapting it to their particular needs.[107] How well they succeeded can be seen in the remarkable diversification and specialization of slave labor. Anyone could use the system, since it was not necessary to own slaves in order to obtain their labor. By renting the services of a bondsman, employers could meet labor needs without tying up large amounts of capital in workers. Moreover, profitability was built right into the system, for the exploitation of the slave could make up any loss caused by the inefficiency of his exploiters. Flexible and mobile, promoting general as well as specific interests, slavery played an indispensable role in the Northern economy.

107. W. Noel Sainsbury, et al., eds., Calendar of State Papers: Colonial Series, America and West Indies, 42 vols. (London: H.M.S.O., 1860–1953), XVII (1699), 152, 176. N.Y. Col. Docs., IV, 588, 707; VII, 889.

4

Race and Status

Slavery promoted economic progress, but it also produced a society lacking in justice and compassion. Since the system sorted people out by race, every black automatically became part of a servile class without any of the rights belonging to the white hegemony. Negroes commanded high prices as slaves because they were exploitable, and the higher the price the more certain their exploitation. As ever larger amounts of capital became tied up in slaves, it was easy to assume that blacks had no rights at all against the power of the masters. Before a decade had passed, Negroes in every colony had begun the dehumanizing descent into the chattel status peculiar to American slavery.[1]

The racial visibility of the Negro made it easy to assume that his blackness somehow justified his enslavement. Long before statutes were enacted equating status with pigmentation, race played a central role in the everyday operation of the system. An early example of how status converged with race occurred in 1642 when the French privateer *La Garce* brought some captured Negroes to New Netherland. Although the captives claimed to be free Spanish subjects, they were summarily sold into slavery without any inquiry about their status under Spanish law.[2] Because of their

1. Lorenzo J. Greene, *The Negro in Colonial New England, 1620–1776* (New York: Columbia University Press, 1942), pp. 65–66; Edward R. Turner, *The Negro in Pennsylvania* (Washington, D.C.: The American Historical Association, 1911), pp. 17–20.
2. David T. Valentine, comp., *Manual of the Corporation of the City of New York*, 28 vols. (New York, 1842–70), (1870), p. 764.

race alone they were presumed to be slaves, and the burden was on them to prove otherwise. Nor did the presumption change when New Netherland became New York after the English occupation. A century later Governor Hunter reported to the Board of Trade that some Spanish prisoners had been sold as slaves "by reason of their colour which is swarthy."[3]

For most of the seventeenth century Negro slaves had an equivocal legal status somewhere between indentured servitude and absolute bondage.[4] Frequently they were referred to as servants rather than as slaves, and in some cases freedom was granted after a limited period of service.[5] What most clearly separated them from white servants was that the latter had contracts defining the terms of their bondage. The difference was that Negroes were purchased as persons, while technically only the indenture or labor obligation of the servant was acquired by the buyer.[6] Thus a slave had only those rights allowed by his master or granted by the law, whereas the servant had all rights except those specifically denied by his indenture.[7] The distinction meant that in everyday practice there were no limits on how far a master might go in exploiting black labor.

Because blacks had no indentures limiting their service, the laws regulating white servants were not relevant to slavery. Whites could be punished for public offenses by imprisonment or additional servitude, but blacks already in permanent bondage had to

3. E. B. O'Callaghan and Berthold Fernow, eds., Documents Relative to the Colonial History of the State of New York, 15 vols. (Albany: Weed, Parsons, 1856–87), V, 342, hereafter cited as N.Y. Col. Docs.

4. Oscar and Mary F. Handlin, "Origins of the Southern Labor System," WMQ, 3d ser., VII (1950), 218.

5. Acts and Resolves, Public and Private, of the Province of the Massachusetts Bay, 5 vols. (Boston: Wright & Potter, 1869–86), I, 154; J. Hammond Trumbull and Charles J. Hoadly, eds., The Public Records of the Colony of Connecticut, 1636–1776, 15 vols. (Hartford: Lockwood & Brainard, 1850–90), I, 349; John R. Bartlett, ed., Records of the Colony of Rhode Island and Providence Plantations in New England, 1636–1792, 10 vols. (Providence: Greene, 1856–65), III, 492–93; E. B. O'Callaghan, ed., Laws and Ordinances of New Netherland (Albany: Weed, Parsons, 1868), pp. 36–37. Hereafter cited as Mass. Acts and Resolves, Conn. Col. Recs., and R. I. Col. Recs. See William L. Stuart, "Negro Slavery in New Jersey and New York," Americana, XVI (1922), 353; Greene, The Negro in Colonial New England, pp. 168, 290–91.

6. Marcus W. Jernegan, Laboring and Dependent Classes in Colonial America (Chicago: University of Chicago Press, 1931), p. 47.

7. Richard B. Morris, Government and Labor in Early America (New York: Columbia University Press, 1946), p. 500.

be controlled by other means. The sharp differentiation that evolved between white and Negro offenders underscored the unique status of blacks. Pennsylvania in an early law for "the better regulation of servants" prescribed additional service for whites who embezzled their master's goods, but ordered that blacks guilty of the same offense should be severely flogged.[8] By the beginning of the eighteenth century similar legislation had created an elaborate network of racial segregation in every Northern colony.

The principal formative influence on slavery came from the West Indies. Since chattel bondage had disappeared in Northern Europe prior to the colonial era, the settlers brought over no legal precedents for dealing with slaves.[9] Indeed, in the beginning the slave status was not automatically tied to race, for even whites were sometimes sold into slavery as a punishment for crime.[10] In the West Indies, however, slavery based on race had become well established by the time the first blacks reached the mainland, and their steady importation from the islands provided impetus for the idea that Negroes could be held as chattels.[11] The North did not adopt the harsh codes of the islands completely, for some changes had to be made for local needs and conditions.[12] Nevertheless, slavery might have developed in different, less brutal ways if the West Indian model had not promoted the conception of the blacks as persons naturally suited to slavery.[13]

That Negroes might have been bound to service in ways different from chattel slavery can be found in the "half-freedom" system developed in New Netherland. This system, under which blacks were conditionally released from bondage, was adopted by the Dutch West India Company as a means of rewarding faithful

8. James T. Mitchell and Henry Flanders, comps., *The Statutes at Large of Pennsylvania from 1682–1801*, 16 vols. (Harrisburg: State Printer, 1896–1911), II, 56, hereafter cited as *Pa. Stat. at L.*

9. John C. Hurd, *The Law of Freedom and Bondage in the United States*, 2 vols. (Boston: Little, Brown, 1858–62), I, 195–228.

10. Nathaniel B. Shurtleff, ed., *Records of the Governor and Company of the Massachusetts Bay in New England, 1628–1674*, 5 vols. (Boston: White, 1853–54), I, 246, hereafter cited as *Mass. Bay Recs.*

11. Winthrop D. Jordan, "The Influence of the West Indies on the Origins of New England Slavery," *WMQ*, 3d ser., XVIII (1961), 243–47.

12. Emma L. Thornbrough, "Negro Slavery in the North: Its Legal and Constitutional Aspects," unpublished Ph.D. dissertation (University of Michigan, 1946), p. 39.

13. Jordan, "The Influence of the West Indies," *WMQ*, 3d ser., XVIII, 248–50.

service. Blacks who earned the status received full personal liberty in return for a yearly tribute and a promise to perform certain labor if the company needed their services. A typical half-freedom grant bound the Negro to pay the company "thirty schepels of maize or wheat and one fat hog, valued at twenty guilders." To distinguish them from ordinary bondsmen, the half-freedmen carried passes certifying them to be "free and at liberty on the same footing as other free people."[14]

The half-freedom system benefited the West India Company as much as the Negroes, for it had been expensive to maintain slaves whose full-time labor was not needed. The system enabled the company to reduce slave costs without relinquishing the right to specific labor when the need arose. Three company slaves who received their half-freedom in 1652 were still obliged to perform certain chores for Director General Stuyvesant.[15] These chores had to be performed faithfully, for the freedom passes provided that any Negro who defaulted would "forfeit freedom and return back into the said Company's slavery."[16]

That the system benefited the company did not make it any less attractive to the slaves. Half-freedom was better than no freedom, and there were few slaves who did not seek it. Indeed, the chief complaint of the half-free Negroes was that the status could not be passed along to their children. The freedom passes were granted "on condition that their children serve the Company whenever it pleased."[17] Although this proviso was never invoked, the half-freedmen bombarded the company with petitions demanding guarantees that their children would not be enslaved.[18] The issue generated so much heat that some of the white settlers joined them in a remonstrance denouncing the proviso as "contrary to the law of every people."[19]

Half-freedom raised fundamental questions about the slave status itself. If slavery consisted only of a labor obligation, as half-

14. O'Callaghan, *Laws and Ordinances of New Netherland*, pp. 36–37.
15. I. N. Phelps Stokes, ed., *The Iconography of Manhattan Island*, 6 vols. (New York: Dodd, 1915–28), IV, 223.
16. O'Callaghan, *Laws and Ordinances of New Netherland*, pp. 36–37.
17. *N.Y. Col. Docs.*, I, 343.
18. E. B. O'Callaghan, ed., *Calendar of Historical Manuscripts in the Office of the Secretary of State*, 2 vols. (Albany: Weed, Parsons, 1866), I, 269.
19. *N.Y. Col. Docs.*, I, 343.

freedom seemingly implied, then the rights of slaveowners were less than absolute. Such a conception of bondage contradicted the prevailing theory that slavery and freedom were mutually exclusive and could not be fused into a composite status.[20] The pragmatic Dutch cared little about such distinctions. All that mattered was that half-freedom provided them with a flexible system of servile labor. Whether it might also have provided an alternative to the West Indian model remains a moot but interesting speculation.

The first official recognition of chattel slavery as a legal institution occurred in the Massachusetts "Body of Liberties" of 1641. The general court legalized the enslavement of "captives taken in just wars, and such strangers as willingly sell themselves or are sold to us."[21] Subsequently incorporated in the "Articles of the New England Confederation," the Massachusetts statute technically legalized slavery in Connecticut and New Plymouth as well.[22] Rhode Island, which was not a member of the confederation, passed a law along similar lines in 1652.[23] These enactments provided the legal basis for New England's slave system, though in some cases technical changes had to be made to deal with special problems. The Massachusetts "Body of Liberties," for example, did not specifically sanction slavery for the children of slaves; it authorized only the enslavement of "strangers" sold into the colony. When the issue was raised in 1670, the word *strangers* was deleted, thereby removing alienage as a condition and legalizing the hereditation of slave status.[24]

Statutory recognition of slavery began in the Middle colonies with the English occupation of New Netherland. During the entire period of Dutch control the enslavement of blacks had been a *de facto* institution based on custom and usage.[25] The "Articles

20. Thomas R. R. Cobb, *An Inquiry in the Law of Slavery in the United States of America* (Philadelphia: Johnson, 1858), pp. 283–88.
21. William H. Whitmore, ed., *The Colonial Laws of Massachusetts* [1660–72] (Boston: Rockwell & Churchill, 1889), p. 53, hereafter cited as *Mass. Col. Laws* [1660–72].
22. Greene, *The Negro in Colonial New England,* p. 125.
23. *R.I. Col. Recs.,* I, 243.
24. George H. Moore, *Notes on the History of Slavery in Massachusetts* (New York: Appleton, 1866), pp. 16–17.
25. Hurd, *The Law of Freedom and Bondage,* I, 277–78.

of Capitulation," however, specifically confirmed Dutch slave titles, and the laws promulgated by the Duke of York the following year recognized slavery as a legal institution.[26] Slavery in New Jersey obtained legal sanction for the first time under the proprietary regime of Berkeley and Carteret.[27] Although slaves had long been used in Pennsylvania by both the English and the Dutch, slaveholding did not receive statutory approval until the turn of the century. A law passed in 1700 for the regulation of servants and slaves made Pennsylvania the last Northern colony to legitimate the institution.[28]

The slave status depended on race, but racial categorization itself could often be misleading. As time passed and the population became racially mixed, physical appearance provided only an approximate index of status. Persons of predominantly Negro ancestry were often free, while persons who obviously had white blood were sometimes slaves. In order to clear up ambiguities the colonies adopted the civil law principle of *partus sequitur ventrem*, which fixed status according to matrilineal descent.[29] Children born to a male slave and a free woman were free, while those of a free man and a slave woman became the property of the woman's owner. Although only New York enacted this rule by statute, custom and judicial decision produced the same result in the other colonies.[30] Thus the slave status was not limited to Negroes alone but technically encompassed anyone with slave blood on the maternal side.

Status theoretically followed matrilineal descent, but in some cases physical appearances made all the difference. Whenever the status of racially mixed persons became an issue, the courts had to decide who would be treated as white and who would be treated as black. How this was decided could be crucial to the

26. *N.Y. Col. Docs.*, II, 250–53; *Colonial Laws of New York from 1664 to Revolution*, 5 vols. (Albany: James B. Lyon, Co., 1894), I, 18, hereafter cited as *N.Y. Col. Laws.*
27. Aaron Leaming and Jacob Spicer, eds., *The Grants, Concessions and Original Constitutions of the Province of New Jersey* (Somerville, N.J.: Honeyman, 1881), pp. 20–23.
28. *Pa. Stat. at L.*, II, 56.
29. Maryland once followed the common-law rule of patrilineal descent primarily to deter miscegenation between white women and Negro Slaves. See *Archives of Maryland*, 69 vols. (Baltimore: Maryland Historical Society, 1883–1961), I, 533.
30. *N.Y. Col. Laws*, I, 597–98.

outcome of particular cases, because all Negroes were presumed to be slaves. The test adopted by the courts was physical appearance, and litigants were treated accordingly in determining the burden of proof.[31] When Thomas Thatcher of New York claimed a predominantly white mulatto as a slave, the court gave him eight days to prove his claim; in the meantime the mulatto was presumed to be free.[32] On the other hand, Negro prisoners of war were subject to sale as prize goods unless they could rebut the presumption of slavery by offering proof that they were free men.[33] The visibility test doubtless caused injustice, but it was the only practical indicator of status in a system predicated on race.

Slave law gave Negroes an indeterminate status somewhere between that of a person and that of a chattel. Massachusetts taxed slaves as both persons and property, while Rhode Island and New Hampshire assessed them as livestock.[34] New Jersey and Pennsylvania included them in the ordinary lists of ratable property, and New York, when it taxed them at all, did so by capitation.[35] In wills and estate accounts slaves were inventoried as chattels in the same manner as tools, household goods, and other personal property.[36] Even the extinction of private rights over slaves

31. Cobb, *Inquiry into the Law of Slavery*, p. 67.
32. O'Callaghan, *Calendar of Historical Manuscripts*, II, 56.
33. Daniel Parish, Transcripts of Material on Slavery in the Public Records Office in London (1729–60), pp. 3, 8–9, 14–15, MS. coll., NYHS, hereafter cited as Parish's Transcripts.
34. *Mass. Acts and Resolves*, I, 615; William H. Whitmore, ed., *The Colonial Laws of Massachusetts* [1672–86] (Boston: Rockwell & Churchill, 1890), p. 24, hereafter cited as *Mass. Col. Laws* [1672–86]; *R.I. Col. Recs.*, III, 308; Nathaniel Bouton, ed., *Provincial Papers: Documents and Records Relating to the Province of New-Hampshire from the Earliest Period of Its Settlement, 1623–1776*, 7 vols. (Concord and Nashua: Jenks, 1867–73), V, 304–305, VI, 175, hereafter cited as *N.H. Provincial Papers*.
35. Samuel Nevill, comp., *The Acts of the General Assembly of the Province of New Jersey*, 2 vols. (Philadelphia and Woodbridge, N.J., 1752–61), I, 429–30; *Pa. Stat. at L.*, V, 118; *N.Y. Col. Laws*, II, 876, 881.
36. George F. Dow, ed., *Records and Files of the Quarterly Courts of Essex County, Massachusetts*, 8 vols. (Salem, Mass.: Essex Institute, 1911–21), IV, 58; V, 65. *The Early Records of the Town of Providence*, 20 vols. (Providence: Snow & Fornbrow, 1892–1909), XVI, 192. *East Hampton Town Records*, 5 vols. (Sag Harbor, N.Y.: John S. Hunt, 1887–1905), I, 412. William S. Pelletreau, ed., *Records of the Town of Smithtown* (Huntington, N.Y.: Long Islander Print, 1898), pp. 39–41. "Abstracts of Wills on File in the Surrogate's Office, City of New York," in NYHS *Colls.*, XXV–XLI (17 vols., 1892–1908), hereafter cited as "N.Y. Abstracts of Wills."

did not alter their status as chattels. If the master died without heirs, his slaves would escheat to the colony along with the rest of his property.[37]

The chattel aspects of slavery reveal themselves most clearly in the buying and selling of slaves. Negroes were bought or hired as personal property, and regular bills of sale were executed to effect the transfer of title.[38] They were also mortgaged and aliened as collateral for the debts of their masters.[39] Any interference with these property rights constituted a trespass for which damages could be recovered. Damages could be had by the masters for enticing Negroes away from their duties and for harboring or helping them to escape.[40] A free man responsible for making a slave woman pregnant was liable for any loss of services or diminution of value suffered by her owner.[41] On the other hand, as property, slaves could be taken from their masters on writs of attachment and sold for the benefit of creditors.[42] A typical forced sale at Newport gave the buyer a sheriff's deed with "all right, title, and property of, in, and to the said Negro . . . forever."[43]

Although technically classed as property, slaves also had some of the attributes of legal personality. They could own and transfer property, receive and bequeath legacies, and work for their own benefit during their free time. The master's property in the slave did not automatically entitle him to the property of the slave. This distinction was peculiar to Northern slavery, and there

37. *Early Records of Providence*, XVI, 10–11, 154, 163.
38. Miscellaneous Slavery Manuscripts, NYHS; Massachusetts Archives, IX, 142, MS. coll., MSL.
39. Newport Town Records, 1743–50, Vault B, MS. coll., NHS; A. J. F. Van Laer and Jonathan Pearson, eds., *Early Records of the City and County of Albany and Colony of Rensselaerswyck*, 4 vols. (Albany: State University of New York, 1915–19), I, 149, 458; A. J. F. Van Laer, ed., *Minutes of the Court of Albany, Rensselaerswyck and Schenectady, 1668–1680*, 2 vols. (Albany: State University of New York, 1926–28), II, 232.
40. *Mass. Acts and Resolves*, I, 535–36; *Mass. Col. Laws* [1672–86], p. 281; *R.I. Col. Recs.*, III, 492–93, VI, 64–65; *Conn. Col. Recs.*, IV, 40; *Pa. Stat. at L.* III, 250; *N.Y. Col. Laws*, I, 520; Samuel E. Morison, ed., "Records of the Suffolk County Court, 1671–1680," in CSM *Colls.*, XXIX–XXX (2 vols., 1933), I, 159.
41. Van Laer, *Minutes of the Court of Albany, Rensselaerswyck and Schenectady*, II, 97, 122, 137, 168, 172, 179, 401, 417–18.
42. Dow, *Essex County Court Recs.*, IV, 233. *New York Weekly Post-Boy*, September 21, 1772. See Greene, *The Negro in Colonial New England*, pp. 172–73.
43. Bill of sale for the slave Prince, August 7, 1770, Box 43, Folder 4, MS. coll., NHS.

are instances where slaves were both heirs and chattels under the wills of their masters.[44] The property privilege had no specific sanction, but it was everywhere protected by custom and usage. Writing to England in 1771, Chief Justice Hutchinson of Massachusetts observed that anyone might have "property in goods, notwithstanding he is called a slave."[45]

Masters who wanted property owned by their slaves had to pay for it. The widow of one Long Island slaveowner had to bargain with her slave over some goods given to him by her late husband.[46] A master who took his slave's property arbitrarily could be sued by a legal proxy for the slave in a form of action known as *prochein ami*.[47] But slaves apparently had little to fear on this account. The numerous legacies that they received make it clear that their right to own property was taken for granted.[48] Such legacies would have been made contingent on the right of enjoyment if there had been any chance that they might be taken by the masters. That testators with firsthand knowledge of slavery did not take this obvious legal precaution is convincing evidence that it was not necessary. Sometimes the slaves themselves made wills leaving their possessions to relatives and friends.[49]

Racial boundaries were blurred somewhat by numerous sexual attachments between whites and blacks. In New England, where white males were outnumbered by their women, the latter not only found sexual compensation with black men but in some cases legitimated the relationship by marriage.[50] Although the shortage of white men was less marked in the Middle colonies,

44. "N.Y. Abstracts of Wills," VII, 129, 380–81, 407; IX, 72; XII, 155–57; XIV, 1–3; XV, 112–13.
45. Josiah Quincy, Jr., *Reports of Cases Argued and Adjudged in the Superior Court of Judicature of the Province of the Massachusetts Bay Between 1761 and 1772* (Boston: Little, Brown, 1865), p. 31n.
46. John Cox, ed., *Oyster Bay Town Records*, 2 vols. (New York: Tobias A. Wright, 1916–24), II, 453.
47. Nathan Dane, *A General Abridgement and Digest of American Law with Occasional Notes and Comments*, 9 vols. (Boston: Cummings, Hilliard, 1823–29), II, 313.
48. Dow, *Essex County Court Recs.*, VIII, 434; *Early Records of Providence*, V, 278–79. "N.Y. Abstracts of Wills," VII, 380–81, IX, 9, XV, 127–28. *Documents Relating to the Colonial, Revolutionary and Post-Revolutionary History of the State of New Jersey*, 42 vols. (Newark: New Jersey Historical Society, 1900–49), XXIII, 14; XXIV, 251; hereafter cited as *N.J. Archives* (binder's title).
49. Register of Manumissions, p. 87, MS. coll., MCNY.
50. "Letters and Documents Relating to Slavery in Massachusetts," in MHS *Colls.*, 5th ser, III (1877), 386; Evarts B. Greene and Virginia D. Harrington,

there were numerous cases of cohabitation and marriage between white women and blacks.[51] But sexual relations between the races more often involved men of the master class, for the defenseless condition of slave women invited exploitation. Visible evidence of such contacts can be seen in the emergence everywhere of large numbers of racially mixed slaves.[52] By the early eighteenth century both Massachusetts and Connecticut officially recognized mulattoes as a separate category of identification.[53]

The growth of a racially mixed population caused much alarm, for it threatened and confused the premises of the white hegemony. Unless the color barrier could be held, it would be difficult to sort people out on the basis of pigmentation. Therefore the most stringent moral and social pressures were exerted to preserve racial purity. Anne Grant reported that white New Yorkers believed that nature had drawn a line between the races "which it was in a high degree criminal and disgraceful to pass; they considered a mixture of such distinct races with abhorrence, as a violation of her laws."[54] The New England colonies enforced their laws against fornication and bastardy with special rigor in interracial cases. White men were flogged for forming liaisons with black women, and many were compelled to pay for the support of their mulatto offspring.[55]

Both Massachusetts and Pennsylvania passed stringent laws against miscegenation. The Massachusetts statute, enacted "for the better preventing of a spurious and mixt issue," prohibited marriage or sexual relations between the races. Any Negro guilty

American Population before the Federal Census of 1790 (New York: Columbia University Press, 1932), pp. 46, 61.

51. Berthold Fernow, ed., *Records of New Amsterdam, 1653–1674,* 7 vols. (New York: The Knickerbocker Press, 1897), VII, 11; Turner, *The Negro in Pennsylvania,* pp. 29–31.

52. Greene and Harrington, *American Population before the Federal Census of 1790,* pp. 16, 70; Greene, *The Negro in Colonial New England,* p. 210; Turner, *The Negro in Pennsylvania,* p. 31.

53. *Mass. Acts and Resolves,* I, 156; *Conn. Col. Recs.,* IV, 40. See Winthrop D. Jordan, "American Chiaroscuro: The Status and Definition of Mulattoes in the British Colonies," *WMQ,* 3d ser., XXIX (1962), 183–200.

54. Anne Grant, *Memoirs of an American Lady,* 2 vols. (New York: Dodd, Mead, 1901), I, 85.

55. Morison, "Suffolk County Court Recs.," I, 185, 232; Dow, *Essex County Court Recs.,* VII, 410.

of fornication with a white woman was to be sold out of the province, both were to be flogged, and the woman bound out to service to support any children resulting from the affair. In the case of a white man and black woman, both were to be flogged; the man in addition was to be fined £5 and held liable for the support of any children, and the woman was to be sold out of the province.[56] Since the statute made no distinction between slaves and free blacks, the latter suffered additional punishment in the loss of their freedom when they were sold out of the colony. Pennsylvania Negroes incurred similar penalties for crossing the racial line. A law passed in 1726 provided that free blacks guilty of sexual relations with whites were to be sold as servants for seven years. Any Negro who married a white person was to be sold as a "slave during life," and the minister or magistrate who performed the marriage was to be punished by a £100 fine.[57]

Racial intermixture ran counter to Puritan concepts of sexual morality. The Massachusetts statute banishing blacks guilty of such relationships was more severe than that of any other continental colony. Next to death or mutilation, it was the punishment most feared by slaves, since it usually meant transportation to the West Indies.[58] Although the other New England colonies did not expressly prohibit miscegenation, stringent enforcement of the ordinary laws against fornication had the same effect. Moreover, blacks who crossed the color line had to be wary of brutal elements in the white population. In 1718 a Connecticut Negro discovered with a white woman was castrated by the white who found them together. Reporting the incident, the March 3, 1718, edition of the *Boston News Letter* noted approvingly that "the Black, now an eunuch, is . . . doubtless cured from any more such wicked attempts."

Puritan antipathy for miscegenation partly reflected a religious bias that blacks belonged to an inferior race. Some New Englanders gave the Calvinist doctrine of election a sociobiological interpretation and argued that Negroes were an accursed people condemned by God to serve the whites. John Saffin, a Negrophobic

56. *Mass. Acts and Resolves*, I, 578.
57. *Pa. Stat. at L.*, IV, 62–63.
58. Greene, *The Negro in Colonial New England*, pp. 208–209.

bigot, declared that God had ordained "different degrees and orders of men, some to be high and honorable, some to be low and despicable."[59] He derogated all blacks as "the spume issue of ingratitude" and argued forcefully that nature had marked them for bondage.[60] Even Cotton Mather, whose racial views were more enlightened, regarded Negroes as the "miserable children of Adam and Noah" relegated to slavery as a punishment for sin.[61]

The derogation of Negroes was so explicit among Puritans that racial intermixture equated with contamination. Richard Baxter, an otherwise generous man who admonished his coreligionists to remember that their slaves had souls, nevertheless concluded that "their sin have enslaved them to you."[62] Thus status and pigmentation easily fused in the Puritan mind as secular manifestations of God's will. Not only did miscegenation weaken such attempts to rationalize slavery, but it also threatened the purity of God's white elect. If racial barriers broke down completely, whites too would be degraded by the blood of the inferior race. As late as 1773 a Massachusetts resident publicly defended slavery on the grounds that the black was "a conglomerate of child, idiot, and madman."[63]

Puritan abhorrence of racial intermixture led to efforts to make slave families more cohesive. In 1705 Massachusetts forbade any master to "deny marriage to his Negro with one of the same nation, any law, usage or custom to the contrary notwithstanding."[64] Slaves were encouraged to regularize their marital ties in the way prescribed for the rest of the population. The consent of both parties was needed, and the marriage bans had to be read or posted in a public place.[65] The masters of course had to be con-

59. John Saffin, *A Brief and Candid Answer to a Late Printed Sheet Entitled the Selling of Joseph* (Boston, 1701), pp. 1–2. See Milton Cantor, "The Image of the Negro in Colonial Literature," *NEQ*, XXXVI (1963), 471.
60. Saffin, *A Brief and Candid Answer*, pp. 4–5. See Moore, *Notes on the History of Slavery in Massachusetts*, p. 256.
61. Cotton Mather, *The Negro Christianized* (Boston, 1706), pp. 2, 5–8.
62. Quoted in Winthrop D. Jordan, *White over Black* (Chapel Hill: University of North Carolina Press, 1968), p. 22.
63. *A Forensic Dispute on the Legality of Enslaving the Africans, by Two Candidates for the Bachelors Degree* (Boston, 1773), p. 28, cited in Greene, *The Negro in Colonial New England*, p. 285.
64. *Mass. Acts and Resolves*, I, 578.
65. George E. Howard, *A History of Matrimonial Institutions*, 3 vols. (Chicago:

sulted because the marriage could not take place if the owner of either party raised reasonable objections.[66] The same procedure applied to free Negroes who wished to marry slaves, for only then could they be reasonably certain that the relationship would not be disrupted.[67]

That New England's leading clergymen and magistrates often officiated at these marriages attests to the importance of the institution in the Puritan scheme of things. Samuel Sewall, Cotton Mather, and Ezra Stiles joined slaves in marriage with the same solemnity the occasion demanded in the case of whites.[68] Moreover, the marital ties bound slaves to the same moral code as whites: they were expected to be faithful to their spouses and to care for their families.[69] The idea that monogamy might not be compatible with slavery was piously ignored. In 1742 Massachusetts granted a divorce to a slave whose wife had been found guilty of "the detestable sin of adultery."[70] The court records abound with the cases of slaves charged with extramarital sexual relations.[71] Both men and women were flogged for such offenses, and in cases of bastardy the men were ordered to support the illegitimate offspring.[72]

Every colony had laws to guarantee white supremacy. There were statutes that subjected blacks to special police controls, disqualified them as witnesses against whites, and recognized the

University of Chicago Press, 1904), II, 145–47; Arthur W. Calhoun, A Social History of the American Family from Colonial Times to the Present, 3 vols. (Cleveland: Clark, 1917–19), I, 59; Joseph B. Felt, The Ecclesiastical History of New England, 2 vols. (Boston: Congregational Library Association, 1862), I, 387.

66. "Diary of Samuel Sewall, 1674–1729," in MHS Colls., 5th ser., V–VII (3 vols., 1878–82), II, 22.

67. Buck Bebee to Samuel Vernon, April 11, 1782, Box 43, Folder 4, MS. coll., NHS.

68. A Report of the Record Commissioners of the City of Boston, 39 vols. (Boston: Rockwell & Churchill, 1881–1909), XXVIII, 2, 5, 29; hereafter cited as Registry Dept. Recs. of Boston (binder's title).

69. Greene, The Negro in Colonial New England, pp. 192–93, 195–96.

70. Massachusetts Archives, IX, 248–50, MS. coll., MSL.

71. Dow, Essex County Court Recs., I, 196, 287; II, 247; V, 316, 409; VI, 73, 135–38, 205; VII, 411, 419–20. Morison, "Suffolk County Court Recs.," II, 233, 809, 841. In Maryland, by way of contrast, Attorney General Daniel Dulany ruled that "a slave is not admonished for incontinence, or punished for fornication or adultery; never prosecuted for bigamy." Thomas Harris, Jr., and John McHenry, eds., Maryland Reports, 3 vols. (New York: Riley, 1809–13), I, 563.

72. Thornbrough, "Negro Slavery in the North," p. 49.

complete power of the masters over them.[73] Some of these laws imposed harsh disabilities on free Negroes. New York excluded freedmen from owning real estate or possessing "any houses, lands, tenements or hereditaments" under penalty of forfeiture.[74] A similar law in New Jersey deprived free blacks of the right to own land, thus making them dependent upon whites for their livelihood.[75] Pennsylvania went furthest in legislating economic dependency by prescribing reenslavement "if any free Negro fit and able to work shall neglect to do so."[76]

The legal status of blacks was somewhat better in New England. All the Puritan colonies were profoundly affected by the biblical idea that the slave was part of the master's family.[77] Connecticut's first statute relating to slavery quoted a passage from *Exodus* on man-stealing.[78] The Massachusetts law of 1641 specifically provided that slaves should "have all the liberties and Christian usages which the law of God, established in Israel concerning such persons, doth morally require."[79] No distinction was made between free persons and slaves in the prosecution of serious crimes.[80] Moreover, the testimony of Negroes against whites was accepted by the courts in both civil and criminal cases.[81] In 1679 the testimony of a Massachusetts Negro played a prominent role in the indictment of a white for witchcraft.[82] That the testimony of a black could put a white person in such jeopardy is striking evidence of the acceptability of Negro testimony in the courts.

73. "Proceedings of the General Court of Assizes, 1680–1682," in NYHS *Colls.*, XLV (1912), 37–38; *N.Y. Col. Laws*, I, 519–21, 597–98, 617–18, 631; *Pa. Stat. at L.*, II, 56, 77–78; *Mass. Acts and Resolves*, I, 154, 156; *Conn. Col. Recs.*, I, 349; *R.I. Col. Recs.*, III, 492–93.
74. *N.Y. Col. Laws*, I, 764–65.
75. Nevill, *N.J. General Assembly Acts*, I, 23.
76. *Pa. Stat. at L.*, IV, 61–62.
77. Greene, *The Negro in Colonial New England*, pp. 167–69.
78. Bernard Steiner, *History of Slavery in Connecticut* (Baltimore: The John Hopkins Press, 1893), pp. 11–12.
79. Hurd, *The Law of Freedom and Bondage*, I, 260. One hundred and thirty years later, Chief Justice Thomas Hutchinson observed: "A slave here is considered as a servant would be who had bound himself for a term of years exceeding the ordinary term of human life." Quincy, *Mass. Superior Court of Judicature Reports*, p. 31n.
80. Thornbrough, "Negro Slavery in the North," p. 40.
81. Dow, *Essex County Court Recs.*, III, 101; V, 179–80. Morison, "Suffolk County Court Recs.," II, 809, 1164.
82. Dow, *Essex County Court Recs.*, V, 329–30.

All the colonies were understandably reluctant to allow blacks to bear arms. An armed Negro was such a dangerous anomaly that stringent restrictions were placed on the possession of weapons by anyone but whites. New Jersey allowed slaves to carry firearms only in the company of their masters, and violators were subject to flogging.[83] A similar law in Pennsylvania forbade any Negro to carry a pistol, club, or musket under penalty of twenty-one lashes.[84] New York slaves were forbidden to use firearms of any sort except under the direction of the master.[85] Most of the towns and counties had special local provisions for keeping the Negroes disarmed. Boston provided that blacks might not carry any stick or cane "fit for quarreling or fighting with or any other thing of that nature."[86] Both New York City and Albany prescribed flogging for slaves who brought weapons within the city limits.[87] Westchester County provided that slaves carrying guns or staffs "when out of their masters' plantations" were to be flogged at the discretion of the magistrates.[88]

The colonial militia laws invariably excluded Negroes from military training. Except during wartime, when manpower of any color was needed, the training of blacks in the martial arts was regarded as an invitation to disaster.[89] In 1656 Massachusetts set the pattern by providing that "henceforth no Negroes or Indians . . . shall be armed or permitted to train."[90] Connecticut and New Hampshire enacted similar exclusions, and Rhode Island, though not barring Negroes completely, used them as watchers and look-

83. Leaming and Spicer, *N.J. Grants, Concessions, and Constitutions*, p. 341; Nevill, *N.J. General Assembly Acts*, I, 444.

84. *Pa. Stat. at L.*, II, 79.

85. *N.Y. Col. Laws*, I, 766.

86. *Registry Dept. Recs. of Boston*, VIII, 224–25.

87. Joel Munsell, ed., *Annals of Albany*, 10 vols. (Albany: Munsell, 1859), VIII, 296; *Minutes of the Common Council of the City of New York, 1675–1776*, 8 vols. (New York: Dodd, Mead, 1905), I, 134, hereafter cited as *N.Y. City Council Min.*

88. Dixon Ryan Fox, ed., *Minutes of the Court of Sessions, 1657–1696, Westchester County* (White Plains, N.Y.: Westchester County Historical Society, 1924), pp. 66–67.

89. Benjamin Quarles, "The Colonial Militia and Negro Manpower," *MVHR*, XLV (1959), 643–44, 648–52.

90. *Mass. Bay Recs.*, III, 397. This reversed the policy of an earlier militia law in 1652 that allowed "Negroes and Indians inhabiting with or servants to the English" to be enrolled for military service; *ibid.*, p. 268.

outs rather than as regular troops.[91] New York provided that nothing in the militia law "shall be construed or taken to allow or give liberty to any Negro . . . to be listed or to do any duty in the militia of this province."[92] No special racial distinctions were made in New Jersey, but the law specified that neither slaves nor servants might enlist without their master's consent.[93] Pennsylvania followed the same policy, except that the Delaware counties categorically forbade Negroes to bear arms "upon any pretense whatsoever."[94]

Blacks barred from military training were sometimes required to perform unarmed militia service. New York allowed the enlistment of blacks as "trumpeters and drummers, if capable, and to work as pioneers and not otherwise." The "not otherwise" proviso specifically excluded combat training for Negro recruits. Another New York law provided that during public emergencies every slaveholder should provide one slave for services to be determined by the local militia commander.[95] Rhode Island specifically required limited duty from blacks as lookouts, and New Hampshire did the same indirectly by omitting them from the list of persons "exempted from military watches and wardings."[96]

Some colonies preferred general labor to unarmed militia service. In 1707 Massachusetts required "free Negroes and mulattoes . . . who are not charged with trainings, watchings and other services" to work at repairing and cleaning the streets.[97] The selectmen of Boston specifically ordered Negroes to perform labor "equivalent to the service of trainings, watchings and other duty required of the rest of his Majesty's subjects."[98] Blacks also had to report to the parade grounds to be formed into labor companies

91. *Conn. Col. Recs.*, I, 349. *R.I. Col. Recs.*, II, 536. *Acts and Laws, Passed by the General Court or Assembly of His Majesty's Province of New Hampshire in New-England* [1696–1725] (Boston: Green, 1726), p. 93; hereafter cited as *N.H. General Court Acts.*

92. *N.Y. Col. Laws*, I, 506.

93. Nevill, *N.J. General Assembly Acts*, II, 267.

94. *Pa. Stat. at L.*, V, 200; *Laws of the Government of New-Castle, Kent, and Sussex upon Delaware* (Philadelphia, 1741–42), p. 178. See Quarles, "The Colonial Militia and Negro Manpower," *MVHR*, XLV (1959), 647–48.

95. *N.Y. Col. Laws*, II, 91; III, 526–27.

96. *R.I. Col. Recs.*, II, 536; *N.H. General Court Acts*, p. 93. Cited in Quarles, "The Colonial Militia and Negro Manpower," *MVHR*, XLV (1959), 647.

97. *Mass. Acts and Resolves*, I, 606–607.

98. *Registry Dept. Recs. of Boston*, XIX, 240.

whenever an emergency required the militia to assemble. Failure to report for ordinary labor was punishable at the rate of five shillings a day, and the penalty was four times greater for not reporting at the parade grounds during an emergency.[99]

All in all, colonial law gave free Negroes a status somewhat higher than that of slaves but decidedly lower than that of free whites. No matter what a Negro did he could never escape the legal disabilites of race. Whether it had to do with his standing as a witness or with his eligibility for militia duty, he was never fully free in the sense that whites were free. While whites turned out for military training, a privilege as much as an obligation in colonial times, blacks were relegated to cleaning and repairing the highways.[100] This sort of racial derogation was as much a part of slavery as the buying and selling of slaves. It served as a constant reminder that so long as some blacks remained slaves no black could be really free.

99. *Mass. Acts and Resolves,* I, 606–607.
100. Thornbrough, "Negro Slavery in the North," pp. 73–74.

5

The Law and Order of Slavery

The management and control of slaves required a large body of repressive legislation. By the early eighteenth century every colony had special laws, judicial procedures, and punishments for the regulation of blacks.[1] Slavery could not have existed very long without this network of controls, for blacks every-

1. *Colonial Laws of New York from 1664 to the Revolution,* 5 vols. (Albany: Lyon, 1894), I, 519–21, 582–84, 598, 765–66. E. B. O'Callaghan and Berthold Fernow, eds., *Documents Relative to the Colonial History of the State of New York,* 15 vols. (Albany: Weed, Parsons, 1856–87), V, 157. James T. Mitchell and Henry Flanders, comps., *The Statutes at Large of Pennsylvania from 1682–1801,* 16 vols. (Harrisburg: State Printer, 1896–1911), II, 56, 77–78, 112; III, 250; IV, 59–64. Samuel Hazard, ed., *Colonial Records of Pennsylvania,* 16 vols. (Philadelphia: Severns, 1852), II, 112. Aaron Leaming and Jacob Spicer, eds., *The Grants, Concessions and Original Constitutions of the Province of New Jersey* (Somerville, N.J.: Honeyman, 1881), pp. 340, 356–57, 642. Samuel Nevill, comp., *The Acts of the General Assembly of the Province of New Jersey,* 2 vols. (Philadelphia and Woodbridge, N.J., 1752–61), I, 18–22. *Acts and Resolves, Public and Private, of the Province of the Massachusetts Bay,* 5 vols. (Boston: Wright & Potter, 1869–86), I, 154, 156, 325, 535–36, 578. J. Hammond Trumbull and Charles J. Hoadly, eds., *The Public Records of the Colony of Connecticut, 1636–1776,* 15 vols. (Hartford: Lockwood & Brainard, 1850–90), I, 349; IV, 40; V, 52. *Charter and the Acts and Laws of His Majesty's Colony of Rhode Island and Providence Plantations in America* (Providence: Sidney & Burnett Rider, 1858), pp. 101–102. John R. Bartlett, ed., *Records of the Colony of Rhode Island and Providence Plantations in New England, 1636–1792,* 10 vols. (Providence: Greene, 1856–65), III, 492–93; IV, 179; V, 52–53. *Acts and Laws of His Majesty's Province of New Hampshire in New England with Sundry Acts of Parliament* (Portsmouth: Daniel & Robert Fowle, 1771), pp. 39–40. *Acts and Laws, Passed by the General Court or Assembly of His Majesty's Province of New Hampshire in New England* [1696–1725] (Boston: Green, 1726), p. 57. Hereafter cited as *N.Y. Col. Laws, N.Y. Col. Docs., Pa. Stat. at L., Pa. Col. Recs., Mass. Acts and Resolves, Conn. Col. Recs., R. I. Charter, Acts, and Laws, R.I. Col. Recs., N.H. Acts and Laws,* and *N.H. General Court Acts.*

where hated and resisted the system. Some tried to escape by malingering or running away, and others sought a way out by working at odd jobs in order to buy their freedom. But whatever form
their resistance took, the bondsmen made it clear that they placed
a high value on liberty. Nothing could conceal the fact that only
the most stringent controls prevented them from breaking their
bonds and shattering the white hegemony.

Slave controls severely restricted the movement of the Negroes. Connecticut required blacks to be off the streets by nine
at night and to remain within the towns to which they belonged.
Any slave found wandering about without a pass was to be arrested as a runaway, and the cost of his detention was to be paid
by his owner. In addition, curfew violators were to be punished
by flogging.[2] Massachusetts prescribed flogging for slaves found
in the streets at night, and slaves who absented themselves from
their master's household without permission received the same
punishment.[3] Rhode Island's curfew applied to free Negroes as
well as slaves, and the law authorized the constables to punish
chronic offenders with unlimited flogging.[4] New Hampshire had
a statute "to prevent disorders at night" that prescribed ten lashes
for slaves who ventured out after dark or who disturbed the public peace at any time.[5]

The Middle colonies enacted the most sweeping restraints on
slave mobility. New York made it a misdemeanor, punishable by
flogging, for more than four slaves to meet unless on some business of their masters.[6] The number of slaves allowed to meet together was later reduced to three, and, to insure enforcement,
very town was required to have a "Negro whipper" to punish offenders.[7] These measures were supplemented by local ordinances
designed to keep blacks immobile and isolated. New York City
forbade slaves to gamble, and slaves over the age of fourteen had

2. *Conn. Col. Recs.*, IV, 40; V, 534.
3. *Mass. Acts and Resolves*, I, 535–36.
4. *R.I. Col. Recs.*, III, 492; *Acts and Laws of His Majesty's Colony of Rhode
Island and Providence Plantations in America* (Newport: James Franklin, 1730),
p. 50, hereafter cited as *R.I. Acts and Laws.*
5. *N.H. Acts and Laws*, p. 52.
6. "Proceedings of the General Court of Assizes, 1680–1682," in NYHS *Colls.*,
XLV (1912), 37–38.
7. *N.Y. Col. Laws*, I, 519–21.

to be off the streets by sunset unless accompanied by a member of the master's family.[8] Kingston provided that any "above the number of three Negroes found together upon the Lord's Day or at any unreasonable hours . . . shall be publicly whipped or the master pay a fine of 8 shillings."[9] Slaves in Westchester County were forbidden to hunt, and at Smithtown, Long Island, they could not travel more than a mile from home without a pass.[10]

Slave controls in Pennsylvania and New Jersey were equally repressive. Pennsylvania forbade blacks to travel more than ten miles from home without a pass, to gather in groups of more than four, or to venture on the streets at night.[11] Philadelphia directed its constables to arrest Negroes found in the streets on Sunday unless they had a pass from their owners. Offenders were to be punished with thirty-nine lashes, and the costs of detention and flogging were to be assessed against their masters.[12] New Jersey forbade slaves to carry firearms, and anyone giving or lending such weapons to a slave was liable for a fine of twenty shillings. Slaves were forbidden to meet on their own time, to appear in the streets at night, or to hunt unless accompanied by their masters.[13]

How well these measures worked depended on the cooperation of the masters. The law recognized this and made slaveholders legally accountable for their bondsmen. Pennsylvania followed the rule that slaves violating any local ordinance were to be flogged and their owners fined for each offense.[14] New Jersey slaves guilty of stealing were to be flogged, and the costs of arrest and detention were charged against their masters.[15] New York

8. *Minutes of the Common Council of the City of New York, 1675–1776*, 8 vols. (New York: Dodd, Mead, 1905), III, 277–78, hereafter cited as *N.Y. City Council Min.*

9. Ulster County Court of Sessions, Kingston, September 3, 4, 1695, HDC, QC.

10. Dixon Ryan Fox, ed., *Minutes of the Court of Sessions, 1657–1696, Westchester County* (White Plains, N.Y.: Westchester County Historical Society, 1924), pp. 66–67; William S. Pelletreau, ed., *Records of the Town of Smithtown* (Huntington, N.Y.: Long Islander Print, 1898), p. 170.

11. *Pa. Stat. at L.*, II, 56, 77–79; IV, 59–64.

12. *Pa. Col. Recs.*, I, 380–81.

13. Leaming and Spicer, *N.J. Grants, Concessions, and Constitutions*, pp. 340–42; Samuel Allinson, comp., *Acts of the General Assembly of the Province of New Jersey* (Burlington, N.J.: Isaac Collins, 1776), pp. 191–92.

14. *Pa. Stat. at L.*, VI, 68.

15. Allinson, *N.J. General Assembly Acts*, pp. 19–20.

provided that masters who failed to report slave offenses were themselves guilty of an offense punishable by a fine.[16] Connecticut held the owners liable for court costs arising from any sort of slave misconduct. A statute passed in 1730 provided that slaves guilty of "speaking defamatory words" were to be arrested, flogged, and then sold at auction "to defray all charges arising thereupon."[17]

Every colony had stringent laws against the sale of liquor to slaves. The Rhode Island statute noted that by selling them strong drink "slaves are induced and tempted to pilfer and steal from their masters."[18] Pennsylvania forbade Negroes to enter public "tippling-houses" under penalty of a whipping for the slave and a fine for the proprietor.[19] A Connecticut law of 1703 prohibited any licensed innkeeper to allow Negroes "to sit drinking in his house, or have any manner of drink there." Violators were to be fined ten shillings or punished with flogging at the discretion of the justice of the peace.[20] In New York, any tavernkeeper guilty of serving slaves was to be deprived of his license for three years.[21] To facilitate enforcement of its anti-drinking statute New Jersey provided that "one creditable witness or a probable circumstance" should be "sufficient evidence" to convict offenders.[22] Rhode Island encouraged spying in such cases by allotting one-half of the heavy fine of £30 to the informer who reported the violation.[23]

The slave controls strictly forbade trading with the slaves without the consent of their masters. Such trade encouraged stealing and pilferage, undermined discipline, and promoted criminal associations. Persons receiving goods stolen by slaves not only had to make restitution, sometimes with double and treble dam-

16. "Proceedings of the General Court of Assizes," pp. 37–38; N.Y. Col. Laws, I, 519–21.

17. John C. Hurd, The Law of Freedom and Bondage in the United States, 2 vols. (Boston: Little, Brown, 1858–62), I, 272.

18. Acts and Laws of His Majesty's Colony of Rhode Island and Providence Plantations in New England from 1745 to 1752 (Newport, 1752), pp. 92–93, hereafter cited as R.I. Acts and Laws, 1745–1752.

19. Pa. Stat. at L., IV, 59–64.

20. Conn. Col. Recs., IV, 437–38.

21. N.Y. Col. Laws, V, 584.

22. Leaming and Spicer, N.J. Grants, Concessions, and Constitutions, p. 512.

23. R.I. Acts and Laws, 1745–1752, pp. 92–93.

ages, but in some cases were punished by flogging.[24] Connecticut had a statute against persons who "for the sake of filthy lucre do receive property stolen by slaves," and provided that anyone guilty of the crime should be sold into servitude in order to indemnify the owner.[25] New York made failure to report violations a misdemeanor, and subjected the masters to a fine for failure to report persons who traded illegally with their slaves.[26] New Jersey required anyone to whom stolen goods were offered to detain and whip the slave, for which service the master was to pay a reward of half a crown.[27] Some courts held that the mere act of dealing with a slave was evidence of criminal intent unless it could be proved that the master had in fact consented to the transaction.[28]

Slave law dealt harshly with whites who intrigued with slaves against the interests of their masters. Thus the hiring of a slave without his owner's consent was strictly forbidden in order to prevent him from being enticed away from his regular duties.[29] Even more serious was the outright theft of slaves by "Negro jockeys" who exported them for sale to other colonies. Massachusetts forbade any ship to carry slaves out of the province without a permit from the governor.[30] Rhode Island made it a misdemeanor for ferrymen to "carry, convey or transport any slave" without a pass.[31] Some owners offered larger rewards for the arrest of the slave stealer than for the return of the slave.[32] Often a slave would be persuaded to run away by a white accomplice who, pretending to be his owner, would sell him in some other place. Slaves could be enticed into such schemes by a promise of

24. *Mass. Acts and Resolves*, I, 156, 325. *Conn. Col. Recs.*, V, 52. *R.I. Charter, Acts, and Laws*, pp. 101–102. *N.H. Acts and Laws*, pp. 39–40. *N.Y. Col. Laws*, I, 519–21; II, 310, 679. Allinson, *N.J. General Assembly Acts*, p. 18. Nevill, *N.J. General Assembly Acts*, I, 242. *Charter to William Penn and Laws of the Province of Pennsylvania Passed 1682–1700* (Harrisburg: Hart, 1879), p. 153; hereafter cited as *Pa. Charter and Laws, 1682–1700*.

25. *Conn. Col. Recs.*, V, 52.

26. *N.Y. Col. Laws*, I, 519–21.

27. Leaming and Spicer, *N.J. Grants, Concessions, and Constitutions*, p. 254.

28. Ulster County Court of Sessions, Kingston, September 7, 8, 1693; September 1, 2, 1698, HDC, QC.

29. *N.Y. City Council Min.*, IV, 85.

30. William H. Whitmore, ed., *The Colonial Laws of Massachusetts* [1672–86] (Boston: Rockwell & Churchill, 1890), p. 281, hereafter cited as *Mass. Col. Laws* [1672–86].

31. *R.I. Charter, Acts, and Laws*, pp. 70–71.

32. *New York Weekly Mercury*, September 22, 1777; August 24, 1778.

eventual freedom and a share of the money collected from the sale.[33] Since the pattern could be repeated many times, the original crime was frequently compounded at the expense of several buyers.

But far more serious than the white offenses regarding slavery were the crimes committed by the slaves themselves. Stealing of course was the most common slave crime and the one most frequently directed against the masters.[34] Even seemingly trustworthy slaves surprised their owners by helping themselves to cash and goods.[35] The hunting restrictions imposed by every colony were partly designed to prevent slaves from stealing stray farm animals. In New Jersey, slaves were not allowed to keep traps without the owner's mark of identification, and whites were not permitted to give or lend such equipment to a slave without his master's consent.[36] Slaves living in New York's Westchester County were forbidden to have "any gun, dog, or staff" when away from home.[37] Pennsylvania slaves were liable to a punishment of twenty-one lashes for carrying firearms without the master's permission.[38] Laws were also passed to prevent slaves from intermingling stolen animals with their own livestock.[39] A Boston ordinance forbade slaves to keep "any hogs or swine whatsoever," and enjoined whites not to rent land to Negroes for the purpose of keeping livestock.[40]

The usual punishment for theft was flogging. In most of the New England colonies this could vary from twenty to thirty lashes for each offense.[41] Rhode Island, however, provided that slaves

33. *New York Weekly Post-Boy*, October 15, 1753. *New York Weekly Mercury*, November 2, 1772; September 22, 1777; August 24, December 21, 1778.

34. Lorenzo J. Greene, *The Negro in Colonial New England, 1620–1776* (New York: Columbia University Press, 1942), pp. 150–53; Henry S. Cooley, *A Study of Slavery in New Jersey* (Baltimore: The Johns Hopkins Press, 1896), pp. 35–36.

35. *New York Weekly Post-Boy*, April 15, 1762; Joel Munsell, ed., *Collections on the History of Albany*, 4 vols. (Albany: Munsell, 1865), II, 380–83.

36. Leaming and Spicer, *N.J. Grants, Concessions, and Constitutions*, pp. 340–42.

37. Fox, *Minutes of the Westchester Court of Sessions*, pp. 66–67.

38. *Pa. Stat. at L.*, II, 235–36.

39. Leaming and Spicer, *N.J. Grants, Concessions, and Constitutions*, p. 340.

40. *A Report of the Record Commissioners of the City of Boston*, 39 vols. (Boston: Rockwell & Churchill, 1881–1909), XIV, 96–97; hereafter cited as *Registry Dept. Recs. of Boston* (binder's title).

41. *Mass. Acts and Resolves*, I, 156, 325; *N.H. Acts and Laws*, pp. 39–40; *Conn. Col. Recs.*, V, 52.

convicted of stealing might be deported as well as flogged, and an appeal from the justices court was allowed only if the owner posted bond.[42] The Middle colonies prescribed even harsher penalties. New Jersey provided that thieves should be given forty lashes, and that the cost of flogging "be paid by the master or mistress of the slave."[43] Pennsylvania punished thefts valued at less than £5 by thirty-nine lashes; thefts of greater amounts were punished by whipping, branding on the forehead with a *T,* and by deportation.[44] New York prescribed both flogging and branding. In 1679 an Albany court ordered a slave to be flogged and then "branded on the right cheek as an example to other rogues."[45]

Although stealing cut deeply into profits, it was arson that caused the most fear and apprehension. Except for insurrection and murder, it was the most harshly punished of all crimes. In 1681 Massachusetts burned a slave at the stake for arson, a punishment not even imposed for witchcraft.[46] The usual penalty imposed in Pennsylvania and New York was death by hanging.[47] New Jersey permitted much more brutal punishments under a statute providing that slaves guilty of arson should suffer death in whatever way the "aggravation or enormity of their crime shall merit and require."[48] Thus in 1735 a Negro was burned at the stake in Bergen County for attempting to burn a house, and in 1741 two slaves were burned at Hackensack for setting fire to several barns.[49]

Slave control was most difficult in the towns, for it was there that daily contacts with every level of society left the slaves with few illusions about white superiority. Moreover, town life encour-

42. *R.I. Charter, Acts, and Laws,* pp. 101–102.

43. Nevill, *N.J. General Assembly Acts,* I, 22.

44. *Pa. Stat. at L.,* II, 235.

45. A. J. F. Van Laer, ed., *Minutes of the Court of Albany, Rensselaerswyck and Schenectady, 1668–1680,* 2 vols. (Albany: State University of New York, 1926–28), II, 430–36. See also E. B. O'Callaghan, ed., *Calendar of Historical Manuscripts in the Office of the Secretary of State,* 2 vols. (Albany: Weed, Parsons, 1866), II, 371. *New York Weekly Post-Boy,* February 4, 1744/45; October 28, 1751; January 29, 1767.

46. John B. Noble, ed., *Records of the Court of Assistants of the Colony of the Massachusetts Bay, 1630–1692,* 3 vols. (Boston: Pub. by Suffolk County, 1901–1908), I, 198–99; II, 100; hereafter cited as *Mass. Assistants Court Recs.*

47. *N.Y. Col. Laws,* I, 765; *Pa. Stat. at L.,* II, 79, 235.

48. Allinson, *N.J. General Assembly Acts,* p. 18.

49. Cooley, *Study of Slavery in New Jersey,* p. 40.

aged an aggressiveness among blacks totally inconsistent with their legal status. In 1696 a group of slaves assaulted Mayor Merritt of New York City when he ordered them to disperse, and one of Governor Cornbury's first impressions when he arrived a few years later was of the "great insolency" displayed by Negroes.[50] Slave disturbances were so common that the streets of most towns were not safe. Citing the frequent disorders in Philadelphia, a grand jury condemned "the great multitude of Negroes who commonly meet together in a riot and tumultuous manner."[51] In 1753 the Massachusetts General Court charged that Negroes continually disturbed the peace of Boston with "horrid profanity, impiety and gross immoralities."[52] Slave tumults in Elizabeth, New Jersey, were so common that in 1754 the assembly prescribed flogging for Negroes guilty of "any misdemeanor or rude or disorderly behavior."[53]

Keeping the peace in the towns was complicated by the fact that slaves could get together under the pretense of serving their masters. Such routine chores as going to a well for water or stabling horses could be used as a pretext for gathering in the streets in violation of the law.[54] Curfew violations became so common in Boston that petitions were sent to the general court for more stringent controls.[55] In 1741 Philadelphia's common council protested that the nightly gathering of slaves in the streets had resulted in "many disorders . . . against the peace and good government of this city."[56] New York City slaves broke the curfew repeatedly with pranks and drunken brawls.[57] Their reputation for

50. I. N. Phelps Stokes, ed., *The Iconography of Manhattan Island*, 6 vols. (New York: Dodd, 1915–28), IV, 397. W. Noel Sainsbury, *et. al.*, eds., *Calendar of State Papers: Colonial Series, America and West Indies*, 42 vols. (London: H.M.S.O., 1860–1953), XXI (1702–1703), 32; hereafter cited as *Cal. State Papers, Col.*

51. Edward R. Turner, *The Negro in Pennsylvania* (Washington, D.C.: The American Historical Association, 1911), pp. 32–33, 33n.

52. *Mass. Acts and Resolves*, III, 647–48.

53. Nevill, *N.J. General Assembly Acts*, II, 29.

54. Thomas F. De Voe, *The Market Book* (New York: the Author, 1862), pp. 265–66.

55. Justin Winsor, ed., *The Memorial History of Boston*, 3 vols. (Boston: Osgood, 1880–81), II, 355.

56. *Minutes of the Common Council of the City of Philadelphia, 1704–1776* (Philadelphia: Crissy & Markley, 1847), p. 405; hereafter cited as *Philadelphia Council Min.*

57. Daniel Parish, Transcripts of Material on Slavery in the Public Records

troublemaking led some towns on Long Island to pass ordinances forbidding them to enter without the consent of the local authorities.[58]

Many of these disorders began in the taverns and public houses patronized by slaves. Despite the stringent laws against entertaining slaves, many tavernkeepers found it profitable to accept their patronage. It was so profitable that some whites turned their homes into clandestine drinking places where slaves could meet and roister at any hour of the day or night.[59] These illegal drinking places and the low groggeries with which they competed undermined discipline and encouraged crime. Slaves who had no money of their own were tempted to steal in order to pay for the entertainment that they provided. New York's "tippling houses" drew the wrath of Lieutenant-Governor Colden, who found them invariably "destructive to the morals of servants and slaves."[60]

Every colony enacted stringent measures against the illegal drinking places.[61] Rhode Island provided that any householder who opened his premises to slaves for "dancing, gaming, or other diversion" was to be fined £50 and imprisoned for one month.[62] The penalty in Connecticut for entertaining slaves was 20 shillings, half of which went to the informer and the other half was used for the benefit of the town.[63] Pennsylvania passed a law "for suppressing idleness, drunkenness, and other debaucheries," which prescribed a flogging for "Negro tipplers" and a fine for their

Office in London (1695–1713), p. 3, MS. coll., NYHS; hereafter cited as Parish's Transcripts. See *New York Weekly Post-Boy*, February 10, 1763.

58. Henry R. Stiles, *A History of the City of Brooklyn*, 3 vols. (New York: Pub. by subscription, 1867–70), I, 208.

59. Ancient Records of Philadelphia, November 3, 1703, J. W. Wallace Manuscript Collection, HSP; Minutes of the General Quarter Sessions of the Peace (N.Y. Court of General Sessions), May 2, 1693, February 3, November 4, 1696, microfilm, HDC, QC. See Richard B. Morris, ed., *Select Cases of the Mayor's Court of New York City, 1674–1784* (Washington, D.C.: The American Historical Association, 1935), p. 745.

60. Charles Z. Lincoln, ed., *Messages from the Governors*, 11 vols. (Albany: James B. Lyon, 1909), I, 659–60.

61. *N.Y. Col. Laws*, I, 519–21. Leaming and Spicer, *N.J. Grants, Concessions, and Constitutions*, pp. 109, 512. *Pa. Stat. at L.*, IV, 59–64. *Mass. Acts and Resolves*, I, 154. *R.I. Acts and Laws, 1745–1752*, pp. 92–93. *N.H. Acts and Laws*, p. 52. *Acts and Laws Passed by the General Court or Assembly of His Majesty's Colony of Connecticut in New England* (New London: Green, 1729), p. 234; hereafter cited as *Conn. Acts and Laws*.

62. *R.I. Acts and Laws, 1745–1752*, p. 93.

63. *Conn. Acts and Laws*, p. 234.

Phillis Wheatley, brought from Africa as a child and purchased by John Wheatley of Boston, gained an international reputation as a poet before the age of twenty. *By permission of The New-York Historical Society, New York City*

A N

Evening THOUGHT.

SALVATION BY *CHRIST*,

W I T H

PENETENTIAL CRIES:

Composed by Jupiter Hammon, a Negro belonging to Mr Lloyd, of Queen's-Village, on Long-Island, the 25th of December, 1760.

SALVATION comes by Jesus Christ alone,
 The only Son of God ;
Redemption now to every one,
 That love his holy Word.
Dear Jesus we would fly to Thee,
 And leave off every Sin,
Thy tender Mercy well agree ;
 Salvation from our King.
Salvation comes now from the Lord,
 Our victorious King ;
His holy Name be well ador'd,
 Salvation surely bring.
Dear Jesus give thy Spirit now,
 Thy Grace to every Nation,
That han't the Lord to whom we bow,
 The Author of Salvation.
Dear Jesus unto Thee we cry,
 Give us thy Preparation ;
Turn not away thy tender Eye ;
 We seek thy true Salvation.
Salvation comes from God we know,
 The true and only One ;
It's well agreed and certain true,
 He gave his only Son.
Lord hear our penetential Cry :
 Salvation from above ;
It is the Lord that doth supply,
 With his Redeeming Love.
Dear Jesus by thy precious Blood,
 The World Redemption have :
Salvation comes now from the Lord,
 He being thy captive Slave.
Dear Jesus let the Nations cry,
 And all the People say,
Salvation comes from Christ on high,
 Haste on Tribunal Day.
We cry as Sinners to the Lord,
 Salvation to obtain ;
It is firmly fixt his holy Word,
 Ye shall not cry in vain.
Dear Jesus unto Thee we cry,
 And make our Lamentation :
O let our Prayers ascend on high ;
 We felt thy Salvation.

Lord turn our dark benighted Souls ;
 Give us a true Motion,
And let the Hearts of all the World,
 Make Christ their Salvation.
Ten Thousand Angels cry to Thee,
 Yea louder than the Ocean.
Thou art the Lord, we plainly see ;
 Thou art the true Salvation.
Now is the Day, excepted Time ;
 The Day of Salvation ;
Increase your Faith, do not repine :
 Awake ye every Nation.
Lord unto whom now shall we go,
 Or seek a safe Abode ;
Thou hast the Word Salvation too
 The only Son of God.
Ho ! every one that hunger hath,
 Or pineth after me,
Salvation be thy leading Staff,
 To set the Sinner free.
Dear Jesus unto Thee we fly ;
 Depart, depart from Sin,
Salvation doth at length supply,
 The Glory of our King.
Come ye Blessed of the Lord,
 Salvation gently given ;
O turn your Hearts, accept the Word,
 Your Souls are fit for Heaven.
Dear Jesus we now turn to Thee,
 Salvation to obtain ;
Our Hearts and Souls do meet again,
 To magnify thy Name.
Come holy Spirit, Heavenly Dove,
 The Object of our Care ;
Salvation doth increase our Love ;
 Our Hearts hath felt thy fear.
Now Glory be to God on High,
 Salvation high and low ;
And thus the Soul on Christ rely,
 To Heaven surely go.
Come Blessed Jesus, Heavenly Dove,
 Accept Repentance here ;
Salvation give, with tender Love ;
 Let us with Angels share.

F I N I S.

Slave burned at the stake in New York City after
the alleged Negro plot of 1741. A total of
thirty-six persons, including four whites, were
executed for complicity in the affair.
By permission of Three Lions, Inc., New York City

Earliest known published writing of a black American.
The religious intensity of the author, a New York slave,
indicates that the Protestant proselytizing effort
profoundly influenced some of the bondsmen.
By permission of The New-York Historical Society, New York City

November 20, 1836, Peter John Lee, a free black resident of Westchester County, New York, was kidnapped by four white men from New York City and sold into slavery. One of the kidnappers pretended that he wanted to shake hands with Lee while the others used the gag and chain. Many Northern blacks were seized in this manner and sold into Southern slavery. *Courtesy of the New York Public Library*

Schools accepting black children as students often became the targets of racist mobs. In the 1830s attacks on schools occurred at Canterbury, Connecticut; Canaan, New Hampshire; and Zanesville, Ohio. *Courtesy of the New York Public Library*

The death of Crispus Attucks, left foreground, while leading the American crowd against British troops in the Boston Massacre, 1770. *Courtesy of the New York Public Library*

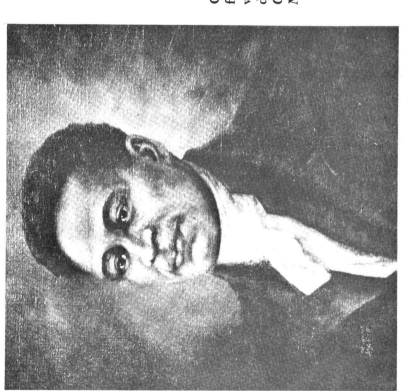

Crispus Attucks, a black sailor from Framingham, Massachusetts, was the first American to die in the Revolution.
Courtesy of the
New York Public Library

Peter Salem, a black militiaman, left, fatally wounding Major John Pitcairn, who led the British marines in the final assault at Bunker Hill, 1775. *Courtesy of the New York Public Library*

hosts.[64] New York imposed a fine of £2 on anyone who knowingly failed to report an illegal drinking place to the authorities.[65] These places were described in the August 9, 1742 edition of the *New York Weekly Journal* as "the principal bane and pest of the city."

Slave control in the towns required special local ordinances to supplement the general laws. Boston slaves "except such as are lame or crippled," were forbidden to carry any sticks or implements that might be used for fighting.[66] Any Negro found guilty of breaking street lights was to be punished by ten lashes for the first offense and twenty for subsequent offenses.[67] New York City prescribed twenty lashes for slaves "playing or making any hooting or disorderly noise" in the streets.[68] Both New York and Philadelphia had special slave patrols to prevent curfew violations. Philadelphia punished slaves found in the streets at night by twenty-one lashes and three days at hard labor in the public workhouse.[69] Any impudence or gesture of rebellion could bring harsh reprisals. For insulting a white New Yorker in 1736, a slave girl was sentenced to be tied to a cart "and carried round some of the wards of this city and receive on the naked back thirty-nine lashes."[70]

Stamping out illegal gatherings had the highest priority of all. New York's slave control law of 1702 was specifically directed against "slaves in the City of New York and Albany and also in other towns . . . guilty of confederating together."[71] The gathering of more than three slaves was outlawed in New York and Albany, and in Kingston the meeting of more than two was illegal.[72] Anything that brought slaves together, particularly at night,

64. *Pa. Stat. at L.*, V, 109–110.
65. *N.Y. Col. Laws*, I, 762–64.
66. *Registry Dept. Recs. of Boston*, VIII, 224–25.
67. *Mass. Acts and Resolves*, III, 645–46.
68. *N.Y. City Council Min.*, I, 276.
69. *Calendar of Council Minutes, 1668–1783* (Albany: State University of New York, 1902), p. 435; *Pa. Stat. at L.*, V, 241–42.
70. Minutes of the General Quarter Sessions of the Peace, February 1, 1736, HDC, QC.
71. *N.Y. Col. Laws*, I, 519–21.
72. *N.Y. City Council Min.*, II, 102; Joel Munsell, ed., *Annals of Albany*, 10 vols. (Albany: Munsell, 1859), VIII, 296. See Edwin Olson, "The Slave Code in Colonial New York," *JNH*, XXIX (1944), 155.

alarmed the authorities. Slaves could not be buried after dark in New York City, nor could more than ten of them assemble for a burial.[73] Philadelphia ordered the constables to disperse any slaves found in the streets more than half an hour after sunset.[74] Implicit in all these measures was the assumption that private discipline was dangerously lax. Boston specifically forbade slaves to remain on the town common at night, even though they had their master's permission to be there.[75]

The hallmark of all slave law was a double standard of justice that kept blacks in subjection to whites. Minor offenses punishable by fine or imprisonment when committed by whites were punished by flogging if the offender happened to be a slave.[76] Since a slave had no freedom and little or no property, some form of corporal punishment had to be imposed regardless of the seriousness of the offense. Frequently summary punishments were meted out by the police without judicial supervision. Rhode Island gave local constables discretion to flog slaves for "incorrigible behavior."[77] Newspaper reports reveal that in New York City drunk or disorderly slaves were dunked in the harbor or forced to swallow "a plentiful dose" of salt water and lamp oil.[78] When such "a plentiful dose" proved fatal to one slave in 1772, no charges were brought against the sheriff. According to the May 11 edition of the *New York Weekly Post-Boy*, he was absolved on the grounds that this was "the usual discipline for such offenses."

Puritan respect for law gave New England the most equitable administration of justice.[79] From indictment to punishment, slaves generally received the same judicial treatment accorded to whites. They had the right to a jury trial in criminal cases and could also bring freedom suits against their masters.[80] Nor did equal justice

73. *N.Y. City Council Min.*, IV, 447.
74. *Philadelphia Council Min.*, p. 405.
75. Robert M. Lawrence, *New England Colonial Life* (Cambridge, Mass.: Cosmos, 1927), p. 97. See Greene, *The Negro in Colonial New England*, p. 140.
76. *Mass. Acts and Resolves*, I, 156; III, 319, 648. *Conn. Col. Recs.*, V, 52–53. *N.H. Acts and Laws*, pp. 39–40. *N.Y. Col. Laws*, I, 617–18. Leaming and Spicer, *N.J. Grants, Concessions, and Constitutions*, pp. 254–55. *Pa. Stat. at L.*, II, 56.
77. *R.I. Col. Recs.*, III, 492.
78. *New York Weekly Post-Boy*, July 11, 1743; May 11, 1772.
79. Robert C. Twombly and Robert H. Moore, "Black Puritan: The Negro in Seventeenth-Century Massachusetts," *WMQ*, 3d ser., XXIV (1967), 226–27.
80. Connecticut Archives: Miscellaneous, II, 10a–18, MS. coll., CSL; Emory

end when a slave was convicted of a serious crime. The circumstances of the crime were generally more important in fixing the punishment than either the race or legal status of the offender. Sometiems slaves convicted of rape were punished by flogging or deportation, whereas whites guilty of the same crime might be put to death.[81] Even the killing of a white did not mean automatic execution. In cases where there were extenuating circumstances, slaves were prosecuted for the noncapital crime of manslaughter.[82]

But even Puritan justice had to bend before the harsh realities of slave control. In Massachusetts, only slaves were flogged for curfew violations, and in Connecticut the mere threat to assault a white brought the same punishment.[83] Rhode Island set up special courts to try slaves accused of stealing, and there was no right to appeal unless the owner agreed to give bond.[84] Another Rhode Island law punished the attempted rape of a white woman by flogging, branding, and sale outside of the colony. The proceeds were to be used to pay the cost of prosecution and the damages awarded to the woman if she also brought a civil suit.[85]

The Middle colonies relied heavily on special courts and punishments to keep their slaves under control. In 1700 Pennsylvania set up parallel county courts consisting of two justices of the peace and six freeholders to "try and determine all such offenses . . . committed by any Negro or Negroes." Witnesses were allowed and blacks could testify, but there was no right of trial by jury.[86] Although the eastern division of New Jersey had special slave courts as early as 1695, it was not until 1713 that separate judicial

Washburne, "The Extinction of Slavery in Massachusetts," in MHS *Colls.*, 4th ser., IV (1858), 336–39; "Sewall's Commonplace Book," in MHS *Colls.*, 5th ser., VI (1879), 16–20.

81. *Mass. Assistants Court Recs.*, I, 50, 74, 199; II, 86. Samuel E. Morison, ed., "Records of the Suffolk County Court, 1671–1680," in CSM *Colls.*, XXIX–XXX (2 vols., 1933), II, 1067. See Twombly and Moore, "Black Puritan," *WMQ*, 3d ser., XXIV, 231–32.

82. Nathaniel B. Shurtleff and David Pulsifer, eds., *Records of the Colony of New Plymouth*, 12 vols. (Boston: White, 1855–61), VI, 141–42; hereafter cited as *Ply. Col. Recs. Mass. Assistants Court Recs.*, I, 304–305, 321.

83. *Mass. Acts and Resolves*, III, 648. *Conn. Col. Recs.*, V, 52–53; VII, 290.

84. *R.I. Charter, Acts, and Laws*, pp. 101–102.

85. *R.I. Acts and Laws, 1745–1752*, pp. 263–64.

86. *Pa. Stat. at L.*, II, 77–79.

procedures were set up for the entire colony.[87] Slaves accused of any crime were to be tried by courts of three justices of the peace and five freeholders. However, a jury trial could be obtained on demand by the slave's owner, and the right to challenge prospective jurors was also guaranteed.[88] These tribunals operated until 1768, when slave offenses were transferred to the regular courts on the grounds that the dual system had "on experience been found inconvenient."[89]

New York had the most complete system of segregated justice. A warrant would be issued by a justice of the peace for the arrest of the accused slave, and witnesses would be ordered to attend a preliminary hearing. If it appeared at the hearing that there was enough evidence to prosecute the slave, the justice then notified two other justices and five freeholders to join him in the trial. Although the slave had no right to demand a regular jury, his owner might do so by paying a nominal fee. But whatever the method of trial, no challenge to jurors or freeholders was allowed, and a grand jury hearing was specifically denied. In the case of an assault on a white, two justices of the peace, sitting without a jury, might impose any punishment short of death or amputation.[90]

The dual administration of justice exposed slaves to brutal, discriminatory punishments. In 1708 New York made flogging mandatory for minor slave offenses, "any law, custom or usage to the contrary . . . notwithstanding."[91] Pennsylvania punished murder, burglary, or the rape of a white woman by death and attempted rape by castration. Later, under pressure from England, castration was changed to flogging, branding on the forehead with the letter *R*, and deportation from the colony.[92] New Jersey prescribed death for slaves convicted of murder, arson, mutilation, or the rape of a white woman, and castration for attempted rape.[93]

87. Leaming and Spicer, *N.J. Grants, Concessions, and Constitutions*, pp. 356–57.
88. Nevill, *N.J. General Assembly Acts*, I, 20.
89. Allinson, *N.J. General Assembly Acts*, p. 307.
90. *N.Y. Col. Laws*, I, 762–66.
91. *Ibid.*, pp. 617–18.
92. *Pa. Stat. at L.*, II, 77–79, 233–36.
93. Nevill, *N.J. General Assembly Acts*, I, 19; Allinson, *N.J. General Assembly Acts*, p. 5. The Lords of Trade denounced such "inhumane penalties on Negroes,"

So that the courts could impose terroristic punishments as a deterrent, the penalties for some capital offenses were deliberately left unspecified. New Jersey gave its courts discretion to determine the method of execution, and New York authorized the judges to punish slaves guilty of conspiracy or murder "in such manner and with such circumstances as the aggravation and enormity of their crime shall merit and require."[94]

These laws provided a mandate for judicial barbarity. Slaves in Pennsylvania were branded, castrated, and hanged for offenses punishable by flogging or imprisonment when committed by whites.[95] New Jersey punished rape with burning at the stake, and slaves were also sent to the stake for arson and assault.[96] New York slaves convicted of capital crimes were broken on the wheel, burned at the stake, and gibbeted alive in chains.[97] The authorities had so much faith in the deterrent effect of terror that gibbeted corpses were left on display for days as an object-lesson to spectators. Sometimes special cruelties were improvised to terrorizes the slaves who witnessed the executions. As the flames consumed a black woman executed by New York in 1708, a horn filled with water was suspended just beyond her reach "as a terror to others."[98]

Some of these terroristic displays rivaled the worst brutalities of the plantation colonies. A New Jersey court sentenced a slave convicted of murder to have his hand "cut off and burned before thine eyes" before being executed by hanging.[99] Two New York slaves convicted of murdering a white family were sentenced to be put to death by "all manner of torment possible." One of them

---

and the Privy Council voted to disallow the law. *Documents Relating to the Colonial, Revolutionary, and Post-Revolutionary History of the State of New Jersey*, 42 vols. (Newark: New Jersey Historical Society, 1900–49), III, 473–74; hereafter cited as *N.J. Archives* (binder's title). W. L. Grant and James Munro, eds., *Acts of the Privy Council: Colonial Series, 1613–1783*, 6 vols. (London: Wyman, 1908–12), II, 848.

94. *N.J. Archives*, XVII, 483–86; Allinson, *N.J. General Assembly Acts*, p. 307; *N.Y. Col. Laws*, I, 631.

95. Turner, *The Negro in Pennsylvania*, p. 111.

96. *Pennsylvania Gazette*, December 14, 1744. See Cooley, *Study of Slavery in New Jersey*, p. 40.

97. Parish's Transcripts (1729–60), p. 34; Stokes, *Iconography of Manhattan Island*, IV, 475.

98. Olson, "The Slave Code in Colonial New York," *JNH*, XXIX, 162.

99. Cooley, *Study of Slavery in New Jersey*, p. 39.

was burned alive over a slow fire, and the other was partially impaled and then hung alive in chains in order to prolong his suffering for hours.[100] Slaves guilty of conspiracy or insurrection met the worst fate. One of the leaders of the New York City slave uprising of 1712 was roasted alive over a slow fire for ten hours before death ended his ordeal.[101]

Brutal punishments to deter wrongdoing were by no means limited to blacks. Control by terror underlay colonial order generally, and free persons as well as slaves were subject to barbarous penalties. New Jersey prescribed death for children who "smite or curse their parents," and in Pennylvania whites as well as Negroes were castrated and burned for rape.[102] Moreover, most courts punished the wrongdoing of slaves against one another almost as harshly as crimes committed against whites. A New York slave convicted of killing another slave in 1696 was sentenced "to be hanged by the neck till he shall be dead, and to be cut with a knife in his throat and after to be hanged in a chain for the example of others."[103] New Jersey made the willful killing of any slave by a "Negro, Indian, or other slave" a capital offense.[104] A slave named Harry was put to death in 1731 for killing a fellow slave, and some years later a Hackensack slave was executed for poisoning three black women.[105]

Frequently slaveholders shielded their bondsmen from the full rigor of the law. From the very beginning they were torn between their interests as owners and the interest of the community in maintaining law and order. The flogging of a slave could mean the loss of his services for a time, and a sentence of death would destroy the master's investment. In 1705 New York took the lead in resolving this dilemma by compensating owners with amounts of up to £30 for every slave put to death.[106] A New Jersey law of 1713 awarded the owners a maximum of £30 for every male

100. David T. Valentine, comp., *Manual of the Corporation of the City of New York,* 28 vols. (New York, 1842–70), (1870), p. 765.
101. Stokes, *Iconography of Manhattan Island,* IV, 475.
102. Marion T. Wright, "New Jersey Laws and the Negro," *JNH,* XXVIII (1943), 170–71; *Pa. Stat. at L.,* II, 7.
103. Special Court of Kingston, January 7, 8, 1695/96, HDC, QC.
104. Nevill, *N.J. General Assembly Acts,* I, 19.
105. Cooley, *Study of Slavery in New Jersey,* p. 39n.
106. *N.Y. Col. Laws,* I, 582–84.

slave executed and £20 for every woman. The money was to be raised by a special assessment on slaveholders in the town or county where the execution took place.[107] Pennsylvania provided unlimited compensation on the grounds that the loss of a slave could put the owner to "so great a hardship that sometimes may induce him to conceal such crimes or to convey his Negro to some other place and so suffer him to escape justice."[108]

New England slaveholders had special reason not to report capital crimes. Since slave offenders had the full protection of judicial due process, no provision was made to indemnify the owners of executed bondsmen.[109] Even crimes affecting the masters directly were concealed or mitigated in order to keep slaves from the gallows. In 1676 a Massachusetts slave sentenced to death for raping his master's daughter was saved from the gallows when the master, Robert Cox, persuaded the jury to reduce the punishment to thirty-nine lashes.[110] Another owner, the Reverend George Beckwith of Connecticut, worked tirelessly to save a slave unjustly condemned for rape. Beckwith gathered so much evidence on behalf of the slave that the general court set aside the sentence of death.[111]

Lax enforcement by the authorities also weakened the machinery of control. Indeed, some of the controls, particularly those restricting movement and assembly, could not be strictly enforced because they ran counter to the human needs of the slaves as social beings. Slaveholding was so widely diffused on a petty scale that most bondsmen had to form their friendships and family attachments outside the premises of their masters. The obvious need for some freedom of movement caused the local authorities to take a tolerant view of peaceable gatherings and violations of the curfew. So much forbearance was shown that the law officers were sometimes threatened with penalties for failure to enforce the controls strictly.[112] In New Jersey and New York the constables

107. Nevill, *N.J. General Assembly Acts*, I, 21.
108. *Pa. Stat. at L.*, IV, 59–60.
109. Emma L. Thornbrough, "Negro Slavery in the North: Its Legal and Constitutional Aspects," unpublished Ph.D. dissertation (University of Michigan, 1946), p. 47.
110. *Mass. Assistants Court Recs.*, I, 74.
111. Greene, *The Negro in Colonial New England*, p. 166.
112. *Philadelphia Council Min.*, p. 405; *N.Y. City Council Min.*, II, 102–103;

could be fined for tolerating slave offenses or for failing to impose the full punishment ordered by the courts.[113]

That a brutal network of repression existed was much more important than the occasional forbearance shown by the authorities. Lax enforcement of the controls might make life more bearable, but it did not alter the pervasiveness of the repression. Any open resistance brought instant, terrible reprisals calculated to bring the slaves back into line. Nor could a rebel hope for mercy, for the masters relied on systematic horror to compel submission. Even when not invoked, the awful deterrents of stake and gallows had enormous psychological impact. They cast a shadow everywhere, reminding slaves that were a caste apart, living on sufferance in a system amply geared for their destruction.

"Minutes of the Supreme Court of Judicature, 1693–1701," in NYHS Colls., XLV (1912), 113.

113. Nevill, N.J. General Assembly Acts, I, 23; New York Gazette, February 9, 1730/31.

6

Life at the Bottom

The slave codes in part protected blacks against cruel and abusive treatment. Since brutality or deprivation could make slaves dangerous to the community, the law imposed certain obligations on the masters. In 1682 the eastern division of New Jersey sought to reduce pilferage and theft by requiring the owners of slaves "to allow them sufficient accommodation of victuals and clothing."[1] New York slaveholders were punished by a fine if their Negroes had to beg for sustenance, and the bondsmen were invited to report cases of maltreatment or neglect to the authorities.[2] The masters were expressly forbidden to abandon slaves who had become too old or sick to be of further service. Massachusetts and Connecticut had laws making the owner responsible for indigent blacks who had been cast adrift under the pretense of freeing them.[3] In Rhode Island, the masters had to reimburse the overseers of the poor for any public assistance given to abandoned slaves.[4]

1. Aaron Leaming and Jacob Spicer, eds., *The Grants, Concessions and Original Constitutions of the Province of New Jersey* (Somerville, N.J.: Honeyman, 1881), p. 109.
2. E. B. O'Callaghan, ed., *Calendar of Historical Manuscripts in the Office of the Secretary of State*, 2 vols. (Albany: Weed, Parsons, 1866), II, 371. See Alexander C. Flick, ed., *History of the State of New York*, 10 vols. (New York: Columbia University Press, 1933–37) II, 300.
3. *Acts and Resolves, Public and Private, of the Province of the Massachusetts Bay*, 5 vols. (Boston: Wright & Potter, 1869–86), I, 520; J. Hammond Trumbull and Charles J. Hoadly, eds., *The Public Records of the Colony of Connecticut, 1636–1776*, 15 vols. (Hartford: Lockwood & Brainard, 1850–90), IV, 375–76. Hereafter cited as *Mass. Acts and Resolves* and *Conn. Col. Recs.*
4. John R. Bartlett, ed., *Records of the Colony of Rhode Island and Providence*

Though a master could use physical force to compel obedience, his power to do so was subject to the ordinary laws against mutilation and murder. Every Northern colony treated the deliberate killing of a slave as a capital crime, and none permitted maiming in the exercise of private discipline. New Hampshire specifically prescribed the death penalty for the murder of a slave, and owners guilty of cruel or inhuman punishments were required to free their bondsmen and to pay damages if permanent injuries were inflicted.[5] Though no other colony legislated so specifically on the subject, the common law everywhere made slave-killing a crime. In 1742 William Bullock of Pennsylvania was sentenced to death for murdering his slave, and six years later another master accused of slave-killing was warned by the magistrates to leave the colony or "be condemned to die according to the laws of the country."[6]

But since the master could legally use whatever force was needed to enforce his commands, the deliberate killing of a slave was almost impossible to prove. The issue in every case was the master's intent, not the degree of brutality employed. If a deadly weapon had been used, the intent to kill could be inferred; but death resulting from a flogging or a beating, no matter how severe, was equivocal. Nathaniel Cane of Massachusetts, though convicted of killing a slave woman by "cruel beating and hard usage," escaped execution because it could not be proved that the killing was intentional. The fine of five shillings imposed by the court was no more than the penalty for minor misdemeanors.[7] Another Massachusetts master was acquitted of flogging his slave to death because the court found that the slave had died by swallowing his tongue during the beating.[8] Juries were reluctant to

---

Plantations in New England, 1636–1792, 10 vols. (Providence: Greene, 1856–65), IV, 415–16; hereafter cited as R.I. Col. Recs.

5. Acts and Laws of His Majesty's Province of New Hampshire in New England with Sundry Acts of Parliament (Portsmouth: Daniel & Robert Fowle, 1771), p. 101; hereafter cited as N.H. Acts and Laws.

6. American Weekly Mercury (Philadelphia), April 29, 1742; Peter Kalm, Travels into North America, John R. Forster, trans., 3 vols. (London: Eyres 1770–71), I, 391–92.

7. George H. Moore, Additional Notes on the History of Slavery in Massachusetts (New York: Bradstreet Press, 1866), p. 7n.

8. Lorenzo J. Greene, The Negro in Colonial New England, 1620–1776 (New York: Columbia University Press, 1942), pp. 234–35.

convict if death resulted from disciplinary action. According to the *New York Weekly Journal*, January 5, 1735/36, an owner who beat his runaway slave to death was acquitted by a New York City jury on the grounds that the death was accidental, having been caused by "the visitations of God."

Although much brutality obviously occurred, Northern slavery exhibited none of the systematic barbarism practiced in the plantation colonies.[9] The odium and expense of being subjected to a public trial deterred Northerners from wanton cruelty. The death of a slave under suspicious circumstances meant a grand jury hearing, with much unfavorable publicity and considerable inconvenience.[10] For beating his slave to death in 1733, John Cooley of New York was held in jail for trial until exonerated by a coroner's jury.[11] Public opinion was a powerful deterrent against brutal punishments, and masters who inflicted them incurred the opprobrium of their neighbors. Newspaper descriptions of runaways reveal that relatively few Northern slaves were physically disfigured; by contrast, those from the plantation colonies were often scarred, branded, and cruelly mutilated.[12] Except for flogging, a punishment also inflicted on indentured servants and free whites, private discipline was about as humane as could be expected under any system of slave control.

Since a large proportion of the slaves were skilled workers, the self-interest of the masters dictated a sensible approach to discipline. The owners of such slaves often found it expedient to ig-

9. The maximum statutory penalty for killing a slave in South Carolina was a fine of £100 sterling. Thomas Cooper and David J. McCord, eds., *Statutes at Large of South Carolina*, 14 vols. (Columbia, S. C.: Johnston, 1836–73), VII, 397–417. See William Goodell, *The American Slave Code* (New York: The American and Foreign Anti-Slavery Society, 1853), pp. 218–20; Thomas R. R. Cobb, *An Inquiry into the Law of Slavery in the United States of America* (Philadelphia: Johnson, 1858), p. 114.

10. George F. Dow, ed., *Records and Files of the Quarterly Courts of Essex County, Massachusetts*, 8 vols. (Salem, Mass.: Essex Institute, 1911–21), II, 121; VIII, 59.

11. *New York Gazette*, December 17, 1733. "Abstracts of Wills on File in the Surrogate's Office, City of New York," NYHS *Colls.*, XXV–XLI (17 vols., 1892–1908), III, 433–35; hereafter cited as "N.Y. Abstracts of Wills."

12. *American Weekly Mercury* (Philadelphia), July 23, 1722; October 16, 23, 1729; August 30, 1733. *Pennsylvania Gazette*, July 4, 1745. Weyman's *New York Gazette*, June 14, 1762. *New York Mercury*, September 5, 1757; July 11, 1763. *New York Weekly Post-Boy*, March 15, 1756; August 29, 1757; June 26, July 31, 1766. *New York Weekly Mercury*, July 20, 1772. See James T. Adams, *History of the Town of Southampton* (Bridgehampton, N.Y.: Hampton Press, 1918), p. 201.

nore minor regulatory infractions in order to obtain the sort of cooperation that could not be extorted by coercion alone. The value of an artisan partly depended on his willingness to work, for no amount of threats or beatings could guarantee the quality of his performance. The most highly skilled slaves therefore had considerable bargaining power, and they used it effectively to obtain special clothing, hiring privileges, and promises of eventual freedom.[13] It was even possible for slaves to avoid unwanted sales by refusing to work for prospective buyers.[14] A slave belonging to Reyer Schermerhorn of New York broke up an auction by declaring his unwillingness to work for any of the bidders.[15]

Slaves generally received adequate food, shelter, and clothing. Peter Kalm reported that generally "they have as good food as the rest of the servants."[16] In Pennsylvania food costs averaged about 20 to 25 percent yearly on the slave's market value.[17] In the rural areas of New York, the slaves had so much food that they were able to sell their surpluses for cash or other goods.[18] How well slaves were housed depended upon the master's accommodations and the size of his holding. In the towns they lived in close proximity with whites, usually in the cellars or garrets of the master's house. But where the holding was large, some had to be quartered in outbuildings at some distance from the main house.[19] This was typically the pattern in rural areas where farms were offered for sale with separate "Negro houses."[20]

13. Massachusetts Archives, IX, 153–54, MS. coll., MSL. Register of New York Manumissions, pp. 65–66, MS. coll., MCNY. "N.Y. Abstract of Wills," XI, 86–87; XV, 114–16. The Early Records of the Town of Providence, 20 vols. (Providence: Snow & Fornbrow, 1892–1909), IV, 71–72; IX, 153.

14. New York Weekly Post-Boy, March 23, 30, 1747; August 30, 1756; January 8, 1758; September 1, 1763. New York Mercury, September 5, 1763; May 27, 1765. New York Weekly Mercury, February 26, June 1, 1772; January 18, April 26, 1773.

15. Reyer Schermerhorn to Governor George Clinton, N.Y., January 13, 1788, in Beekman Papers, Box 32, Folio 1, MS. coll., NYHS.

16. Kalm, Travels into North America, I, 394.

17. Israel Acrelius, A History of New Sweden, William M. Reynolds, trans. (Philadelphia: Historical Society of Pennsylvania, 1874), p. 168.

18. Thomas F. De Voe, The Market Book (New York: the Author, 1862), pp. 344–45.

19. Edward R. Turner, The Negro in Pennsylvania (Washington, D.C.: The American Historical Association, 1911), pp. 39–40; Greene, The Negro in Colonial New England, pp. 223–41.

20. Pennsylvania Gazette, June 26, 1746. New York Weekly Post-Boy, April 29, May 6, November 18, 1751; October 21, November 18, 1754; November 17, 1768.

The variety and quality of slave clothing is best revealed in newspaper advertisements describing the apparel worn by runaways. Though much of the clothing was obviously homespun, the advertisements make it clear that slaves were well clad for all sorts of weather.[21] The winter season was so harsh for slaves who had recently arrived that their owners sometimes provided them with better clothing than that worn by white servants.[22] Household accounts and diaries reveal that clothes were a considerable expense of slaveholding, in some cases amounting to 5 percent annually of the slave's value.[23] Some masters provided their slaves with "Sunday clothes" for special occasions besides ordinary working clothes for the job.[24] John Brown of Providence furnished his household retainers with shoes of about the same quality and price as those ordered for members of his family.[25] Thomas Penn of Philadelphia spent over £7 yearly on shoes for his slaves, and Hendrick Denker of New York City spent over £5 on one complete set of clothing for a bondsman.[26]

Slaves took considerable pride in their clothing and went to great lengths to dress well. Some tailors and bootmakers did a profitable business fitting them out with all sorts of expensive apparel.[27] The desire for such clothing caused much petty crime, for

21. *American Weekly Mercury* (Philadelphia), January 24, October 5, 1721; November 23, 1722; April 25, August 22, 1723; March 12, May 7, July 30, October 15, 22, 1724; June 3, 10, 17, July 1, December 28, 1725; January 18, September 19, October 13, 1726; May 15, June 8, 29, 1727. *Pennsylvania Gazette,* July 31, September 11, August 1, October 31, 1745; June 5, July 3, 1746; October 22, 1747; February 16, May 5, 1748; August 28, 1755; April 16, 1761. *New York Weekly Post-Boy,* September 4, 1749; February 11, 1750/51; May 11, 1752; May 24, August 30, 1756; August 1, 1757; July 3, 17, 24, 1758; June 16, 1760; June 18, 23, 1761. *New York Mercury,* July 18, 1757; May 22, 1758; August 13, September 24, 1759; April 14, May 5, 1760; July 20, 1761; December 12, 1763. *New England Weekly Journal,* May 27, December 9, 1728; November 10, 1729; August 24, 1730; March 29, May 10, August 9, 16, October 11, 1731; February 14, 21, 28, June 12, 1732; October 28, November 11, 1735; October 26, 1736; October 11, 18, 1737.
22. Greene, *The Negro in Colonial New England,* p. 225.
23. Acrelius, *History of New Sweden,* p. 169.
24. "Papers of the Lloyd Family of the Manor of Queens Village," in NYHS *Colls.,* LIX–LX (2 vols., 1926–27), II, 725; hereafter cited as "Lloyd Papers."
25. John Steven's Book, 1705, p. 15, MS. coll., JCBL.
26. Turner, *The Negro in Pennsylvania,* p. 39n; Hendrick Denker's Account Book, 1752–72, p. 119, MS. coll., NYHS.
27. Charles Nicoll's Account Book, 1753–58, January 27, October 24, 1756; October 2, 1760; March 21, 1761. Charles Nicoll's Ledger, 1759–65, pp. 4, 9, 11,

slaves unable to raise the necessary money by hiring their free time sometimes resorted to theft and pilferage.[28] Both men and women dressed with color and variety, perhaps finding in distinctive attire relief from the drudgery and boredom of slave life. According to the *Pennsylvania Gazette*, August 28, 1755, a runaway belonging to Jonathan Sergeant of Newark was reported wearing "a beaver hat, light grey jacket, tow trousers, new pumps, and a purple colored waistcoat." The October 28, 1735 edition of the *New England Weekly Journal* reported that Binah, a slave woman of Boston, ran away wearing "a cinnamon colored cloak and yellow-colored hat, a red and white quilted callico petticoat, blue yarn stockings, and red shoes." Such clothes not only relieved the drabness of everyday life but also provided a means of individual expression.

The sort of medical care available to slaves varied in quality, but in the main it compared favorably with that of the white population. Only the meanest owners would deny sick slaves professional treatment or risk giving them the cheap nostrums advertised specifically for Negroes.[29] Humane considerations apart, the property value of a slave was a powerful motive for providing adequate medical care. Nor was the treatment of slaves a discount form of medical practice, for the fees charged by physicians varied according to the difficulty of the case, sometimes exceeding the fees charged for treating whites.[30] "Sundry medicines, dressing, and attendance" for one of his slaves cost Elisha Tillinghast of Providence over £20.[31] Frequently slaves were attended by the same physician who cared for the owner's family. Henry Lloyd of New York paid annual fees of about £7 to his family physician for treating his slaves.[32]

Despite favorable standards of medical care, slave mortality was high. The cold, damp northern climate caused much respira-

---

13–16, 33. Both in MS. coll., NYHS. John Stevens's Book, 1705, p. 15, MS. coll., JCBL.

28. Joel Munsell, ed., *Collections on the History of Albany*, 4 vols. (Albany: Munsell, 1865), II, 382–83; *New York Weekly Post-Boy*, April 15, 1762.

29. *New York Weekly Post-Boy*, March 11, 1762.

30. David Vanderlight's Ledger, 1751–55, pp. 1, 43, 47, 49, 98, MS. coll., JCBL.

31. *Ibid.*, p. 43.

32. "Lloyd Papers," I, 309–10, 341; II, 719.

tory illness, particularly among slaves imported during the winter season.[33] The heaviest mortality was caused by smallpox, measles, pneumonia, and mumps, and these diseases attacked whites as well as blacks with achromatic impartiality. In the case of small-pox, however, slaves fared somewhat better than their masters. Exposure to mild forms of the disease aboard slave ships resulted in a natural immunity that saved them during the worst epidemics. During the Boston epidemic of 1721 white mortality was about double that of the black population.[34] Although blacks accounted for about 20 percent of New York City's population during the epidemic of 1730, their mortality rate was only 12 percent of all deaths.[35] Except for the respiratory ailments to which they were particularly vulnerable, slaves resisted disease as well or better than the masters.

Since most slaves worked alongside their masters and shared similar working conditions, they had about the same free time for rest and recreation. When the day's work was done, they were usually free to spend their time as they pleased. Although public controls technically restricted their activities, slaves who stayed out of trouble were seldom interfered with by the authorities. How they used this freedom depended on personal disposition and motivation. Some used their leisure time for relaxation, while others worked hard at odd jobs to buy their way out of slavery.[36] But in all their activities the desire to separate themselves from the control of the masters is clearly discernible. Whether they gathered together in clandestine drinking places or worked to earn their freedom, slaves sought to escape the constant surveillance and domination of whites.

Sunday usually meant a full day off, and in this regard the slaves were more fortunate than many white indentured servants. Richard Cain, a New York City servant, complained that slaves "universally almost have one day in seven whether to rest or to

33. Darold D. Wax, "The Negro Slave Trade in Colonial Pennsylvania," unpublished Ph.D. dissertation (University of Washington, 1962), pp. 94–96.

34. "Table of Burials," *Boston Gazette*, January 23, 1753.

35. John Duffy, *Epidemics in Colonial America* (Baton Rouge: Louisiana State University Press, 1953), pp. 78–80.

36. George Sheldon, *Negro Slavery in Old Deerfield* (reprint from *New England Magazine*, March, 1893; Boston, 1893), pp. 55–56; Turner, *The Negro in Pennsylvania*, p. 42.

go to church or see their country folks—but we are commonly compelled to work as hard every Sunday."[37] Although the New England colonies forbade Sunday amusements, slaves could use the day to visit friends and relatives or to engage in approved activities which allowed them to meet together.[38] In the Middle colonies Sabbath regulations were less strict, so slaves could celebrate with more exuberance. Their noisy gatherings and pranks in Philadelphia led to demands that the authorities "suppress the unruly Negroes of this city accompanying together on the first day of the week."[39]

New England slaves annually celebrated elections at which they chose black "governors" and other officials. The masters encouraged and subsidized these contests, for the success or failure of a candidate reflected on the standing of his owner.[40] While the elections varied as to time and detail in the different colonies, the canvass for votes was everywhere intense and often extended over several weeks of hard campaigning. Rhode Island slaves elected their own local officials, and in New Hampshire and Connecticut black "kings" and "governors" were chosen respectively for the entire colony.[41] Election day itself was a festive affair, with Negroes turning out in their best clothing for the reception and games that followed the counting of the ballots. In Massachusetts, slaves were traditionally given a three-day holiday to celebrate the event.[42]

These elections created a subgovernment of black governors, sheriffs, and judges. In Connecticut the governor settled disputes among slaves and prescribed penalties for minor offenses; in Rhode Island, there were black magistrates and judges who tried

37. Richard Cain to William Kempe, October 23, 1754, in John Tabor Kempe Papers, Box IV, Folio A–C, MS. coll., NYHS.
38. Greene, *The Negro in Colonial New England*, p. 247.
39. Ancient Records of Philadelphia, April 4, 1717, J. W. Wallace MS. coll., HSP.
40. Bernard Steiner, *History of Slavery in Connecticut* (Baltimore: The Johns Hopkins Press, 1893), pp. 78–79; William Johnston, *Slavery in Rhode Island, 1755–1776* (Providence: Rhode Island Historical Society, 1894), pp. 31–32. See Orville H. Platt, "Negro Governors," *New Haven Historical Society Papers*, VI (1900), 319–28.
41. Joseph B. Felt, *The Ecclesiastical History of New England*, 2 vols. (Boston: Congregational Library Association, 1862), II, 419; Johnston, *Slavery in Rhode Island*, p. 31; Platt, *New Haven Historical Society Papers*, VI, 319, 321.
42. Greene, *The Negro in Colonial New England*, pp. 250–51.

charges against slaves and imposed punishments.[43] The system became an effective instrument of slave control, for blacks who gained power over their fellow slaves generally collaborated with the masters. Owners could report slave offenses to the black magistrates, certain that the delinquent would be severely punished.[44] Free Negroes, of course, were strictly excluded; only blacks under white control were trusted with power over other Negroes. By coopting potential slave leaders into the power structure, the masters reduced the possibility of resistance to their own rule.

Although Northern slaves had sufficient opportunities to form personal attachments, they had great difficulty maintaining stable family ties—not that such relationships were deliberately disrupted, for the masters sometimes went to great lengths to keep slave families together. John Waite of Boston subsidized the marriage of his slave Sebastian with an allowance of £5 yearly for Sebastian's wife and family.[45] The towns often relaxed their curfews to enable spouses to visit in the evening, and men occasionally got time off to visit with their wives and children in other households.[46] Some masters tried to stabilize family relationships by making testamentary restrictions against the separate sale of spouses.[47] Others tried to keep families together when offering slaves for sale.[48] One New Jersey slaveholder sold a husband and wife together, though he actually wanted to sell only one of them.[49] In advertising a black family for sale in the *Pennsylvania Gazette*, April 4, 1751, Isaac Roberts of Philadelphia put prospective buyers on notice that he was "not inclined to sell them separate."

43. Steiner, *History of Slavery in Connecticut*, p. 79; Platt, *New Haven Historical Society Papers*, VI, 324.

44. Platt, *New Haven Historical Society Papers*, VI, 324.

45. "Diary of Samuel Sewall," in MHS *Colls.*, 5th ser., V–VII (3 vols., 1878–82), II, 22.

46. William S. Pelletreau, ed., *Records of the Town of Smithtown* (Huntington, N.Y.: Long Islander Print, 1898), p. 170; Turner, *The Negro in Pennsylvania*, p. 42; David Humphreys, *An Account of the Endeavours Used by the Society for the Propagation of the Gospel in Foreign Parts to Instruct the Negro Slaves in New York* (London, 1730), p. 7.

47. "N.Y. Abstracts of Wills," V, 99–100; VI, 97–98; XII, 374–75.

48. *American Weekly Mercury* (Philadelphia), March 28, 1734. *New York Weekly Post-Boy*, March 23, 1746/47; March 21, November 28, 1765. *New York Weekly Mercury*, March 5, November 19, 1770; February 15, 1779.

49. John Bartow to David Humphreys, November 15, 1725, SPG Transcripts, B1, p. 217, LC.

Nothing, however, could prevent the disintegration of slave families. Slavery was not structured for permanent relationships, and no amount of good will could obviate this fact or mitigate its consequences. Slave families that somehow kept together inevitably burdened owners with unwanted children. One New York City master advertising a husband and wife for sale in the *New York Weekly Post-Boy*, November 28, 1765, informed the public that "they are sold for no fault, save getting of children." Another problem was that slave spouses often belonged to different owners. If either of them moved or had to sell one of the partners, the marriage was over and the family disrupted. Even though one of the owners might be willing to keep the family together, he was powerless to do so without the cooperation of the other. It was inevitable that for most slaves family ties should be casual and impermanent.

The absence of normal social reinforcement weakened family stability almost as much as the threat of physical disruption. Men did not support their families, for slavery preempted their time and energy for the benefit of the masters. Most of them in fact had no desire to provide support, for they understood this to be the master's responsibility. Whatever cohesion the slave family had depended almost entirely upon the women. Except for their biological contribution, the men played almost no role in the raising of children. It was the mother who provided food and clothing, and it was she who served as a symbol of authority and protection.[50] Indeed, women with dependent children were commonly regarded as complete family units. Sales notices advertising "a likely Negro woman and child" without mention of the father abound in the newspaper files of every colony.[51]

Disruption of the slave family created a bad climate of sexual morality. Men and women formed temporary, casual attachments, knowing that the relationship could end at any time by the sale of either partner. Nor did the population distribution promote

50. Kenneth M. Stampp, *The Peculiar Institution* (New York: Knopf, 1956), pp. 343–44; E. Franklin Frazier, *The Negro Family in the United States* (Chicago: University of Chicago Press, 1939), p. 57.

51. *American Weekly Mercury* (Philadelphia), June 4, 1724; January 16, November 7, 1728; April 13, 20, August 10, 1732; April 10, 17, 1735. *Boston News Letter*, August 25, 1718. *New England Weekly Journal*, August 19, 26, September 2, 1728; May 8, 1732; April 9, 1733; August 25, 1741.

morality, for the shortage of black women in every colony resulted in intense competition for sexual partners.[52] This meant that there were thousands of black men unable to form monogamous relationships and for whom temporary, shifting attachments were the only alternative. The numerous morals offenses recorded in counties where men heavily outnumbered women make it clear that sexual promiscuity among slaves was inevitable.[53] Even if other factors had been more favorable, the imbalance between the sexes would have undermined stable relationships.

Although the darker pigmentation of their skin excluded Negroes from the mainstream of colonial life, it raised no barriers to them in the hereafter. The religious leaders of every colony saw no reason why slaves could not be converted into conventional Christians. In New England, the Puritan clergy took the lead in the Christianizing effort. The Reverend John Eliot regarded the proselytization of slaves as a religious duty, and he admonished the masters to act accordingly "lest the God of Heaven . . . be provoked into a vengeance."[54] As early as 1641 a black woman of Dorchester, Massachusetts, having been "well approved by divers years experience for sound knowledge and true godliness," was baptized into the church.[55] Cotton Mather, a leading proponent of proselytization, reminded Puritan masters that some of the slaves might be "the elect of God placed in their hands by Divine Providence."[56]

The proselytization of slaves received strong support from the Church of England. The Society for the Propagation of the Gospel in Foreign Parts (SPG), a powerful Anglican missionary organization, appointed catechists and teachers to work for the con-

52. Evarts B. Greene and Virginia D. Harrington, *American Population before the Federal Census of 1790* (New York: Columbia University Press, 1932), p. 101; Greene, *The Negro in Colonial New England*, pp. 93–96.
53. Samuel E. Morison, ed., "Records of the Suffolk County Court, 1671–1680," in CSM *Colls.*, XXIX–XXX (2 vols., 1933), II, 233, 809, 841. Dow, *Essex County Court Recs.*, I, 196, 287; II, 247; V, 316, 409; VI, 73, 135–38, 205; VII, 411, 419–20.
54. Cotton Mather, *The Life of the Rev. Mr. John Eliot* (London: Printed for J. Dunton, 1694), p. 109.
55. John Winthrop, *History of New England from 1630–1649*, James Savage, ed., 2 vols. (Boston: Little, Brown, 1853), II, 26, quoted in Greene, *The Negro in Colonial New England*, p. 257.
56. Cotton Mather, *The Negro Christianized* (Boston, 1706), pp. 4–5.

version of blacks. Since literacy facilitated proselytization, the missionary effort gave impetus to education. Bishop Edmund Gibson of London, who directed the SPG, sent out thousands of letters admonishing slaveholders that they had "a religious duty to teach their slaves and domestics to read and write."[57] Many Anglican clergymen and catechists provided secular as well as religious instruction during their proselyting sessions.[58] In 1758 a school for black children was opened under Anglican auspices in Philadelphia, and two years later others were started in Newport and New York City. The children were taught reading, writing, and arithmetic; in addition, the girls were trained in sewing and knitting. The Newport school provided continuous instruction for slaves until the Revolution.[59]

Virtually every religious denomination supported proselytization. As early as 1693 George Keith, the leader of the Philadelphia Quakers, urged his followers to provide their slaves with a Christian education. In 1696 the Pennsylvania Yearly Meeting urged slaveholders to bring their Negroes to meetings and to instruct them in the Christian religion.[60] The Newport Friends enjoined Quakers to instruct their slaves and to bring them to religious meetings.[61] Secular education was also encouraged as a means of promoting conversion. Benjamin Lay urged Pennsylvania Quakers to give their slaves "some learning, reading, and writing," and Anthony Benezet started a night school for slaves in Philadelphia.[62] The New England Yearly Meeting urged slaveholders "to

57. Quoted in Greene, The Negro in Colonial New England, p. 240.
58. Francis L. Hawks's Records of the General Convention of the Protestant Episcopal Church of New York, II, 9–10, MS. coll., NYHS.
59. Marcus W. Jernegan, "Slavery and Conversion in the American Colonies," AHR, XXI (1916), 510; Edgar L. Pennington, "The Work of the Bray Associates in Pennsylvania," Pennsylvania Magazine of History, LVII (1934), 7; Morgan Dix, A History of the Parish of Trinity Church, 5 vols. (New York: The Knickerbocker Press and Columbia University Press, 1898–1950), I, 294–95; New York Mercury, September 15, 1760.
60. Jernegan, "Slavery and Conversion in the American Colonies," AHR, XXI (1916), 512.
61. Greene, The Negro in Colonial New England, p. 275.
62. Benjamin Lay, All Slave-Keepers That Keep the Innocent in Bondage, Apostates . . . (Philadelphia: the Author, 1737), pp. 30, 53–54; George S. Brookes, Friend Anthony Benezet (Philadelphia: University of Pennsylvania Press, 1937), pp. 45–52.

give such as are young at least as much learning that they may be capable of reading."[63]

Most of the Lutheran, Baptist, and Presbyterian clergy also favored proselytization, and baptism was seldom refused because of race or slavery. The Reverend Heinrich Muhlenberg of Pennsylvania not only gave religious instruction but personally baptized slaves into the Lutheran faith.[64] In Rhode Island most of the Baptist churches accepted black converts regardless of their legal status.[65] Although the Presbyterian synods did not officially endorse proselytization, individual clergymen worked hard to Christianize the slaves.[66] The period of the Great Awakening gave added impetus to all these efforts, for the emotional gospel of the evangelists attracted black converts to every denomination. Reporting on his visit to Pennsylvania in 1740, the Reverend George Whitefield wrote that "near fifty Negroes came to give me thanks under God for what has been done to their souls."[67]

The most serious opposition to the missionary effort came from slaveholders who feared that proselytization might jeopardize their property interests. Many believed that heathenism justified slavery, and that baptism or conversion would automatically free a slave.[68] Writing to the Board of Trade in 1699, Governor Bellomont of New York reported that a bill to encourage conversion "would not go down with the Assembly, they having a notion that the Negroes' being converted to Christianity would emancipate them from their slavery."[69] Frequently slaveholders refused to al-

63. Allan C. Thomas, "The Attitude of the Society of Friends toward Slavery in the Seventeenth and Eighteenth Century," *Papers of the American Society of Church History*, VIII (1897), 279.

64. Henry E. Jacobs, *A History of the Evangelical Lutheran Church in the United States* (New York: The Christian Literature Co., 1893), p. 231.

65. Greene, *The Negro in Colonial New England*, p. 275.

66. Jernegan, "Slavery and Conversion in the American Colonies," *AHR*, XXI (1916), 514.

67. George Whitefield, *A Continuation of the Reverend Mr. Whitefield's Journal, after His Arrival at Georgia, to a Few Days after His Second Return thither from Pennsylvania* (London: Printed for J. Hutton, 1741), pp. 65–66, cited in Turner, *The Negro in Pennsylvania*, p. 45n.

68. Humphreys, *Account of the Endeavours by the S.P.G.*, p. 27. See Jernegan, "Slavery and Conversion in the American Colonies," *AHR*, XXI (1916), 504–506.

69. W. Noel Sainsbury, *et al.*, eds., *Calendar of State Papers: Colonial Series, America and West Indies*, 42 vols. (London: H.M.S.O., 1860–1953), XVII (1699), 176; hereafter cited as *Cal. State Papers, Col.*

low Negroes to attend religious instruction, and some even threatened their slaves with sale if they became Christians.[70] An SPG catechist for New York City's slaves reported that the work often had to be done secretly "against the will and without the knowledge of their masters, because they fear lest by baptism they should become temporally free."[71]

Colonial officials worked hard to convince slaveholders that black souls could be saved without emancipating their bodies. In 1704 New Jersey provided by statute that "the baptizing of any Negro, Indian, or Mulatto slave shall not be any reason or cause for setting them or any of them at liberty," and two years later New York enacted similar legislation "to put an end to all such doubts and scruples."[72] When the Massachusetts general court failed to provide statutory reassurance, Cotton Mather pointed out that owners could protect themselves by making "sufficient indentures" with their slaves. Thus baptized Negroes could be kept in contractual bondage regardless of any change in their legal status.[73] Even stronger reassurance came from the attorney-general and solicitor-general of England who ruled in 1729 that a converted slave remained a slave because "baptism doth not bestow freedom on him nor make any alteration in his temporal condition."[74]

But the masters also feared that proselytization might undermine discipline, even if it did not legally free the slaves. Writing in 1748, Peter Kalm noted that the owners opposed conversion "partly through fear of the Negroes growing too proud on seeing themselves upon a level with their masters in religious matters."[75] There was always the danger that too much emphasis on the

70. Ernest Hawkins, *Historical Notices of the Missions of the Church of England in the North American Colonies* (London: Fellowes, 1845), p. 271.

71. Elias Neau to John Chamberlayne, April 30, 1706, SPG Transcripts (translation), No. 167, pp. 392–93, LC.

72. Nicholas Trott, comp., *The Laws of the British Plantations in America, Relating to the Church and the Clergy, Religion and Learning* (London: Clarke, 1725), p. 257; *Colonial Laws of New York from 1664 to the Revolution*, 5 vols. (Albany: James B. Lyon, 1894), I, 597–98.

73. *Mass. Acts and Resolves*, VII, 537; Mather, *The Negro Christianized*, p. 26.

74. John C. Hurd, *The Law of Freedom and Bondage in the United States*, 2 vols. (Boston: Little, Brown, 1858–62), I, 186n.

75. Kalm, *Travels into North America*, I, 397. See Jernegan, "Slavery and Conversion in the American Colonies," *AHR*, XXI (1916), 517.

Christian idea of the equality of all men under God might make the slaves more restive. Slaveholders could never forget that Christian Negroes had played leading roles in the bloody uprising of 1730 in Virginia.[76] One master in New York City frankly admitted his fear that religious instruction would inspire the slaves with "dangerous conceits."[77] In the Delaware counties of Pennsylvania, slaves were not only forbidden to attend religious services, but some were threatened with flogging for taking or answering to Christian names.[78]

The clergy went to great lengths to convince the masters that religious indoctrination posed no threat to their property or security. In a catechism prepared for slaves in 1693, Cotton Mather taught that bondsmen "must be patient and content with such conditions as God has ordered," and that only "faithful and honest servants" could hope for salvation.[79] Slaves proselytized by the SPG heard similar exhortations about Christian submissiveness and the need to look to God for a reward in the hereafter. Writing to the SPG in 1750, the Reverend Samuel Auchmuty of New York reported that besides providing the slaves with religious instruction he also endeavored "to make them sensible . . . of the duty and obligation they are under to live as Christians."[80] Whether they also had any rights as Christians apparently never entered into their instruction.

Far from causing discontent, conversion tended to make slaves more submissive than those who remained outside the Christian fold. Reporting on his New York City converts in 1764, the Reverend Auchmuty noted that "not one single black that has been admitted by me . . . has turned out bad, or been in any shape a disgrace to our holy profession."[81] Christian slaves took no part in the New York City uprising of 1712, which was led by uncon-

76. Francis L. Hawks's Records of the General Convention of the Protestant Episcopal Church of New York, II, 33–34, MS. coll., NYHS.
77. Ibid., I, 639.
78. Frank J. Klingberg, "The African Immigrant in Colonial Pennsylvania and Delaware," Historical Magazine of the Protestant Episcopal Church, XI (1942), 147.
79. Mather, The Negro Christianized, pp. 32, 41–42.
80. Quoted in Frank J. Klingberg, Anglican Humanitarianism in Colonial New York (Philadelphia: The Church Historical Society, 1940), p. 148.
81. Samuel Auchmuty to Daniel Burton, March 29, 1764, SPG Transcripts, No. 16, pp. 20–21, LC.

verted blacks who used heathen spells to make themselves invulnerable. The Reverend John Sharpe drew a direct link between the uprising and heathenism, pointing out that "the persons whose Negroes have been found guilty are such as are declared opposers of Christianizing Negroes."[82] Frequently the leading collaborators under slavery were black Christians who had so assimilated white values that they rationalized their own bondage. " 'Twas mercy brought me from my pagan land," wrote Phillis Wheatley of her devotion to Christianity and the teachings of her masters.[83] New York's slave poet Jupiter Hammon went even further and urged his fellow slaves to accept their bondage "as the servants of Christ doing the will of God."[84]

The masters, however, remained unconvinced, and those who did not actively oppose proselytization did nothing to assist it. John Eliot accused the slaveholders of Massachusetts of "such prodigious wickedness as to deride, neglect, and oppose all due means of bringing their own poor Negroes unto the Lord."[85] Dean Berkeley charged that Rhode Island masters treated their slaves "as creatures of another species, who had no right to be instructed or admitted to the sacraments."[86] Nor were slaveholders willing to have their Negroes proselytized by missionaries of other denominations. Elias Neau, an SPG catechist in New York City, attributed most of his difficulties to anti-Anglican "Arians, Socinians, Quakers, deists."[87] Another SPG worker reported that the Quakers refused to have their slaves instructed by Anglicans, and that the Presbyterians, though permitting instruction, would not allow their slaves to be baptized.[88]

82. John Sharpe to the Secretary, June 23, 1712, SPG Transcripts, A7, p. 216, LC. See Daniel Parish, Transcripts of Material on Slavery in the Public Records Office in London (1688–1760), pp. 15–16, MS. coll., NYHS; Hawkins, *Historical Notices of the Missions of the Church of England*, pp. 9–10, 272.

83. Quoted in Greene, *The Negro in Colonial New England*, p. 287.

84. Jupiter Hammon, *An Address to the Negroes of the State of New York* (New York: Carroll & Patterson, 1787), p. 7.

85. Mather, *The Life of John Eliot*, p. 109.

86. Wilkins Updike, *A History of the Episcopal Church in Narragansett, Rhode Island*, 3 vols. (Boston: Updike, 1907), I, 212–13, cited in Greene, *The Negro in Colonial New England*, p. 260.

87. Elias Neau to the Secretary, April 2, 1722, SPG Transcripts, A16, p. 196, LC.

88. James Wetmore to the Secretary, February 20, 1727/28, SPG Transcripts, A20, p. 218, LC.

Missionaries had great difficulty reaching slaves in the rural areas. One SPG worker in Jamaica, New York, found it impossible to estimate the number of slaves in his parish, and another in Hempstead reported that population dispersion made missionary work almost impossible.[89] Only fifty-three slaves were baptized in Huntington over a period of fifty-six years, a conversion rate of about one slave per year.[90] Even in New York City no more than 10 percent of the slaves had been converted by 1731, despite a decade of intensive efforts by the SPG to proselytize them.[91] Results were just as meagre elsewhere. Although Governor Bradstreet probably exaggerated when he estimated that no slaves had been baptized in Massachusetts before 1680, the number actually converted must have been negligible.[92] As late as 1776, at the end of the colonial era, most of New England's Negroes had no religious connections, and of those who were nominally Christian only a few had regular ties with the churches.[93]

Black apathy probably hindered the missionary effort even more than the antipathy shown by the whites. The emphasis placed upon submission and obedience by the proselytizers must have convinced many slaves that Christianity was but another device for keeping them subservient. Cotton Mather taught that slaves owed their first loyalty to their masters, and that they had a religious duty to inform on their fellow slaves who were guilty of misconduct.[94] Another Massachusetts clergyman admonished slaves that to run away or even to be dissatisfied with their bondage would be to the "dishonor of religion and the reproach of Christianity."[95] Even less vocal apologists of slavery never questioned the premises of the system or concerned themselves about

89. Francis L. Hawks's Records of the General Convention of the Protestant Episcopal Church of New York, I, 634, MS. coll., NYHS; Klingberg, Anglican Humanitarianism in Colonial New York, p. 158.

90. Ebenezer Prime, comp., Records of the First Church of Huntington, Long Island, 1723–1779 (Huntington, N.Y.: Scudder, 1899), passim.

91. "Revolutionary and Miscellaneous Papers," in NYHS Colls., XI–XIII (3 vols., 1878–80), III, 356.

92. Cal. State Papers, Col., X (1677–80), 530.

93. Ezra Stiles, Literary Diary, F.B. Dexter, ed., 3 vols. (New York: Scribner's, 1901), I, 213–14. See Greene, The Negro in Colonial New England, p. 289.

94. "Diary of Cotton Mather, 1681–1708," in MHS Colls., 7th ser., VII (1911), 177.

95. George Sheldon, A History of Deerfield, Massachusetts, 2 vols. (Deerfield, Mass.: Hall, 1895–96), II, 901–902.

the rights of slaves as human beings. The Reverend Richard Charlton of New York believed that "imprudence and indiscretion directed his pen" when George Whitefield published a letter critical of slaveholders who abused their Negroes.[96] But this was precisely what concerned slaves the most, and the failure of the clergy to face the issue must have weakened their influence.

Conversion not only failed to improve everyday life, but it subjected slaves to a moral code incompatible with their status. To expect slaves to practice monogamy when their marital ties might be broken at any time was an obvious hypocrisy that even the proselytizers could not rationalize.[97] Although privileged slaves like Phillis Wheatley and Jupiter Hammon found no contradiction between Christianity and slavery, most blacks were more discerning. They saw, for example, that black Christians were excluded from voting on church matters, barred from church offices, and segregated from the rest of the congregation at religious meetings.[98] Instead of inculcating respect for religion, proselytization more often nurtured contempt for white hypocrisy. The Reverend Samuel Hopkins of Newport found that the misconduct and brutality of Christian masters instilled slaves "with the deepest prejudices against the Christian religion."[99]

Despite its failure to win converts, the missionary effort forced the whites to face more squarely the fact that Negroes were persons as well as property. Although none of the proselytizers questioned the premises of slavery, some were bold enough to admonish the masters that they had a religious duty to treat their slaves humanely.[100] And by asserting the spiritual equality of blacks as moral beings they struck a powerful blow against the idea that slavery was justified by a natural inferiority of race. Spiritual equality of course did not mean temporal emancipation, but it

96. Richard Charlton to Philip Bearcroft, October 30, 1741, SPG Transcripts, No. 62, pp. 1–2, LC. See Klingberg, *Anglican Humanitarianism in Colonial New York*, p. 145.

97. Robert Jenney to the Secretary, March 19, 1725, SPG Transcripts, B1, p. 293, LC. See also John Bartow to the Secretary, November 15, 1725, *ibid.*, p. 217.

98. Greene, *The Negro in Colonial New England*, pp. 282–84.

99. [Samuel Hopkins], A *Dialogue Concerning the Slavery of the Africans* (Norwich, Conn.: Spooner, 1776), p. 20, quoted in *ibid.*, p. 288.

100. Humphreys, *Account of the Endeavours by the S.P.G.*, pp. 28–30.

closed somewhat the gap between the races.[101] The open hostility of most slaveholders to the missionaries sprang precisely from the fact that religious conversion undercut racial stereotypes and blurred the line between freedom and bondage. The proselytizers never attacked slaveholding directly, but they steadfastly insisted upon the equality of all races under God. This insistence proved far more important in the long run than their failure to win converts. It became, as the masters feared it would, a moral cutting edge against which slavery had no defense.

101. Klingberg, *Anglican Humanitarianism in Colonial New York*, pp. 122–23.

7

Fugitive Slaves

Blacks who fled slavery by the hundreds were a costly reminder to slaveholders that freedom was foremost in the mind of the bondsmen. So prevalent was the problem that an almost unbroken run of fugitive notices can be found in the newspaper files of every colony. Except for acts of violence and economic sabotage, running away was the clearest protest that Negroes could register against slavery. It cut deeply into profits and put the masters on notice that neither repression nor paternalism could reconcile blacks with bondage. Any slave might run away, and the owners were often surprised to find that even the most favored, docile bondsmen would defect when the chances of gaining freedom seemed favorable.[1]

Some runaways fled to the forest where they sought refuge among the Indians. The Senecas and Onondagas of northern New York assisted numerous fugitives, and the Minisinks of eastern Long Island not only provided help but also welcomed many blacks into the tribe.[2] Evidence of the assistance fugitives received can be found in the recovery clauses included in almost every colonial treaty with the tribes.[3] In 1732 the Pennsylvania authorities urged the Indians not to harbor Negroes, who were "the sup-

1. "Papers of the Lloyd Family of the Manor of Queens Village," in NYHS *Colls.*, LIX–LX (2 vols., 1926–27), I, 144; hereafter cited as "Lloyd Papers."
2. Evert Wendell's Account Book, 1695–1726, pp. 56, 89; Versteeg's Notes, pp. 14, 16; both in MS. coll., NYHS. See Kenneth W. Porter, "Relations between Negroes and Indians," *JNH*, XVII (1932), 308.
3. Porter, "Relations between Negroes and Indians," *JNH*, XVII (1932), 308.

port and livelihood of their masters, and get them their bread."[4] Though rewards were offered to induce the Indians to surrender runaways, there is no evidence that such cooperation was forthcoming.[5] Even Indians as closely allied with the English as the Iroquois refused to return blacks who took refuge among them.[6]

How many slaves found freedom among the Indians cannot be determined precisely, but the number was large enough to alarm the authorities. Since the Indians already had serious grievances of their own, there was an obvious danger that rebellious blacks might stir up trouble against the whites.[7] The eastern division of New Jersey became so alarmed about this possibility in 1682 that the council sought a meeting with the local sachems "to confer with them about their entertainment of Negro servants."[8] The presence of restive blacks among the tribes was particularly disturbing to British military authorities responsible for Indian relations.[9] One of the runaways living among the Mohawks stirred up so much trouble in western New York that the army had to reinforce its frontier garrisons.[10] When the Negro was finally captured in 1765, General Thomas Gage ordered him to be sold out of the province "so that he may never have an opportunity of getting among the Indians again."[11]

4. George E. Reed, ed., *Pennsylvania Archives*, 4th ser., 12 vols. (Harrisburg: State Printer, 1900–1902), II, 657–58. See Edward R. Turner, *The Negro in Pennsylvania* (Washington, D.C.: The American Historical Association, 1911), p. 50n.

5. "Letters and Papers of Cadwallader Colden, 1711–1775," NYHS *Colls.*, L–LVI, LXVII–LXVIII (9 vols., 1917–23, 1934–35), VII, 29–31; hereafter cited as "Colden Papers."

6. Franklin B. Hough, ed., *Proceedings of the Commissioners of Indian Affairs Appointed by Law for the Extinguishment of Indian Titles in the State of New York*, 2 vols. (Albany: Munsell, 1861), I, 76–77.

7. *Papers of Sir William Johnson*, 11 vols. (Albany: State University of New York, 1921–53), IX, 37.

8. *Documents Relating to the Colonial, Revolutionary, and Post-Revolutionary History of the State of New Jersey*, 42 vols. (Newark: New Jersey Historical Society, 1900–49), XIII, 22, hereafter cited as *N.J. Archives* (binder's title). See Henry S. Cooley, *A Study of Slavery in New Jersey* (Baltimore: The Johns Hopkins Press, 1896), p. 32.

9. J. Wickham Case, ed., *Southold Town Records*, 2 vols. (New York: Green's, 1882–84), I, 154; II, 74–75, 179. *Southampton Town Records*, 4 vols. (Sag Harbor, N.Y.: John S. Hunt, 1874–78), IV, 9. *Papers of Sir William Johnson*, IX, 37. "Colden Papers," IV, 166–68.

10. "Colden Papers," VII, 46–47.

11. *New York Weekly Post-Boy*, July 18, 1765.

Many fugitives tried to reach Canada in the hope of finding refuge with the enemies of their masters.[12] Those who succeeded were potentially dangerous, for they often brought information about frontier defenses and the size of the British garrisons. Some slaves ran away determined to help the French in any manner possible. According to the *Pennsylvania Gazette*, July 31, 1746, a fugitive from Kent County confided to a friend that "he would go to the French and Indians and fight for them." In 1756 John Harris of Philadelphia reported that one of his slaves had run away "in order to join the French and Indians."[13] So serious was the problem that New York imposed the death penalty on slaves trying to reach Canada. The law, first passed during Queen Anne's War in 1705, and reenacted in 1715 and 1745, provided that fugitives found forty miles north of Albany were to be hanged and their masters reimbursed by the county.[14]

But most runaways headed not for Canada but to the cities where the anonymity of urban life made it easier to avoid detection. The ports in particular attracted fugitives, for they provided opportunities to escape from the colony completely. Ship officers seldom asked too many questions, particularly if their crews were undermanned, so slaves could often sign aboard without much difficulty. Both men and women were drawn to the docks in the hope of putting themselves permanently beyond the reach of their masters.[15] The October 15, 1770, edition of the *Pennsylvania Chronicle* reported that a slave from Somerset, New Jersey, had been apprehended with false papers while trying to get aboard a ship in Philadelphia. Slaves from as far away as Ulster County looked to New York City as the springboard to freedom.[16] Indeed, it was almost automatically assumed that a runaway would at-

12. Daniel Parish, Transcripts of Material on Slavery in the Public Records Office in London (1729–60), p. 3, MS. coll., NYHS; hereafter cited as Parish's Transcripts.

13. Edward Shippen to Joseph Shippen, June 19, 1756, Shippen Papers, MS. coll., APS, cited by Darold D. Wax, "The Negro Slave Trade in Colonial Pennsylvania," unpublished Ph.D. dissertation (University of Washington, 1962), p. 156.

14. *Colonial Laws of New York from 1664 to the Revolution*, 5 vols. (Albany: James B. Lyon, 1894), I, 582–84, 880; III, 448; Hereafter cited as *N.Y. Col. Laws*.

15. *New York Weekly Post-Boy*, July 26, 1756. *New York Mercury*, February 20, 1764. *New York Weekly Mercury*, May 4, 1778.

16. *New York Weekly Post-Boy*, September 16, 1751; June 18, 1753; February 27, July 3, October 3, 1758.

tempt to escape by sea. Newspaper notices for fugitives repeatedly warn ship officers "not to carry off said servant at their peril, as they will answer as the law directs."[17]

Runaways fleeing to the cities often obtained food, shelter, and concealment from local blacks. The ease with which they slipped into the black population led New York to pass a law penalizing free Negroes ten shillings for every day a runaway was harbored.[18] A similar law in Pennsylvania provided that free Negroes entertaining slaves without the master's consent were to forefeit five shillings for the first hour and one shilling for every hour thereafter.[19] By denying fugitives the natural cover afforded by other blacks, the authorities hoped to isolate and discourage defection. But whether such measures had much deterrent effect is doubtful, for few blacks would willingly submit to laws protecting slavery.

Blacks who made the break for freedom tended to be young and aggressive, predominantly males, and mostly under the age of forty. Advertisements in New York reveal that about 80 percent of the runaways described by age and sex were men between the ages of eighteen and thirty.[20] The newspaper files of Pennsylvania show a similar youth-runaway correlation. More than 80 percent of all fugitives listed in the *American Weekly Mercury* and the *Pennsylvania Chronicle* were under the age of thirty-one, 18 percent were between thirty-one and forty, and less than 2 percent were more than forty.[21] Statistics on New England con-

17. *Ibid.*, July 31, 1766. See also *New York Mercury*, December 23, 1754; January 6, 13, 1755; June 4, August 13, September 24, 1759; March 17, April 14, May 5, August 4, September 15, December 19, 1760; February 16, July 20, August 3, November 30, December 7, 1761. *Pennsylvania Chronicle*, August 10, 17, 24, September 7, 1767; October 12, 31, November 7, 14, 1768; July 24, 31, September 11, 18, October 2, 1769; March 4, 11, 18, 1771. *New England Weekly Journal*, March 24, 1728/29; February 14, 21, 28, June 12, 1732; October 26, 1736; October 11, 18, 1737; February 7, 14, October 10, 1738; April 24, 1739; October 21, 1740; August 11, 1741.

18. *N.Y. Col. Laws*, I, 764.

19. James T. Mitchell and Henry Flanders, comps., *The Statutes at Large of Pennsylvania from 1682–1801*, 16 vols. (Harrisburg: State Printer, 1896–1911), IV, 61–62; hereafter cited as *Pa. Stat. at L.*

20. *New York Gazette*, 1726–34; *New York Weekly Journal*, 1734–43; *New York Weekly Post-Boy*, 1743–73; *New York Mercury*, 1752–68; *New York Weekly Mercury*, 1768–83.

21. *American Weekly Mercury* (Philadelphia), 1719–46; *Pennsylvania Chronicle*, 1767–74.

firm this pattern. Notices in eleven newspapers published between 1718 and 1784 reveal that two-thirds of all runaways were under the age of twenty-six, five-sixths were thirty-five or younger, and only one was as old as fifty.[22]

Generally women had fewer chances of escaping than men, for their household chores kept them under closer surveillance. Moreover, many of them lacked the strength to endure the hardships of running away, and others were burdened with young children who complicated even the most determined break for freedom. Of twenty-nine fugitives listed in one New England newspaper between 1727 and 1741, only one was a woman; a similar sample of forty runaways in Pennsylvania reveals that only four were women.[23] Nor were young children any likelier to run away, for they had no compelling motive to become fugitives. Only in the late eighteenth century, when the Revolutionary War had strained slave relations to the breaking point, did the number of children trying to escape become significant.[24] But even then only those old enough to fend for themselves ran away.[25] During the whole of the eighteenth century only two slaves under the age of eleven were recorded as fugitives.[26]

Aged slaves were even less likely to run away. Of all the fugitives recorded in the Northern press, only eight were over forty-nine years of age.[27] Even discounting those not advertised because they lacked market value, the scarcity of notices for older fugitives is striking. The most probable explanation is that older slaves had neither the stamina nor the motivation to take on the hard-

22. Lorenzo J. Greene, "The New England Negro as Seen in Advertisements for Runaway Slaves," *JNH*, XXIX (1944), 127–28, 131.

23. *New England Weekly Journal*, 1727–41; *American Weekly Mercury* (Philadelphia), 1719–35.

24. *New York Mercury*, 1752–68; *New York Weekly Mercury*, 1768–83; *New York Gazetteer*, 1783–87.

25. *Pennsylvania Chronicle*, September 7, 1767; June 26, 1769; December 23, 1771; January 25, 1773. *New York Weekly Mercury*, October 11, 1773; August 26, 1776; February 10, 17, September 22, 1777; September 27, December 20, 1779; August 28, October 23, 1780; July 16, October 8, 1781.

26. *American Weekly Mercury* (Philadelphia), July 30, 1724. *New York Weekly Mercury*, January 27, 1777.

27. *American Weekly Mercury* (Philadelphia), June 8, 1725. *New York Mercury* August 24, 1761; October 17, 1763; August 5, 1765. *New York Weekly Mercury*, March 17, 1777. *Frothingham's Long Island Herald*, June 7, 1791. *New York Journal & Patriotic Register*, August 15, 1795. See Greene, "The New England Negro," *JNH*, XXIX (1944), 131.

ships of running away. Since bondsmen over forty were seldom sold, those over fifty had usually had a decade of service with the same master. The relative comfort of their lot and long-standing habits of subordination tended to reconcile them to servitude. There were of course exceptions, for the desire to be free might flare up at any time. According to a report in *Frothingham's Long Island Herald,* June 7, 1791, a slave belonging to Lemuel Peirson of New York ran away at the age of ninety. But such defections were unusual, for the evidence is clear that older slaves seldom made the break for freedom.

Skilled artisans and craftsmen were just as likely to become fugitives as were the less-skilled field hands and common laborers. The runaway advertisements span every category of slave workers—sailors, shipbuilders, iron workers, coopers, waiters, carpenters, butchers, tailors, bakers, tanners, goldsmiths, bricklayers, plasterers, blacksmiths, farmers, and chimney sweeps.[28] There is no evidence that slaves of any particular economic level were more prone to flight than others. Nor is there any evidence that runaways were starved, overworked, or otherwise abused. What apparently motivated most was a deep revulsion for slavery as a way of life. Indeed, one New Englander expressed dismay that his slave had defected "without the least provocation."[29] What he failed to grasp was that slavery itself was provocation enough for running away.

Frequently slaves had a clear-cut reason for defecting. A beating or even a reprimand could turn an otherwise docile Negro into a fugitive. A slave belonging to Richard Fry of Pennsylvania ran away after being "whipped and pilloried . . . for horse stealing," and another Negro, also in Pennsylvania, became a fugitive

28. *Boston News Letter,* August 4, 1718. *New England Weekly Journal,* October 26, December 14, 1736; October 11, 1737. *Boston Gazette,* February 2, 1748; January 15, 1754. *Continental Journal* (Boston), August 6, 1778. *American Weekly Mercury* (Philadelphia), January 20, 1734. *Pennsylvania Gazette,* January 29, 1738/39; August 1, 1745. *Pennsylvania Chronicle,* August 17, 24, September 7, 1767; July 10, 24, 31, August 7, 1769; May 21, June 4, 25, 1770; August 5, September 2, 1771; July 20, 1772. *New York Weekly Journal,* May 10, 1736. *New York Weekly Post-Boy,* September 4, 1749; February 11, 1750/51; May 11, 1752; August 30, 1756; May 8, July 24, 1758. *New York Mercury,* July 18, 1757; May 22, 1758; December 12, 1763; May 16, 1774; March 17, 1777; August 29, September 6, 27, 1779. *New York Journal and State Gazette,* July 15, 1784. *New York Morning Post,* October 15, 1787.
29. *New England Weekly Journal,* August 9, 1731.

after being "much cut in the back by often whipping."[30] Such brutality could make a lifetime rebel regardless of how the slave was
treated by subsequent masters. Moreover, if past mistreatment
could be a factor, prospective punishment could be decisive in
motivating a slave to defect. A Massachusetts Negro named Jack
broke jail and ran away when arrested for stealing, and another,
in Pennsylvania, made a break for freedom after attacking his
master with a knife.[31] The prospect of punishment in such cases
was a compelling motive for running away.

Slaves often ran away in order to avoid being sold to buyers
in another town or colony. So repugnant was the idea of being
sold out of the colony that slaves marked for export had to be
watched carefully by the masters.[32] Such slaves could be a risky
investment for the buyer, for the urge to return to familiar locales
often proved irresistible. Many who became fugitives in order to
revive old relationships with friends and families returned to the
neighborhood of their former masters.[33] A runaway from Chester,
Pennsylvania, was reported "gone towards Newtown in this county
as he lived there several years ago," and another from Philadelphia was reported on his way back to New Jersey to rejoin his
"free mulatto wife . . . and two children."[34] According to the
New York Weekly Mercury, December 4, 1780, runaways made
their way back to their old neighborhoods from as far away as
Virginia and South Carolina.

How much some slaves valued their family attachments is a
recurring theme in notices for fugitives. A slave on Long Island reportedly ran away in pursuit of a wife who had been sold to a
distant buyer, and another in New York City was believed to have
returned to the neighborhood "where he had a wife and children."[35] Frequently male fugitives brought along their women and

30. Pennsylvania Gazette, July 4, 1745. Pennsylvania Chronicle, July 25, 1768.
31. New England Weekly Journal, January 2, 1738/39; Pennsylvania Chronicle,
October 12, 1767.
32. Anne Grant, Memoirs of an American Lady, 2 vols. (New York: Dodd,
Mead, 1901), I, 82–83.
33. New York Weekly Post-Boy, January 14, 1750/51. New York Weekly
Mercury, September 16, 1771; January 11, 1773. New York Journal & Patriotic
Register, May 7, 1794.
34. Pennsylvania Chronicle, September 21, 1767; August 1, 1772.
35. New York Weekly Post-Boy, April 23, 1753. New York Weekly Mercury,
September 16, 1771.

children, though this seriously reduced their chances of getting away.[36] One slave in Westchester, New York, burdened himself with his wife and two children, and another fled from Pelham Manor with his wife and four children.[37] The October 21, 1755, edition of the *New York Mercury* carried an advertisement for an intrepid slave who made his break for freedom with a wife "in an advanced state of pregnancy."

For a fugitive to remain at liberty for more than a short time required both luck and ingenuity. Since unknown blacks automatically aroused suspicion, a runaway had to be prepared to give a plausible account of himself as he moved from place to place. The passage of time brought no security, for slaves continued to be sought long after they had run away.[38] Fugitives unable to speak English had almost no chance of getting away, and in many cases they were arrested for this reason alone.[39] The *American Weekly Mercury* (Philadelphia) reported in its April 20, 1727, edition that a black had been jailed in Monmouth County, New Jersey, because his poor English rendered him incapable of explaining where he came from. Slaves able to speak the language of the masters were at least able to fabricate cover stories when questioned by the authorities.

Slaves of mixed blood comprised a fairly large proportion of all fugitives. A sample of New England runaways shows that about one-sixth were described in the newspapers as mulattoes.[40] The proportion was about the same in the Middle colonies.[41] Of

36. *American Weekly Mercury* (Philadelphia), July 8, 1725. *Pennsylvania Chronicle*, August 1, 8, 15, 22, 1772. *New York Weekly Post-Boy*, November 14, 1748; May 31, July 5, 1756. *New York Mercury*, October 8, 1759. *New York Weekly Mercury*, November 12, 1781.
37. *New York Weekly Post-Boy*, November 14, 1748. *New York Weekly Mercury*, June 30, 1777.
38. *Pennsylvania Chronicle*, September 21, 1767; July 4, 1768. *New York Weekly Post-Boy*, January 8, 1762. *New York Weekly Mercury*, July 1, 1776.
39. *American Weekly Mercury* (Philadelphia), October 27, November 3, 1720; September 15, 1726; April 27, 1727; November 13, 20, 27, December 16, 23, 1729; August 6, 13, 1730. *New York Weekly Post-Boy*, August 19, 1751. *New York Mercury*, November 9, 1761; October 11, 1762; June 17, 1765. *New York Weekly Mercury*, October 29, 1770.
40. Greene, "The New England Negro," *JNH*, XXIX (1944), 134.
41. *American Weekly Mercury* (Philadelphia), September 6, 1722. *Pennsylvania Gazette*, July 31, 1740; August 1, 1745; July 31, 1746. *Pennsylvania Chronicle*, June 15, August 10, 1767; July 10, 17, 24, 31, August 7, 1769; August 5, 11, 19, 26, 1771; July 20, 1772. *New York Weekly Post-Boy*, August 27, 1759; June 18,

sixty-one fugitives advertised in one Pennsylvania newspaper, about 20 percent had varying degrees of white blood.[42] In 1772 Philadelphians were warned that a runaway named Jem "is a cunning fellow and will probably endeavor to pass for a free man." Another fugitive in New York was reportedly trying "to pass for a white or free man, as he is of the whitish sort of mulattoes."[43] Even those not quite able to pass for white had an advantage, for any mixture of white blood made a claim of freedom more plausible.

To improve their chances of getting away, some slaves bided their time until they could obtain passes enabling them to travel without arousing suspicion.[44] Such passes provided excellent cover, and slaves unable to obtain real ones often falsified whatever papers they needed before running away. Notices for fugitives show an unmistakable correlation between literacy and the possession of counterfeit passes. In an advertisement in the *Pennsylvania Gazette*, August 28, 1755, an owner warned that since his fugitive "can write . . . it is likely he may have a counterfeit pass." Another slaveholder warned the public that his runaway would probably falsify a pass "as he can read and write."[45] Slaves unable to read or write sometimes obtained bogus passes from accomplices.[46] In 1773 John Foster of Southampton advertised a larger reward for the arrest of such an accomplice than he offered for the return of the runaway.[47]

The slaves who somehow managed to remain at liberty owed their success to superior intelligence and resourcefulness. The masters admitted as much in their advertisements. Richard Broekden of Philadelphia warned the public that his runaway was "very subtle," and another master in Dover advertised that his Negro

1761; March 18, 1771. *New York Mercury*, July 17, 1758; June 15, 1761; May 10, August 30, 1762; October 10, 1763; November 19, 1764. *New York Weekly Mercury*, July 20, 1772; October 12, 1776.

42. *Pennsylvania Chronicle*, 1767–73.

43. *Ibid.*, July 20, 25, 1772.

44. *New York Weekly Post-Boy*, January 24, May 9, 1757; August 21, 1758; October 23, 1760. *New York Mercury*, April 23, 1753; June 24, 1754; May 22, 1758; January 19, 1761; January 23, September 3, 1764. *New York Weekly Mercury*, June 8, 1772; July 29, 1776.

45. *Pennsylvania Chronicle*, April 13, 1772.

46. *New York Weekly Post-Boy*, December 5, 1765.

47. *New York Weekly Mercury*, April 5, 1773.

was "a sly fellow" able to fabricate a plausible cover story.[48] Runaways were frequently fluent in several languages, including French, Spanish, Dutch, and Swedish as well as English.[49] Some owners made a point of advertising a runaway as "a very sensible fellow" or "very fluent in his talk."[50] Others informed the public that their runaways were "sly," "genteel," "insinuating," "plausible," and "bright."[51] If these descriptions are correct, and there is no reason to doubt their accuracy, many of the fugitives were able to give a good account of themselves.

Most runaways timed their break for freedom with the most favorable weather. Winter was the worst possible time for running away, for the harsh northern climate foreclosed foraging for food and sleeping in open fields. A sample of sixty-two notices in the New England press shows that almost two-thirds of all fugitives chose warm or hot weather for running away.[52] Advertisements in one Boston newspaper during the period 1727–41 reveal that less than 23 percent of the defections occurred between November and March. The best time was between June and October, a period favored by almost 60 percent of the fugitives.[53] There was the same correlation between season and flight in the Middle colonies. A sample of ninety-one fugitives in Pennsylvania shows that five-sixths fled between April and October. When the weather was coldest, fugitives were fewest. Only one slave ran away in January and only two in February, about 3 percent of the total sample.[54]

Fugitives often helped themselves to money and extra clothes before running away.[55] A runaway belonging to Daniel Watts of

48. *American Weekly Mercury* (Philadelphia), December 4, 1726; *Pennsylvania Chronicle*, August 10, 1767.

49. *Pennsylvania Gazette*, July 31, 1740; September 24, 1741; August 1, 1745. *Pennsylvania Chronicle*, June 12, 26, July 3, 24, 1769; April 20, May 7, 1770. *New York Weekly Post-Boy*, February 26, 1750; August 21, 1766. *Continental Journal* (Boston), November 14, 1776.

50. Weyman's *New York Gazette*, November 10, 1760. *Pennsylvania Gazette*, June 21, 1744.

51. *American Weekly Mercury* (Philadelphia), March 20, 1732/33. *Pennsylvania Chronicle*, March 11, 1771. *New York Mercury*, January 18, 1762; July 4, 1763. *New York Weekly Mercury*, January 20, 1772.

52. Greene, "The New England Negro," *JNH*, XXIX (1944), 131–32.

53. *New England Weekly Journal*, 1727–41.

54. *American Weekly Mercury* (Philadelphia), 1719–36; *Pennsylvania Chronicle*, 1767–74.

55. *New England Weekly Journal*, October 10, 24, 1738. *New York Weekly Post-Boy*, July 11, 1748; July 1, 1751; September 16, 1754; April 14, 1755;

Massachusetts reportedly carried away "a morning suit, cinnamon colored coat with brass buttons, two hats, a pair of stockings, and a gun with a new rammer."[56] Horses were sometimes stolen to facilitate flight.[57] A resourceful slave belonging to John Lasker of New York rented a horse, which he charged to Lasker, in order to speed his escape.[58] Skilled artisans usually took along their tools in order to earn a living if they managed to gain permanent freedom.[59] Other slaves showed their determination not to return to slavery by taking along knives, firearms, and other weapons.[60] John Kirke of Pennsylvania reported that his two runaways "have with them a smart gun, well fixed," and Henry Nelson, also of Pennsylvania, warned that his slaves had taken along "two guns with some powder and shot."[61]

But some fugitives burdened themselves with possessions that must have hindered their flight. About one-third of all New England runaways analyzed in one sample carried away personal property of some sort.[62] In 1761 Ephraim Swift of Massachusetts reported that his slave had run away with a coat, cape, greatcoat, and two jackets as well as "a bundle of clothes and a violin."[63] Charles Read of Philadelphia advertised for a fugitive carrying "a bundled dog."[64] A slave in Brooklyn, New York, reportedly ran away with two sheep and a beehive full of honey, and another on Long Island reportedly took along his bed.[65] The desire not to

February 27, 1764; November 5, 1770. *American Weekly Mercury* (Philadelphia), March 4, 21, April 4, 18, 1728. *Pennsylvania Chronicle*, July 10, 17, 24, 31, August 7, 1769; April 30, May 7, 1770.

56. *New England Weekly Journal*, December 9, 1728.

57. *American Weekly Mercury* (Philadelphia), September 2, 23, 1731. *Pennsylvania Gazette*, October 8, 1747. *Pennsylvania Chronicle*, July 31, 1769; July 8, 15, 22, 29, 1771.

58. *New York Weekly Post-Boy*, June 21, 1764.

59. *American Weekly Mercury* (Philadelphia), March 20, 1733. *Pennsylvania Chronicle*, December 23, 1771. *New York Gazette*, August 27, 1733.

60. *New England Weekly Journal*, October 10, 1738. *American Weekly Mercury* (Philadelphia), May 15, June 8, 1727; September 23, 1731; June 20, 1734. *Pennsylvania Chronicle*, September 28, October 5, 12, 26, 1767; April 18, May 16, 1768; *New York Weekly Post-Boy*, April 3, 1749; November 15, 1764.

61. *American Weekly Mercury* (Philadelphia), October 5, 1721; September 2, 1731.

62. Greene, "The New England Negro," *JNH*, XXIX (1944), 140–41.

63. *Boston Gazette*, July 6, 1761.

64. *American Weekly Mercury* (Philadelphia), September 6, 1722.

65. *New York Weekly Post-Boy*, August 26, 1751. *Poughkeepsie Journal*, December 22, 1789.

abandon personal possessions is understandable, but it severely reduced the chances of getting away. Beehives, violins, beds, and
bundles of extra clothes were conspicuous impediments in an enterprise requiring a low level of visibility.

Despite harsh laws against harboring fugitives, there is evidence that runaways received assistance from whites and blacks
alike. In 1767 Alexander Runan of Philadelphia advertised that
his runaway was "well acquainted with most of the Negroes in
town, and it is thought some of them entertain him."[66] Another
master published a warning to the free Negroes of New York City
that anyone assisting his runaway would be prosecuted to the
fullest extent of the law.[67] Frequently fugitives were harbored by
white employers who provided them with false papers and profited
from their labor.[68] Sometimes white servants and black slaves ab-
sconded together, thereby providing one another with cover as
master and bondsman.[69] Since the white might eventually try to
sell the Negro, buyers were warned not to purchase any slave
without positive proof of ownership.[70]

Since young, vigorous blacks were the most likely to become
fugitives, the property loss alone must have been considerable.
New England slaveholders tried to cut their losses by offering rewards that ranged from four pence to £10 sterling, and from $1
to $500 in Spanish currency.[71] The average payment in New York
was 40 shillings, but in some cases rewards of £10 to £25 were
offered for particularly valuable runaways.[72] Although currency

66. *Pennsylvania Chronicle*, September 7, 1767.
67. *New York Weekly Mercury*, July 26, 1779.
68. *New England Weekly Journal*, February 14, 21, 28, June 12, 1732; October
26, 1736; October 11, 18, 1737; February 7, 14, 1738; October 21, 1740; August
11, October 6, 1741. *New York Weekly Post-Boy*, May 24, 1756; August 1, 1757;
July 3, 17, 1758; April 2, August 20, 1759; June 16, 1760; January 1, June 18,
July 23, 1761; January 14, September 2, 1762; December 5, 1765. *New York
Mercury*, October 8, 1759; February 9, 1761. *New York Weekly Mercury*, April
5, 1773; October 27, 1783. *American Weekly Mercury* (Philadelphia), April 25,
May 9, 1723. *Pennsylvania Chronicle*, August 10, 17, 24, September 7, 1767;
October 12, November 7, 14, 1768; July 10, 17, 24, 31, August 7, September 11,
18, October 2, 1769.
69. *Pennsylvania Gazette*, October 31, 1745; October 8, 1747. *Pennsylvania
Chronicle*, June 15, 1767; December 23, 1771. *New York Mercury*, July 18, 1757.
70. *American Weekly Mercury* (Philadelphia), April 25, May 9, 1723; May 9,
June 13, 1728.
71. Greene, "The New England Negro," *JNH*, XXIX (1944), 142–43.
72. *New York Mercury*, January 29, 1759; Weyman's *New York Gazette*, August
11, 1760.

fluctuations make it difficult to determine the actual purchasing power of these payments, some comparative conclusions are possible. A slaveholder in Philadelphia offered seven hundred pounds of tobacco for the return of a runaway, and a master in Trenton offered twice as much for a runaway as for the return of a horse.[73] Slaves almost always commanded higher rewards, sometimes five to six times greater, than those offered for the return of runaway indentured servants.[74]

The loss of slaves by flight had more than economic impact, for runaways were also rebels against the system. Every successful escape set off tremors that undermined discipline and encouraged others to defect. Indeed, mere contact with a fugitive might provide the spark that lit the desire for freedom. In 1764 a Philadelphia master reported that his slave had defected after being seen in the company of a black "supposed to be a runaway."[75] The likelihood of such subversion was real, for fugitives sometimes achieved remarkable mobility. Runaways from Maryland and Virginia continually slipped into Pennsylvania, and those from more distant places like Bermuda, Halifax, Jamaica, and St. Croix made their way to New England and New York.[76] Ship-jumping by slaves was common, and the major ports probably attracted more fugitives than they lost. These runaways mingled with the black population, and their apparent success in getting away provided an impetus to local defections.

The authorities tried to cope with the problem by requiring slaves to carry passes while away from home.[77] Any slave entering

73. *American Weekly Mercury* (Philadelphia), September 13, 1733. *Pennsylvania Chronicle*, July 8, 1771.

74. *American Weekly Mercury* (Philadelphia), July 30, 1724. *Pennsylvania Chronicle*, August 17, September 7, October 5, 1767; December 23, 1771.

75. *Pennsylvania Gazette*, September 20, 1764.

76. *American Weekly Mercury* (Philadelphia), December 29, 1719; January 5, 1719/20; September 6, 27, 1722; December 17, 24, 1723; May 7, 1724; July 9, 1730; March 20, 1733; September 25, October 2, 1735. *Pennsylvania Chronicle*, July 31, September 11, October 16, 1769; July 19, 1773. *New York Gazette*, June 11, August 6, September 24, 1733; May 6, 1734. *New York Mercury*, June 20, October 3, 1757; November 10, 1760; August 8, 1763; May 7, 1764. *New York Weekly Mercury*, October 17, 1774.

77. *Acts and Resolves, Public and Private, of the Province of the Massachusetts Bay*, 5 vols. (Boston: Wright & Potter, 1869–86), I, 535–36; J. Hammond Trumbull and Charles J. Hoadly, eds., *The Public Records of the Colony of Connecticut, 1636–1776*, 15 vols. (Hartford: Lockwood & Brainard, 1850–90), IV, 40; John R. Bartlett, ed., *Records of the Colony of Rhode Island and Providence Planta-*

New Jersey without a pass was to be flogged, and in Rhode Island the regulation applied to free Negroes.[78] Ship officers and ferrymen were subject to heavy fines for transporting slaves without permission, and they were also liable for civil damages if the slave was lost.[79] Any sudden crisis or public emergency brought a tightening of the controls. During Queen Anne's War, New Jersey provided that any slave found more than five miles from home without a pass was to be flogged, and that the person reporting the offense was to receive a mandatory reward from the master.[80] In 1755, during the French and Indian War, New York prescribed the death penalty for any slave older than fourteen who was found more than one mile from home without a pass. The law specifically authorized New Yorkers "to shoot or otherwise destroy such a slave . . . without being impeached, censured, or prosecuted for the same."[81]

Blacks suspected of being runaways were subject to summary arrest and detention. The authorities could act without warrants in such cases because runaways had to be taken by surprise if they were to be taken at all. Nor was there any redress for blacks seized by mistake. In Connecticut free Negroes stopped without a pass were required to pay court costs if brought before a magistrate.[82] The usual procedure was to clap suspects into jail while advertisements were run requesting their owners to claim them.[83] Any suspicion at all could lead to detention. In 1727 the sheriff of

tions in New England, 1636–1792, 10 vols. (Providence: Greene, 1856–65), III, 492–93; "Proceedings of the General Court of Assizes, 1680–1682," in NYHS Colls., XLV (1912), pp. 37–38; Samuel Nevill, comp., The Acts of the General Assembly of the Province of New Jersey, 2 vols. (Philadelphia and Woodbridge, N.J., 1752–61), I, 19; Pa. Stat. at L., IV, 63–64. Hereafter cited as Mass. Acts and Resolves, Conn. Col. Recs., R.I. Col. Recs., and "Proceedings of the N.Y. Assizes."

78. Nevill, N.J. General Assembly Acts, I, 19; R.I. Col. Recs., III, 492–93.

79. William H. Whitmore, ed., The Colonial Laws of Massachusetts [1672–86] (Boston: Rockwell & Churchill, 1890), p. 281; Charter and the Acts and Laws of His Majesty's Colony of Rhode Island and Providence Plantations in America (Providence: Sidney & Burnett Rider, 1858), pp. 70–71. Hereafter cited as Mass. Col. Laws [1672–86] and R.I. Charter, Acts, and Laws.

80. Nevill, N.J. General Assembly Acts, I, 18.

81. N. Y. Col. Laws, III, 1061.

82. Conn. Col. Recs., IV, 40.

83. New York Weekly Post-Boy, February 12, April 16, 1750; November 19, 1759; January 8, February 26, 1770. American Weekly Mercury (Philadelphia), September 15, 1726; July 5, 1733; September 25, October 2, 1735. Pennsylvania Chronicle, July 31, October 16, 23, 1769.

Monmouth County, New Jersey, jailed a Negro simply because he "speaks little English and can give no account of where he came from."[84] Another black was detained in New York City "because he had curious marks on his back."[85]

The sweeping power to arrest and detain suspected runaways could also be used to deprive free Negroes of their liberty. Since colonial law regarded all blacks as presumptively slaves, those unable to prove their freedom were always in danger of losing it.[86] There were no judicial safeguards; it was sufficient for a claimant to identify the suspected fugitive and to reimburse the sheriff and jailer for their expenses.[87] Even the failure of a claimant to come forward did not mean automatic release, for the authorities would then lose the costs of detention. Once arrested, a Negro had great difficulty ever regaining his freedom. So arbitrary was the police power that unclaimed suspects were sometimes sold into bondage to cover the cost of their detention.[88] When repeated advertisements failed to produce claimants for "a strange Negro man" in Newcastle, Pennsylvania, the sheriff finally gave public notice that "the said Negro is to be sold for payment of his prison charges."[89]

Most breaks for freedom probably ended in failure, for the racial visibility of the runaway naturally attracted suspicion. Nor could a fugitive consider himself safe even if he managed to reach another colony. Notices for runaways crossed colonial frontiers, and agents were available to claim fugitives arrested in distant places.[90] A slave belonging to Sir William Pepperell escaped to

84. *American Weekly Mercury* (Philadelphia), April 20, 1727.
85. *New York Weekly Mercury,* April 12, 1773.
86. Thomas R. R. Cobb, *An Inquiry into the Law of Slavery in the United States of America* (Philadelphia: Johnson, 1858), p. 67.
87. *American Weekly Mercury* (Philadelphia), September 15, 1726; April 20, 27, 1727; July 5, 1733. *Pennsylvania Chronicle,* January 25, 1773. *Pennsylvania Gazette,* July 31, 1776. *New York Weekly Post-Boy,* February 12, April 16, 1750; November 19, 1759; January 8, February 26, 1770. *New York Mercury,* November 9, 1761. *New York Weekly Mercury,* March 5, 1770; March 8, 1773.
88. *Pennsylvania Chronicle,* October 26, 1767; January 25, 1773. *New York Weekly Mercury,* October 22, 1770; March 8, April 12, 1773. *New York Gazetteer,* March 31, 1784.
89. *American Weekly Mercury* (Philadelphia), November 13, 20, 27, December 16, 23, 1729; August 6, 1730.
90. *New England Weekly Journal,* November 10, 1729; October 10, 1738. *Boston Gazette,* May 19, 1760. *Boston Evening Post,* May 23, 1763. *Boston News Letter,* August 4, 1768. *Connecticut Courant,* March 9, 1779. *New York Gazette,*

South Carolina in 1705, but was captured and returned to Massachusetts the following year.[91] Since every colony had some slaves, there was no disposition anywhere to give asylum to runaways. Slaveowners as a matter of self-interest cooperated in the return of fugitives, and nonslaveholders were kept in line by the penalties for harboring runaways. Unless a slave could escape from British jurisdiction completely, he was never really beyond the reach of the system.

Many slaves took advantage of the Intercolonial Wars to facilitate their escape. In 1756 Robert Benson of New York City advertised that his fugitive had been "skulking about the docks . . . ever since his running away, and wants to go privateering."[92] Slaves with maritime experience were naturally attracted to this means of escape, for privateer officers could be counted on not to ask too many questions. Others sought to escape by joining the militia. New York made extensive use of black manpower during the French and Indian War, and in Connecticut Negroes served in no fewer than twenty-five militia companies.[93] The enlistment of blacks naturally attracted runaways to the armed forces. A New York slave who fled to New Jersey in 1760 let it be known that "he would enlist in the provincial service."[94]

But the best chance of gaining permanent freedom came during the American Revolution when both sides bid for the support of the blacks. In 1779 Sir Henry Clinton, the British commander-in-chief, offered asylum and freedom "to every Negro that shall

June 11, September 24, 1733; May 6, 1734. *New York Weekly Post-Boy*, July 18, 1748. Weyman's *New York Gazette*, August 11, 1760. *New York Mercury*, May 7, 1764. *American Weekly Mercury* (Philadelphia), September 27, November 23, 1722; December 17, 24, 1723; July 30, October 15, 22, 1724; June 3, 10, 1725; September 19, 1726; July 9, 1730; October 24, 1734. *Pennsylvania Gazette*, September 11, 1740; September 24, 1741; June 21, 1744; August 1, 1745; August 28, 1755. *Pennsylvania Chronicle*, April 18, May 16, 1768; June 12, July 3, 10, 17, 24, September 11, October 2, 1769; May 21, June 4, 1770; July 8, 15, 22, August 5, 12, September 2, 1771; April 13, 20, May 4, June 1, July 13, 20, 1772; May 31, June 7, 1773.
   91. Elizabeth Donnan, ed., *Documents Illustrative of the History of the Slave Trade to America*, 3 vols. (Washington, D.C.: Carnegie Institute, 1930–35), III, 28n.
   92. *New York Weekly Post-Boy*, July 26, 1756.
   93. Benjamin Quarles, "The Colonial Militia and Negro Manpower," *MVHR*, XLV (1959), 651–52.
   94. Weyman's *New York Gazette*, August 11, 1760.

desert the rebel standard."[95] Although the Americans could not match this sweeping offer, individual officers helped slaves along the way to freedom. During the Saratoga campaign General Horatio Gates was accused by a New York slaveowner of harboring runaways in his army.[96] The greater difficulty of recovering fugitives during wartime can be seen in the declining valuation put on runaways. By 1777 the chances of getting a fugitive back had become so remote that the rewards offered for otherwise valuable slaves fell to as little as sixpence.[97]

More slaves gained freedom during the Revolution than in any comparable period. So many escaped when the British occupied New York City and Philadelphia that the slave populations there were permanently reduced.[98] Nor did the masters find it easy to recover slaves after the war, for the newly independent states made no provision for the return of runaways. Each state was free under the Articles of Confederation to make its own policy on fugitives without regard to the laws of the other states. Even after the extradition of runaways became legally possible under federal law, the task of recovery remained an unpopular and dangerous undertaking. One slave-catching service in New York went out of business after advertising for customers only once.[99]

That slaves used the Revolution to break their shackles is not surprising. So long and so deeply had blacks hated slavery that the sudden crisis of their masters set off shock waves against the system. "A desire of obtaining freedom," reported the *New York Weekly Mercury*, November 27, 1780, "unhappily reigns throughout the generality of slaves at present." But there was nothing new about this desire, only that the war gave it greater urgency and prominence. Whether they deserted to the British or served with the Americans in return for manumission, slaves used the conflict to gain for themselves the freedom that whites proclaimed as a natural right.

95. *New York Weekly Mercury*, September 27, 1779.
96. Winslow C. Watson, *Pioneer History of the Champlain Valley* (Albany: Munsell, 1863), pp. 182–84.
97. *Continental Journal* (Boston), March 12, 1777.
98. Evarts B. Greene and Virginia D. Harrington, *American Population before the Federal Census of 1790* (New York: Columbia University Press, 1932), pp. 102, 104; Turner, *The Negro in Pennsylvania*, p. 50.
99. *New York Journal & Patriotic Register*, January 16, 1799.

8

The Black Resistance

From the very beginning rebellious blacks made slavery expensive and dangerous for the masters. Besides those who opposed bondage by running away, many resisted by anti-social conduct and economic reprisals. Stealing and malingering became under slavery acts of sabotage against the system. Indeed, most slaves did not regard stealing as criminal at all, but rather as a form of self-help to mitigate their exploitation. Not that every theft was a conscious blow for freedom, but rather that crime itself was a logical response to slavery. The ordinary social conventions of honesty and respect for law were not virtues at all to the slave but only devices to facilitate his exploitation. By rejecting what white society esteemed, the blacks served notice that they were implacably at war with the system.

Frequently slave resentment flared into brutal reprisals against the master class. In 1708 a white New Yorker named Hallett, his wife, and their three children were murdered by two family slaves.[1] So shocking was the crime that the assembly gave the courts discretion to inflict terroristic punishments on slaves guilty of murder or conspiracy.[2] In 1729 a Negro was hanged in chains at Marlborough, Massachusetts, for killing his owner and her two children. The murders strained judicial sensibilities to the break-

1. E. B. O'Callaghan and Berthold Fernow, eds., *Documents Relative to the Colonial History of the State of New York*, 15 vols. (Albany: Weed, Parsons, 1856–87), V, 39; hereafter cited as *N.Y. Col. Docs.*
2. *Colonial Laws of New York from 1664 to the Revolution*, 5 vols. (Albany: James B. Lyon, 1894), I, 631; hereafter cited as *N.Y. Col. Laws.*

ing point, for in the end the slave was tried and condemned without a grand jury indictment. The governor personally waived the grand jury hearing because it was feared that the slave, being ill, might die and thereby escape public execution.[3]

Poison was often used to strike at unpopular masters. A slave in Salem, Massachusetts, was flogged for slipping ratsbane into his owner's milk, and another in Sherburne was jailed for attempting to buy arsenic for use against a white who had struck him.[4] Some of the most brutal crimes were obviously acts of vengeance against the masters. In 1735 the Scarlett family of Pennsylvania was wiped out by a slave who put ratsbane into the skillet where chocolate was boiling for their breakfast.[5] Sometimes the children of the master class provided targets for reprisals. In 1752 a Boston slave poisoned an infant, and another in Middletown, Connecticut, castrated his master's son.[6] Slaves committed such acts fully aware that their own lives would be forfeit. After killing his master, a black in Hopewell, Pennsylvania, hanged himself the following night.[7]

Every act of violence increased white fears of insurrection. Tensions ran highest during wartime when the absence of local militia led many to fear that the slaves might revolt.[8] In the districts of Long Island where some of the French exiles from Acadia enjoyed friendly relations with the blacks, military officials urged that the tightest security measures be taken to prevent insurrection.[9] The September 5, 1747, edition of the *New York Weekly Post-Boy* reported that a French-speaking slave caused so much anxiety that his owner had to sell him out of the province. Such fears usually waned in peacetime only to flare up again when hostilities resumed. In 1755, during the French and Indian War, Lieu-

3. *New England Weekly Journal*, June 23, 1729.
4. Joseph B. Felt, *The Ecclesiastical History of New England*, 2 vols. (Boston: Congregational Library Association, 1862), II, 460; Lorenzo J. Greene, *The Negro in Colonial New England, 1620–1776* (New York: Columbia University Press, 1942), p. 156.
5. *American Weekly Mercury* (Philadelphia), August 7, 1735.
6. Greene, *The Negro in Colonial New England*, pp. 155–56.
7. *Pennsylvania Chronicle*, October 26, 1767.
8. *New York Weekly Post-Boy*, September 29, 1755.
9. Daniel Parish, Transcripts of Material on Slavery in the Public Records Office in London (1729–60), pp. 16–17, MS. coll., NYHS; *Calendar of Council Minutes, 1668–1783* (Albany: State University of New York, 1902), p. 435. Hereafter cited as Parish's Transcripts and *Cal. of Council Min.*

tenant Governor De Lancey warned that the slaves were likely to revolt if the French attacked New York City.[10] Special patrols were organized to guard the city during the emergency.[11]

The whites had good reason to fear insurrection. As early as 1657, rebellious blacks and Indians destroyed some buildings in Hartford.[12] Again, in 1690, a plot was discovered to have Negroes and Indians join the French in an attack on the Massachusetts frontier. The plot was organized by an antislavery white named Isaac Morrill, who planned to lead a force of French and Indians against Massachusetts. The blacks would then rise, join in the attack, and return with the French to Canada. Before anything could be done, however, Morrill was arrested and sent to Ipswich for trial.[13] This effectively smashed the conspiracy, for the whole scheme apparently depended upon his ability to get French support. Nevertheless, that both blacks and Indians had been involved in the plot had frightening implications for the whites.

In 1712 some desperate slaves in New York City formed a conspiracy to win their freedom by armed rebellion. The leaders were fearless Coromantees whose involvement guaranteed that the outcome would be deadly.[14] "There never was a rascal or coward of that nation," wrote Governor Christopher Codrington of the Leeward Islands, "not a man of them but will stand to be cut to pieces without a sigh or a groan."[15] Since New York's population was almost one-fifth black, the plotters had no difficulty recruiting a vengeful band of rebels. A fierce cohesiveness bound the con-

10. *New York Weekly Post-Boy*, February 10, 1755.
11. *Cal. of Council Min.*, p. 435.
12. "Wyllys Papers, Correspondence and Documents: Chiefly of Descendants of Governor George Wyllys, 1590–1796," in CHS *Colls.*, XXI (1924), 137–38; hereafter cited as "Wyllys Papers."
13. Joshua Coffin, *A Sketch of the History of Newbury and Newburyport, and West Newbury from 1635 to 1845* (Boston: Drake, 1845), pp. 153–54; Greene, *The Negro in Colonial New England*, p. 160.
14. *Boston News Letter*, April 14, 1712.
15. W. Noel Sainsbury, *et al.*, eds., *Calendar of State Papers: Colonial Series, America and West Indies*, 42 vols. (London: H.M.S.O., 1860–1953), XX (1701), 721; hereafter cited as *Cal. State Papers, Col.* The Coromantees were not a particular ethnic or tribal group but probably belonged to the Ashanti nation. They were miscalled Coromantees from the fort at Coromantine, where they were assembled for shipment to America. See James Pope-Hennessy, *Sins of the Fathers: A Study of the Atlantic Slave Traders, 1441–1807* (New York: Capricorn Books, 1969), pp. 58–59.

spirators together in what can best be described as a brotherhood of rage. Recruits were bound by ceremonial oaths, including the drinking of one another's blood, and powders were distributed by a sorcerer to make them invulnerable.[16]

Shortly after midnight, on April 6, 1712, the plotters gathered in an orchard outside the town and armed themselves with muskets, pistols, and other weapons that had been cached there.[17] After about twenty-four of them had assembled, they set fire to a building and concealed themselves among the trees to await the whites. As the latter hurried toward the blaze, the slaves attacked, killing nine and wounding seven.[18] But the shouts and firing gave away the ambush and the town was soon awake and in arms. Even before the troops arrived, the townspeople had counterattacked and driven the hopelessly outnumbered blacks from the field. In their flight some committed suicide, and one of them killed his wife before taking his own life.[19]

Although the uprising had been defeated, no one could be certain that the danger had passed or how many slaves had been involved. Some feared that the uprising was only the opening blow of a general insurrection. Every able-bodied man was put under arms, and militia were brought in from nearby towns to reinforce the local garrison.[20] Having ordered the arrest of any Negro found without a pass, Governor Hunter requested the authorities in Connecticut and Massachusetts to block the escape of rebels attempting to reach New England.[21] Meanwhile, the militia of Westchester and New York City swept Manhattan Island for fugitives.[22] In the end, six of the ringleaders committed suicide, and the rest, desperate from hunger, finally surrendered.

16. Herbert Aptheker, *American Negro Slave Revolts* (New York: Columbia University Press, 1943), p. 172.

17. Kenneth Scott, "The Slave Insurrection in New-York in 1712," NYHS *Quarterly*, XLV (1961), 47.

18. *Boston News Letter*, April 14, 1712. Other accounts differ on the number of casualies. The Reverend John Sharpe, chaplain of the New York garrison in 1712, reported that the rebels "murdered about 8 and wounded about 12 more." SPG Transcripts, A7, pp. 215–18, LC.

19. Aptheker, *American Negro Slave Revolts*, p. 172; Scott, "The Slave Insurrection in New-York in 1712," NYHS *Quarterly* XLV (1961), 49.

20. *Boston News Letter*, April 14, 21, 1712. See Scott, NYHS *Quarterly*, XLV (1961), 51.

21. Parish's Transcripts (1695–1713), p. 27.

22. Scott, "The Slave Insurrection in New-York in 1712," NYHS *Quarterly*, XLV (1961), 49.

Counting those seized outside the city, a total of seventy blacks were arrested within two weeks of the uprising.[23]

It became clear from the outset that the judicial machinery would be used to terrify the slaves into submission. Although procedural formalities were technically observed, Attorney General Bickley believed that getting convictions was more important than getting at the truth. His principal witnesses were two slaves who had been charged with at least two murders during the uprising. Presumably in return for immunity, for neither was ever prosecuted, they testified against most of the defendants.[24] Writing to England, Governor Hunter reported that "without [their] testimonies very few could have been punished."[25] Actually, such testimony was legally insufficient to convict anyone. The two witnesses were admitted accomplices, and their testimony therefore required corroboration that the prosecution failed to provide. The defendants, however, knew nothing about rules of evidence and so did not challenge the sufficiency of the prosecution's case. In the end, twenty-five of them were convicted and sentenced to death.[26]

Since the law authorized terroristic punishments in such cases, New Yorkers witnessed the spectacle of blacks being burned at the stake, racked and broken on the wheel, and gibbeted alive in chains.[27] Robin, a slave who had been convicted of murdering Adrian Hoghlandt, was sentenced to "be hung up in chains alive and so to continue without any sustenance until he be dead."[28] Two other blacks convicted as accomplices also suffered horrible deaths. One was ordered "to be broke upon a wheel and so to continue languishing until he be dead," and the other to "be burnt with fire until he be dead and consumed."[29] Tom, a slave convicted of murdering Adrian Beekman and Henry Brasier, was sen-

23. David T. Valentine, comp., *Manual of the Corporation of the City of New York*, 28 vols. (New York, 1842–70), (1870), p. 766.
24. *N.Y. Col. Docs.*, V, 341–42, 357.
25. *Ibid.*, pp. 341–42.
26. Scott, "The Slave Insurrection in New-York in 1712," NYHS *Quarterly*, XLV (1961), 58–59.
27. *N.Y. Col. Laws*, I, 631.
28. Minutes of the General Quarter Sessions of the Peace, April 11, 1712, MS. in New York Supreme Court (formerly Court of General Sessions), New York City. According to the Reverend John Sharpe, Robin lasted for five days "though often delirious by long continuance in that posture, through hunger, thirst and pain." SPG Transcripts, A7, pp. 215–18, LC.
29. Minutes of the General Quarter Sessions of the Peace, April 11, 1712.

tenced to be "burned with a slow fire that he may continue in
torment for eight or ten hours."[30] Nothing reflected the spirit of
the proceedings better than the calculated barbarity of the sen-
tences.

Some of the defendants were the victims of malicious prosecu-
tions designed to embarrass their owners. Governor Hunter, a
fair-minded man who wanted justice done, reported that the trials
sometimes degenerated into "a party quarrel and the slaves fared
just as the people stood affected to their masters."[31] What particularly outraged his sense of justice was the "infamous proceeding"
against a slave named Mars, who belonged to an owner with
whom the attorney general had a private quarrel.[32] After two ac-
quittals the case was transferred to another court which finally
brought in a verdict of guilty. This was too much for Hunter, who
reprieved and later pardoned the persecuted slave.[33] If Hunter
had not also intervened in several other cases, the death toll would
certainly have been greater. "There has been too much blood shed
already," he wrote to justify his intervention, "and the people are
calm now."[34]

The assembly was determined to improve security by increasing repression. A law "for preventing, suppressing, and punishing
the conspiracy and insurrection of Negroes" placed slaves suspected of such crimes under the jurisdiction of special courts.
There was to be no grand jury hearing, and a trial jury could be
obtained only if the owner of the slave agreed to pay the costs.
This provided a swifter method of prosecution than was possible
in the regular courts, particularly in conspiracy cases involving
many suspects. Restrictions were also placed on free Negroes and
on the right of the masters to manumit their slaves. Freedmen
were forbidden to own "any houses, lands, tenements, or hereditaments," and a manumitting owner was henceforth required to
post a bond of £200 for every slave set free.[35]

30. *Ibid.*, April 15, 1712. See Samuel McKee, *Labor in Colonial New York,
1664–1776* (New York: Columbia University Press, 1935), p. 152.
31. *Cal. State Papers, Col.* XXVI (1711–12), 307.
32. *N.Y. Col. Docs.*, V, 356–57.
33. Scott, "The Slave Insurrection in New-York in 1712," NYHS *Quarterly*,
XLV (1961), 57–59.
34. *N.Y. Col. Docs.*, V, 356–57, 371.
35. *N.Y. Col. Laws*, I, 764–66.

So pervasive was the panic that even the missionary work of the SPG suffered a sharp setback. "This barbarous conspiracy," the Reverend John Sharpe wrote to the society, "opened the mouths of many against Negroes being made Christians."[36] Demonstrations were held against Elias Neau, the catechist for New York City, and the masters refused to allow their slaves to attend his classes.[37] Governor Hunter, whose good sense stands out through the whole affair, went to Neau's school in the company of several missionaries and publicly endorsed its aims.[38] He also issued a proclamation urging every clergyman to support proselytization, and, as a sign of confidence, he sent his own slaves to Neau's classes.[39] Nevertheless, the suspicion persisted that proselytization had somehow abetted the uprising. Fourteen years later an SPG worker on Long Island reported that slaveholders continued to oppose the instruction of their slaves because they feared another outbreak of violence.[40]

The New York City uprising sent a wave of apprehension through the North. Massachusetts reacted by passing an outright prohibition on slave imports, and Rhode Island required ship captains to register every black brought into the province.[41] Noting the "divers plots and insurrections" in neighboring colonies, Pennsylvania imposed a prohibitory duty of £20 on slave imports and authorized customs officers to break into any house or dwelling suspected of harboring smuggled blacks.[42] New Jersey set up spe-

36. SPG Transcripts, A7, pp. 215–18, LC.
37. David Humphreys, *An Account of the Endeavours Used by the Society for the Propagation of the Gospel in Foreign Parts to Instruct the Negro Slaves in New York* (London, 1730), pp. 9–10.
38. Scott, "The Slave Insurrection in New-York in 1712," NYHS *Quarterly*, XLV (1961), 68–69.
39. Elias Neau to New York City clergy, February 28, 1713/14, SPG Transcripts, A8, pp. 292–93, LC.
40. Thomas Standard to David Humphreys, Brookhaven, October, 1726, SPG Transcripts, A19, pp. 404–405, LC.
41. John C. Hurd, *The Law of Freedom and Bondage in the United States*, 2 vols. (Boston: Little, Brown, 1858–62), I, 265. John R. Bartlett, ed., *Records of the Colony of Rhode Island and Providence Plantations in New England, 1636–1792*, 10 vols. (Providence: Greene, 1856–65), IV, 131–35; hereafter cited as *R.I. Col. Recs.* The Massachusetts law was later construed to apply only to Indians, and so did not affect the trade in Negroes.
42. James T. Mitchell and Henry Flanders, comps., *The Statutes at Large of Pennsylvania from 1682–1801*, 16 vols. (Harrisburg: State Printer, 1896–1911), II, 433; hereafter cited as *Pa. Stat. at L.* The law was subsequently disallowed by

cial courts for the trial of slave offenders and denied Negroes the right to a grand jury hearing.[43] Moreover, a heavy duty of £10 was placed on imported slaves in order to attract white servants "for the better peopling of the country."[44]

New Jersey's security measures failed to prevent a conspiracy dangerously similar to the New York plot. In 1734 a group of slaves in Burlington County somehow became convinced that England had outlawed slavery and that they were being illegally kept in bondage. The rumor spread that Governor Cosby's bad relations with the legislature stemmed from colonial resistance to emancipation. Thus enraged against the masters, a large number of slaves formed a plot to gain their freedom by armed rebellion.[45] "Every Negro and Negress in every family was to rise at midnight," a Philadelphia newspaper reported, "cut the throats of their masters and sons, but not meddle with the women, whom they intended to plunder and ravish the day following."[46] When the massacre was over, the rebels intended to seek refuge among the French and Indians.[47]

Only luck saved the white inhabitants from a possible blood bath. While arguing with a white, one of the plotters asserted that he was as good as any of the masters and that the latter would soon have cause to know it. These remarks were reported to the authorities, and an investigation soon uncovered the plot.[48] Although most of the slaves in the county were suspected of complicity, only thirty of the ringleaders were brought to trial. Since no white had actually been harmed, the denouement was less bloody than the New York affair. Only one slave was hanged, several had their ears cut off, and the rest were severely flogged.[49]

England. See W. L. Grant and James Munro, eds., *Acts of the Privy Council: Colonial Series, 1613–1783*, 6 vols. (London: Wyman, 1908–12), II, 582.

43. Samuel Nevill, comp., *The Acts of the General Assembly of the Province of New Jersey*, 2 vols. (Philadelphia and Woodbridge, N.J., 1752–61), I, 20.

44. Samuel Allinson, comp. *Acts of the General Assembly of the Province of New Jersey* (Burlington, N.J.: Isaac Collins, 1776), p. 31. See Marion T. Wright, "New Jersey Laws and the Negro," *JNH*, XXVIII (1943), 166.

45. *New England Weekly Journal*, April 8, 1734.

46. *American Weekly Mercury* (Philadelphia), February 26, 1733/34.

47. *New England Weekly Journal*, April 8, 1734.

48. Henry S. Cooley, *A Study of Slavery in New Jersey* (Baltimore: The Johns Hopkins Press, 1896), pp. 42–43.

49. *Documents Relating to the Colonial, Revolutionary and Post-Revolutionary History of the State of New Jersey*, 42 vols. (Newark: New Jersey Historical

In 1741 a second wave of terror hit New York when slaves were again suspected of plotting to burn the city and massacre the whites. The whole affair grew out of a commonplace burglary committed by two slaves, Caesar and Prince, at the shop of Robert Hogg. During the investigation the authorities were informed that a white tavernkeeper named John Hughson had been an accomplice.[50] The information came from Mary Burton, an Irish servant belonging to Hughson, who accused her master, his wife, and their daughter Sarah, and also Peggy Kerry, a prostitute living at the tavern, of receiving property stolen by slaves. Part of Hogg's property was returned by Hughson, who denied knowing that it had been stolen, and the remainder was found under the floor of a building belonging to Prince's master. Caesar and Prince were arrested and charged with burglary, and Hughson, his wife, daughter, and Peggy Kerry were charged with receiving stolen property.[51]

A sudden outbreak of fires temporarily distracted New Yorkers from the charges pending against Hughson and the slaves. The fort, the governor's house, some government offices, and the troop barracks as well as several private buildings were struck by a series of inexplicable fires. Even more distracting was the growing insolence of the blacks as the fires multiplied. Some suspected that the fires had been set deliberately and that a slave conspiracy was in the making.[52] This suspicion was seemingly confirmed when a Negro was caught looting a burning building.[53] So charged with fear was the atmosphere that many whites began to leave the city for the safety of the country. The common council abetted the panic by offering rewards for the detection of "persons lately concerned in setting fires," though there was not a scrap of

Society, 1900–49), XI, 333, 340–42; hereafter cited as *N.J. Archives* (binder's title). The talkative slave who gave the conspiracy away was sentenced to death but managed to escape. *American Weekly Mercury* (Philadelphia), February 26, 1733/34.

50. Daniel Horsmanden, *The New York Conspiracy, History of the Negro Plot, 1741–1742* (New York: Southwick & Pelsue, 1810), pp. 15–16.

51. Since burglary was not one of the crimes transferred to the jurisdiction of the slave courts in 1712, the usual judicial procedures were followed. *N.Y. Col. Laws*, I, 765–66. See Horsmanden, *The New York Conspiracy*, pp. 20–23; Walter F. Prince, "New York Negro Plot of 1741," pp. 7–9, typescript in NYHS.

52. Horsmanden, *The New York Conspiracy*, pp. 23–30.

53. *New York Weekly Journal*, April 27, 1741.

evidence that arson had been committed. Any white providing information was to receive £100, and any slave who came forward was to be freed, pardoned, and given a £25 reward.[54]

Information came somewhat unexpectedly eleven days later when Mary Burton appeared before the grand jury to testify about the Hogg burglary. In the course of her testimony she hinted that she knew something about the fires. Urged to tell everything, she charged that the fires had been set by slaves on orders from Hughson. In a lurid, rambling tale Burton accused the Hughsons and Peggy Kerry of plotting with blacks to burn the city and massacre the white inhabitants. Numerous slaves had allegedly joined the conspiracy, including Caesar and Prince, who were among the ringleaders. She charged that the plotters planned to set up a new government under Hughson and Prince, and that any white women who survived the massacre were to be divided among the rebels as wives and concubines.[55]

Before pursuing these new accusations, the authorities first prosecuted the burglary and stolen property charges. Both were capital crimes, and once convictions had been obtained the accused might then be persuaded to confess their involvement in the conspiracy in order to save themselves. Caesar and Prince were found guilty of burglary, and the Hughsons and Peggy Kerry were convicted of receiving stolen property.[56] Offers of clemency were made to induce Caesar and Prince to confess their roles in the plot and cooperate with the authorities. All these overtures were rejected. Both slaves denied knowing anything about a plot, and both went to the gallows without implicating others.[57]

Two other slaves, Quack and Cuffee, were the first of the alleged conspirators to be tried on the charges made by Mary Burton. What happened to them set precedents for the trial of other defendants. By far the worst precedent of all was set by the New York Bar, which refused to a man to assist the defense.[58] Also

54. *Minutes of the Common Council of the City of New York, 1675–1776,* 8 vols. (New York, 1905), V, 17–18; hereafter cited as *N.Y. City Council Min.*
55. Horsmanden, *The New York Conspiracy,* pp. 37–40.
56. *Ibid.,* pp. 41, 48.
57. I. N. Phelps Stokes, ed., *The Iconography of Manhattan Island,* 6 vols. (New York: Dodd, 1915–28), IV, 562; Horsmanden, *The New York Conspiracy,* p. 60.
58. Valentine, *Manual* (1856), pp. 448–50.

despicable was the conduct of Attorney General Bradley, who used a convicted thief named Arthur Price to spy on the defendants in prison. Predictably, for his life depended on cooperating with Bradley, Price testified that Quack and Cuffee had admitted that they had set several fires on orders from Hughson. This was denied by both slaves who insisted that no admissions had been made and that they were innocent of any wrongdoing.[59] The cards, however, had been stacked against them. Despite testimony by their masters that they had been at home when the alleged arsons occurred, both were convicted, and sentenced to be burned at the stake.[60]

Quack and Cuffee were offered clemency if they would disclose what they knew about the conspiracy. Although the pressure on them must have been tremendous, they insisted upon their innocence almost until the end. Only when chained to the stake did they make confessions that implicated others and named Hughson as "the first contriver of the plot."[61] But the confessions came too late, for the mob that had gathered threatened to riot when it appeared that the executions might not take place. When the sheriff reported that there would be "great difficulty if not danger in an attempt to take the criminals back," Lieutenant Governor Clarke authorized him to carry out the executions.[62] Thus Quack and Cuffee died anyway, but the confessions that failed to save them would help to bring others to the same fate.[63]

When the turn of the Hughsons and Peggy Kerry came, the outcome was never really in doubt. Mary Burton repeated her now familiar charges, and Arthur Price testified that Peggy and Mrs. Hughson had confessed their guilt to him in prison.[64] Attorney General Bradley then called several witnesses who testified about the confessions made by Quack and Cuffee. Except for Mary Burton's testimony, none of this evidence was legally admissible. Arthur Price, a convicted felon, had no standing as a witness, and the testimony about the confessions violated both the

59. Horsmanden, *The New York Conspiracy*, pp. 61–62.
60. *Ibid.*, pp. 79–96.
61. Valentine, *Manual* (1866), pp. 816–17.
62. Horsmanden, *The New York Conspiracy*, p. 100.
63. *Ibid.*, pp. 96–102.
64. *Ibid.*, pp. 109–20.

hearsay rule and a statute barring the use of slave testimony against whites.[65] The defendants, however, knew nothing about rules of evidence and so let the damaging testimony stand unchallenged. Their helplessness against such tactics made the verdict a foregone conclusion. They were all found guilty and sentenced to be hanged. Hughson, his wife, and Peggy Kerry were executed a week later. Sarah Hughson, however, was reprieved in the expectation that she could be persuaded to confess.[66]

The summer of 1741 was a season of bloody repression. Blacks were condemned daily, and executions averaged about two each week. Mary Burton was the nemesis throughout, and her power grew as the trials progressed. The judges and the attorney general hung on her every word, indicting and prosecuting anyone she accused in testimony that grew steadily wilder. Many of the accused in turn implicated others, for it was clear by now that no other course would save them.[67] By the end of August, 154 Negroes and 24 whites had been jailed for complicity in the conspiracy.[68] As accusations multiplied it seemed that the plot had tentacles everywhere. "If the truth were ever known," Lieutenant Governor Clarke wrote to England, "there are not many innocent Negro men."[69]

The growing web of incrimination slowed down the prosecution and brought the proceedings themselves into question. With slaves confessing in droves, the authorities had to sort out a mass of wildly conflicting stories.[70] Moreover, some New Yorkers were becoming openly critical of the proceedings, particularly those whose slaves had been implicated. They feared that if the trials continued and accusations multiplied at the current rate, not a slave in the city would escape incrimination.[71] To make an example of a few ringleaders might be sound policy, but to purge the slave population indiscriminately was economically wasteful. Justice Daniel Horsmanden, who presided at the trials, com-

65. N.Y. Col. Laws, I, 597–98.
66. Horsmanden, The New York Conspiracy, pp. 122–40.
67. Valentine, Manual (1856), pp. 448–50.
68. Cal. of Council Min., p. 338.
69. N.Y. Col. Docs., VI, 196.
70. New York Weekly Journal, July 27, 1741.
71. Horsmanden, The New York Conspiracy, p. 370.

plained that the masters quickly closed ranks against the proceedings "when it comes home to their own houses and is like to affect their own properties in Negroes."[72]

The hunt for conspirators took a final, bizarre turn when a warning arrived from Governor Oglethorpe of Georgia that Spain was sending priests into the colonies to foment rebellion.[73] The warning breathed new life into the proceedings, giving them an added dimension of religious and national animosity. The idea itself seemed plausible. Spain and England were at war; moreover, the Spaniards had already used priests to subvert Indians and blacks on the Southern frontier.[74] In any case, suspicions soon focused on a Latin teacher named John Ury, who had arrived a few months before and who had a talent for theological disputation. Most New Yorkers had simplistic ideas about priests, and Latin and religious casuistry were part of the stereotype. It was Mary Burton, however, who brought about Ury's arrest by charging that he was a "popish priest" and the real leader of the conspiracy.[75]

However, Burton's accusations against Ury could not be reconciled with her earlier testimony. Originally she had named Hughson as the leader of the plot; she made no charges at all against Ury, nor did she say anything to indicate that the conspiracy had religious implications.[76] Glossing over these contradictions, Attorney General Bradley lined up two corroborating witnesses of dubious credibility. The first was a soldier named William Kane, who had already been accused by Burton of complicity in the plot. Kane told a wild story of being admitted to the conspiracy by Hughson and Ury, and that the latter had performed Catholic rites to bind the plotters together.[77] The second witness was Sarah Hughson, already under sentence of death, who had been promised a pardon if she cooperated. The terrified

72. "Letters and Papers of Cadwallader Colden, 1711–1775," NYHS *Colls.*, L–LVI, LXVII–LXVIII (9 vols., 1917–23, 1934–35), II, 226; hereafter cited as "Colden Papers."

73. Valentine, *Manual* (1856), p. 769.

74. Joseph C. Carroll, *Slave Insurrections in the United States, 1800–1865* (Boston: Chapman & Grimes, 1938), pp. 122–23.

75. Stokes, *Iconography of Manhattan Island*, IV, 569; Valentine, *Manual* (1870), p. 770.

76. Valentine, *Manual* (1870), p. 770.

77. Horsmanden, *The New York Conspiracy*, p. 295.

girl answered in the affirmative to some leading questions and haltingly confirmed that Mary Burton had told the truth.[78] This was the whole of the prosecution's case, but it took the jury only fifteen minutes to bring in a verdict of guilty.[79]

A few days after Ury's execution Mary Burton suffered an irreparable loss of credibility. Intoxicated by self-importance, she began to accuse highly placed New Yorkers of complicity in the plot. With their star witness making ridiculous charges, the authorities had to stop the proceedings or risk losing their own reputations. Even Judge Horsmanden, whose credulity had previously been boundless, now urged "a little relaxation from this intricate pursuit."[80] Fourteen slaves had been burned at the stake, eighteen hanged, and seventy-two deported from the province; in addition, four whites, two of them women, had been hanged.[81] The death toll had been too great for the authorities to admit that they had been hoodwinked. The provincial council put a good face on things by proclaiming a day of thanksgiving "for deliverance from the said conspiracy."[82] Moreover, when Mary Burton claimed the reward for exposing the plot, she got not only her money but also a vote of gratitude from the council "for the great service she had done."[83]

The New York conspiracy trials stand as almost classic examples of judicial murder. Except for the testimony of Mary Burton and William Kane, all the prosecution evidence was legally inadmissible. Neither Arthur Price nor Sarah Hughson was a qualified witness, for in colonial times convicted felons could not testify. And the testimony about the confessions of Quack and Cuffee violated a statute as well as the rule against hearsay. But because the defendants had to stand trial without counsel, the inadmissible evidence went unchallenged. When Ury, who was better educated than the rest, challenged Sarah Hughson's standing as a witness, Attorney General Bradley craftily procured a pardon to remove her felon's disability.[84] What Bradley and other officials

78. *Ibid.*, pp. 138, 162, 183, 223, 246, 295.
79. "Colden Papers," II, 225.
80. *Ibid.*, p. 227.
81. Parish's Transcripts (1729–60), p. 34.
82. *Cal. of Council Min.*, p. 338.
83. Parish's Transcripts (1740–47), p. 10.
84. Horsmanden, *The New York Conspiracy*, p. 295.

wanted was not justice for the accused but mass repression through judicial terror. The refusal of the entire New York Bar to defend any of the accused is convincing evidence of how the ruling class regarded the proceedings.[85]

Some of the panic spilled over into other colonies, and incidents involving slaves were magnified out of all proportion. A series of fires in New Jersey brought a warning from Lieutenant Governor Clarke that "some Negroes . . . are accomplices and were to act their part there."[86] When a slave was arrested near a burning building, the rumor quickly spread that a conspiracy had been formed.[87] "The people thereabouts are greatly alarmed," reported the *New England Weekly Journal*, May 12, 1741, "and keep under arms every night." Two blacks were convicted of arson and burned at the stake, though many more were suspected of complicity in setting the fires.[88] As tensions grew during the summer of 1741, even crimes unrelated to plotting evoked brutal reprisals. In July a slave was hanged at Kingston, New York, for assault, an offense usually punished by flogging.[89] In Roxbury, Massachusetts, a Negro suspected of stealing was seized and beaten to death by an enraged mob.[90]

The fierce conflicts that preceded the American Revolution inevitably produced rumors that the British planned to use the slaves against the patriot party. In 1768 a British army captain named John Wilson was arrested in Boston for inciting Negroes to rise against their masters. According to a report in the *Pennsylvania Chronicle*, November 14, 1768, Wilson urged the slaves "to cut their masters' throats," assuring them that with the army's support "they should be able to drive all the Liberty Boys to the devil." The authorities were so alarmed by the affair that the town watch was ordered to seize any slave found on the streets at night.[91] In 1774 some Boston slaves offered General Gage their services in return for freedom. Though the details of the offer

85. Prince, "New York Plot of 1741," pp. 12–13.
86. *N.Y. Col. Docs.*, VI, 196.
87. *N.J. Archives*, XII, 88–92, 98–99.
88. Cooley, *Study of Slavery in New Jersey*, p. 43.
89. Justices Court, Ulster County, Kingston, July 1, 1741, HDC, QC.
90. *New England Weekly Journal*, July 21, 1741.
91. *New York Weekly Post-Boy*, November 14, 1768.

remain unclear, it must have been obvious to the masters that the blacks were becoming both restive and dangerous. In reporting the affair to her husband in Philadelphia, Abigail Adams expressed the wish that "there was not a slave in the province."[92]

When the confrontation with Great Britain turned into armed conflict, the subversion of slaves became a deadly serious business. Even as the militia marched to Lexington in 1775, rumors spread that the slaves would massacre the noncombatants left behind. In Framingham, people armed themselves with axes, clubs, and pitchforks, and waited behind locked doors until the troops returned.[93] The British of course worked hard to drive a wedge between the slaves and their patriot masters. During the bloody Tory raids in central New York the blacks were treated as neutrals unless they took arms to defend their masters.[94] Word that disloyalty to one side would be rewarded by the other spread rapidly through the slave population. "The Negroes have a wonderful art of communicating intelligence," John Adams observed, and what they communicated as the war deepened was hardly to the liking of their masters.[95]

Slaveholders particularly feared that the enlistment of blacks in the loyalist militia might create a nucleus for armed rebellion. So many slaves were armed by the Tories on Long Island that Governor Trumbull of Connecticut believed that a foray into New England was imminent.[96] The situation was also dangerous in eastern New Jersey and northern New York, where British sympathizers tried to stir up discontent.[97] Frequently fear of slave subversion pinned down local militia badly needed on the fight-

92. Charles F. Adams, ed., *Letters of Mrs. Adams, the Wife of John Adams*, 2 vols. (Boston: Little, Brown, 1840), II, 24, cited in Greene, *The Negro in Colonial New England*, p. 163.

93. Josiah H. Temple, *History of Framingham, Massachusetts* (Framingham, Mass.: the Town, 1887), p. 275.

94. Jeptha R. Simms, *The Frontiersmen of New York*, 2 vols. (Albany: George C. Riggs, 1882–83), II, 176.

95. Charles F. Adams, ed., *The Works of John Adams*, 10 vols. (Boston: Little, Brown, 1850–56), II, 428.

96. Peter Force, ed., *American Archives*, 5th ser., 9 vols. (Washington, D.C.: M. St. Clair Clarke & Peter Force, 1848–53), II, 252.

97. V. H. Paltsits, ed., *Minutes of the Commissioners for Detecting and Defeating Conspiracies in the State of New York*, 2 vols. (Albany: State University of New York, 1909–10), II, 699–700, 741, 750, 762; Edwin F. Hatfield, *History of Elizabeth, New Jersey* (New York: Carlton & Lanahan, 1868), p. 476.

ing front. The Albany Committee of Safety refused to release the county militia while the slaves were restive. A tight curfew was placed on the city, and troublesome blacks were deported to New England as a preventive measure.[98] The Schenectady Committee of Correspondence regarded even minor slave offenses as evidence of British subversion. The town watch was strengthened, and slaves found in the streets at night were severely flogged.[99]

Although preoccupation with internal security diverted energy and manpower from the war effort, black rebelliousness left the Americans no alternative.[100] In 1776 a slave in Bucks County, Pennsylvania, declared that he would "burn the houses and kill the women and children of the Associators when they marched out."[101] Tory agents in northern New York were particularly dangerous, for British prisoners were available in the Albany area to join in an uprising.[102] The danger did not end until the town council ordered all prisoners of war to be moved out of the district.[103] Such precautions were well taken, for slaves had repeatedly shown their willingness to help the British. In 1779 a black was arrested in Albany for "seducing a number of Negroes to join the enemy." Another slave was ordered out of the county for trying "to stir up the minds of the Negroes against their masters and raise insurrection among them."[104]

The Revolution brought all the dangers of slave discontent into final focus. Actually the disintegration of discipline during the war was consistent with the whole history of slavery. Blacks had always resisted the system by any means possible. By running away by the hundreds and by repeated outbreaks of violence they made it clear how much they hated bondage. In the New York

98. Force, ed., *American Archives*, 5th ser., III, 226; *Minutes of the Albany Committee of Correspondence, 1775–1778*, 2 vols. (Albany: State University of New York, 1923–25), I, 585, 954.

99. *Minutes of the Albany Committee of Correspondence*, II, 1090.

100. Paltsits, *Minutes of the Commissioners for Detecting Conspiracies*, I, 142–43; II, 454–55, 702–703, 705–706.

101. Samuel Hazard, ed., *Pennsylvania Archives*, 1st ser., 12 vols. (Philadelphia: Severns, 1852–56), IV, 792.

102. Paltsits, *Minutes of the Commissioners for Detecting Conspiracies*, II, 699–700, 741, 750, 762.

103. Joel Munsell, ed., *Collections on the History of Albany*, 4 vols. (Albany: Munsell, 1865), I, 282.

104. Paltsits, *Minutes of the Commissioners for Detecting Conspiracies*, I, 304.

City uprising of 1712 they killed or wounded at least sixteen whites. The same proportion of casualties to the population today would be more than four thousand. Slaves not only wanted freedom, but they were prepared to kill and be killed in order to get it. If they did not always achieve their goal, they nevertheless succeeded in making their bondage troublesome and sometimes deadly for the masters.

9

Breaking the Chains

Blacks hated bondage so desperately that far-sighted masters sometimes obtained loyal service by promising them eventual freedom. Godfrey Wenwood, a Newport baker, agreed to free his slave Bob "if the said Bob shall well, truly, honestly and faithfully perform and discharge the duty of a slave . . . during the full term of nine years."[1] Frequently slaves paid for their freedom with the money they earned by working nights or hiring their free time.[2] Benjamin Mifflin of Pennsylvania agreed "to sell his Negro man Cuff to himself for sixty pounds if he can raise the money."[3] Other masters allowed their slaves to earn their way to freedom by paying installments over a period of time. Hannah Cornell of Hempstead, New York, agreed to manumit her slave "if he can pay my son or his heirs the sum of £4 for eighteen years." Another owner, also in Hempstead, promised freedom to a Negro "provided he will return to my executors yearly the sum of £3 for the use of my wife and children."[4]

Slaves sometimes convinced their masters of the wisdom of such arrangements by malingering until they got what they

1. Godfrey Wenwood manumission, June 18, 1781, Box 43, Folder 4, MS. coll., NHS.
2. Josephine C. Frost, ed., *Records of the Town of Jamaica, Long Island, New York 1656–1751*, 3 vols. (New York: Long Island Historical Society, 1914), III, 346–47, 349–55.
3. Miscellaneous Manuscript Collection, Negroes, Box 10, HSP.
4. "Abstracts of Wills on File in the Surrogate's Office, City of New York," in NYHS *Colls.*, XXV–XLI (17 vols., 1892–1908), X, 63–64, 271–72; hereafter cited as "N.Y. Abstracts of Wills."

wanted. But in most cases this was not necessary, for slaveholders generally recognized that the prospect of freedom could make slaves more valuable workers. This was particularly true of black artisans who could not be managed efficiently by coercion alone. Those with the highest skills could often bargain effectively for manumission and were even able to prevent unwanted sales by refusing to work for prospective buyers.[5] Threats which might be sufficient to compel compliance could not guarantee the quality of a slave's performance. When a Rhode Island slave named Jack Davis was hired out as a seaman in 1778, his master promised him freedom "provided he behaves well and there is no well-founded complaint against him by any officer."[6]

Not every manumission served economic ends, for some were motivated by antislavery sentiment. Moses Brown of Providence manumitted his slaves after becoming convinced that "the buying and selling of men of what colour soever as slaves is contrary to the Divine Mind."[7] Another master in Westchester County, New York, freed his slaves "believing it to be consistent with the will of kind Providence, who hath created all nations with one blood."[8] Numerous freedom certificates were recorded by masters who made it clear that they had manumitted their slaves "in order to serve the cause of humanity."[9] Even nonslaveholders took a hand in manumission. In 1769 a public subscription in Philadelphia among "sundry well-disposed people" drew numerous pledges of support for buying a Negro's freedom.[10] In other cases the entire freedom price was paid by some philanthropist. For example, Samuel Rodman of Newport advanced $120 in lieu of two years of service that a slave named Cato owed his master in return for manumission.[11]

Most of the moral opposition to slavery came from Quakers who found the system incompatible with the tenets of their reli-

5. Reyer Schermerhorn to Governor George Clinton, N.Y., January 13, 1788, in Beekman Papers, Box 32, Folio 1, MS. coll., NYHS.

6. A. Cary & Son manumission, November 10, 1778, Box 43, Folder 4, MS. coll., NHS.

7. Moses Brown manumission, November 10, 1773, Moses Brown Papers, II, 331, MS. coll., RIHS.

8. "N.Y. Abstracts of Wills," X, 8.

9. Register of Manumissions, pp. 63, 65–66, MS., coll., MCNY.

10. Miscellaneous Manuscript Collection, Negroes, Box 10, HSP.

11. Abraham Rivera manumission, November 24, 1794, Box 43, Folder 4, MS. coll., NHS.

gion. As early as 1688 Quaker settlers in Germantown, Pennsylvania, sent a remonstrance to their monthly meeting condemning slavery as a form of stealing, and urging that Negroes "be delivered out of the hands of the robbers and set free."[12] In 1693 George Keith, the leader of a schismatic group of Quakers, published a pamphlet urging his followers to free their slaves within a reasonable time. Keith's pamphlet, the first antislavery tract printed in the colonies, denounced slaveholding as an affront to Christianity and humanity, and declared that no Friend should buy slaves except to set them free.[13] Three years later the orthodox Quakers moved toward Keith's position. The Philadelphia Yearly Meeting officially condemned the slave trade, and Friends were admonished "not to encourage the bringing in of any more Negroes."[14]

For many Quakers the observable brutality of slavery was reason enough to be against it. In 1711 a Rhode Island Monthly Meeting expelled a member for "hardness of heart" in beating a Negro slave.[15] So repugnant was violence in any form that Quaker merchants sometimes felt constrained to disclaim any interest in the slave trade.[16] By the middle of the eighteenth century manumissions among Quakers had become very frequent. Finally, in 1758, the Pennsylvania and New Jersey Yearly Meeting officially condemned slaveholding and exhorted "such Friends who may have any slaves to set them at liberty."[17] Taking an even stronger stand a decade later, the New York Yearly Meeting declared that Negroes "are by nature born free, and when the way opens liberty ought to be extended to them."[18]

The way to liberty, however, could not be opened by good will alone. Since aged or infirm Negroes might become a public charge, almost every colony regulated the conditions under which they could be freed. Connecticut took the lead in 1702 with a law

12. "The Germantown Protest," *PMHB*, IV (1880), 28–30.
13. George Keith, *An Exhortation and Caution to Friends Concerning Buying or Keeping of Negroes* (New York: William Bradford, 1693), copy in JCBL.
14. Minutes of the Philadelphia Yearly Meeting (1681–1746), p. 57, microfilm copy in Friends Historical Library, Swarthmore College.
15. Rufus M. Jones, *The Quakers in the American Colonies* (New York: Russell & Russell, 1962), pp. 156–57n.
16. Jonathan Dickinson's Letter Book, May 12, 1715, MS. coll., HSP.
17. Minutes of the Philadelphia Yearly Meeting (1747–79), pp. 121–22, microfilm copy in Friends Historical Library, Swarthmore College.
18. Quoted in Jones, *The Quakers in the American Colonies*, p. 257.

that required the masters to obtain the consent of their local selectmen before granting manumission.[19] The following year Massachusetts passed a similar law forbidding anyone to manumit a
slave without posting a bond of £50 to reimburse the town in
case the slave became indigent. Masters who manumitted without
posting security incurred unlimited liability for the support of
their freedmen.[20] By 1728 every Northern colony except New
Hampshire had legal restrictions to prevent masters from aban-
doning slaves under the pretext of freeing them.[21]

These restrictions kept some in slavery who otherwise would
have obtained freedom. John Thurston of Rhode Island refused
to free a faithful slave because he feared "to leave it in the power
of any authority to throw him upon me either in sickness or old
age."[22] Others, however, simply ignored the statutory requirements
on the assumption that their Negroes would make a go of freedom. So many Quakers manumitted their slaves without posting
bond that New York finally validated such grants of "Quaker freedom" retroactively.[23] In some cases slaveholder pressure forced a
relaxation of the restrictions. In 1717 New York sharply reduced
the amount of the manumission bond to only a nominal security
that the slave would not become a public charge.[24] Moreover, the
law allowed the local authorities to waive the bond completely if
satisfied that the Negro was capable of self-support.[25]

Some masters took special precautions to keep their freedmen

19. J. Hammond Trumbull and Charles J. Hoadly, eds., *The Public Records of
the Colony of Connecticut, 1636–1776*, 15 vols. (Hartford: Lockwood & Brainard,
1850–90), IV, 375, hereafter cited as *Conn. Col. Recs.*

20. *Acts and Resolves, Public and Private, of the Province of the Massachusetts
Bay*, 5 vols. (Boston: Wright & Potter, 1869–86), I, 519, hereafter cited as *Mass.
Acts and Resolves.*

21. John R. Bartlett, ed., *Records of the Colony of Rhode Island and Providence
Plantations in New England, 1636–1792*, 10 vols. (Providence: Greene, 1856–65),
IV, 415–16; *Colonial Laws of New York from 1664 to the Revolution*, 5 vols.
(Albany: James B. Lyon, 1894), I, 764–65; James T. Mitchell and Henry Flanders,
comps., *The Statutes at Large of Pennsylvania from 1682–1801*, 16 vols. (Harrisburg: State Printer, 1896–1911), IV, 61; Samuel Nevill, comp., *The Acts of the
General Assembly of the Province of New Jersey*, 2 vols. (Philadelphia and Woodbridge, N.J., 1752–61), I, 18. Hereafter cited as *R.I. Col. Recs., N.Y. Col. Laws*,
and *Pa. Stat. at L.*

22. John Thurston to Moses Brown, November 14, 1782, Moses Brown Papers,
No. 951, IV, 25, MS. coll., RIHS.

23. *Laws of New York, 1798*, XXVII.

24. *N.Y. Col. Laws*, I, 922.

25. Kingston Records, Manumissions, HDC, QC.

off the poor rolls. Slaves might be required to obtain their own sureties or else remain in service long enough to pay for the manumission bond.[26] Others were obliged to contribute to private systems of social security set up and managed by the masters. Moses Brown required his freedmen to "deposit in my hands such a part of your wages . . . for your support when through sickness or otherwise you may be unable to support yourselves."[27] Another Rhode Islander postponed granting manumission until his slave had earned enough to post his own security against becoming a public charge.[28] James Thorne of Flushing, New York, required his freedmen to contribute £3 annually to a fund to provide for their old age. Another owner, James Griffen of Scarsdale, manumitted several slaves "on condition that they pay to my executors forty shillings, which sum my executors are to put to interest for their support at any time when thought necessary."[29]

Provisions against indigence were automatic in the manumission of slave children. In some cases the manumission did not become effective until the slave was fully grown and had provided service equivalent to the security bond. Even Quakers who manumitted for religious reasons sometimes postponed the grant of freedom until they had obtained several years of service.[30] Nathan Browne of Philadelphia delayed emancipation until his Negro had learned the trade of blacksmith.[31] The most generous provisions for young freedmen were usually made by the slaveholders who manumitted by will. Thomas Hadden of Scarsdale, New York, directed his executors to have his young slaves taught to read, and David Hunt of Westchester instructed his heirs to take charge of his "little Negroes and bring them up to a good business."[32]

26. Edward R. Turner, *The Negro in Pennsylvania* (Washington, D.C.: The American Historical Association, 1911), pp. 59–60.
27. Moses Brown manumissions, November 10, 1773, Moses Brown Papers, II, 331, MS. Coll., RIHS.
28. *The Early Records of the Town of Providence*, 20 vols. (Providence: Snow & Fornbrow, 1892–1909), IX, 153.
29. "N.Y. Abstracts of Wills," XII, 374–75; XIII, 354–57.
30. Minutes of the Exeter Monthly Meeting (1765–1785), p. 354, MS. coll., Friends Historical Library, Swarthmore College.
31. Thomas E. Drake, *Quakers and Slavery in America* (Gloucester, Mass.: Peter Smith, 1965), p. 73.
32. William S. Pelletreau, ed., *Early Wills of Westchester County* (New York: Francis P. Harper, 1898), p. 179; "N.Y. Abstracts of Wills," VIII, 322–23.

Frequently help was also given to adult Negroes trying to make a go of freedom. Mary Brown of Providence enjoined her family to treat an ex-slave woman kindly "and on all occasions assist and support her with the needful comforts of this life."[33] Another master on Long Island set aside a tract of land for his freedman and directed his executors to provide any other assistance that might be needed. Joseph Murray of New York City left his two freedmen annuities of £20 each, and Thomas More, also of New York City, ordered his executors to invest £300 for the benefit of an ex-slave.[34] Some masters kept track of their freedmen, and the latter often turned to them for assistance when in trouble.[35] William Varnum received an appeal from one of his freedmen imprisoned for debt in Newport for "as much money as will pay the small debt and cost that I stand committed here for."[36]

Despite many instances of generosity, most masters practiced a selective sort of philanthropy. Frequently one or two slaves were singled out for special consideration, and the favored ones were usually chosen as a reward for faithful service. John Merrett of Rhode Island instructed his executors to treat an ex-slave woman "with all humanity and tenderness, she having been a very faithful servant."[37] But those who resisted the role of faithful servant could expect neither freedom nor humanity, for few slaveowners who were not Quakers regarded the system as morally wrong. John Bouiness of New York City sold five bondsmen into Virginia the same year that he freed a favored slave. Another master in Westchester manumitted three slaves while ordering the sale of a fourth who had "behaved contrary to the rule of a good servant."[38]

Slaves were invariably eager to obtain manumission regardless

33. Mary Brown manumission, November 4, 1773, Moses Brown Papers, II, 331, MS. coll., RIHS.
34. "N.Y. Abstracts of Wills," V, 61–62, 165–66; X, 92–93.
35. William Morris to Moses Brown, October 4, 1782, Moses Brown Papers, No. 942, IV, 22, MS. coll., RIHS.
36. Cato to William Varnum, August 24, 1793, Box 43, Folder 4, MS. coll., NHS.
37. Quoted in William Johnston, Slavery in Rhode Island, 1755–1776 (Providence: Rhode Island Historical Society, 1894), p. 52.
38. "N.Y. Abstracts of Wills," IX, 103–104; XII, 182–83.

of the conditions imposed by the masters. Indeed, many no sooner became freedmen than they set to work to buy their wives, children, and friends out of slavery.[39] How much they valued liberty can be gauged by the numerous freedom suits that they brought against whites who tried to re-enslave them. In some cases unscrupulous employers claimed that black workers were their slaves, and in others sharpers tried to sell them in order to satisfy nonexistent debts. The detention of a free Negro in Providence by a white employer brought several prominent townspeople to his assistance. "Debt is the pretended occasion of his commitment," Joseph Allen wrote to Moses Brown, "but a wicked design of enslaving him appears to be the real motive."[40] In another case a New York City Negro won a suit against an employer who falsely claimed him as a slave. Some not only regained their freedom through the courts but recovered damages as well for unlawful detention.[41]

Frequently the outcome of a freedom suit depended upon technicalities that varied from place to place. In some colonies failure to follow the statutory procedures voided the manumission, while in others the slave became free subject only to the owner's liability for his support.[42] And there were numerous pitfalls in the manumission agreements themselves. One Boston Negro had to spend two years in the courts in order to obtain freedom from a master who refused to manumit him after the agreed term of service.[43] Moreover, the Negro was lucky to have sued in Massachusetts because in most colonies such an agreement would have been unenforceable. New York held that a slave's labor belonged to the master and therefore could not be used as legal consideration to enforce a promise of manumission.[44] On the other hand, a postdated deed of emancipation brought automatic free-

39. Records of the Pennsylvania Society for Promoting the Abolition of Slavery, I, 67, MS. coll., HSP; Register of Manumissions, pp. 65–66, 73, MS. coll., MCNY.
40. Joseph Allen to Moses Brown, July 19, 1775, Moses Brown Papers, II, 393, MS. coll., RIHS.
41. Minutes of the New York Manumission Society, June 20, 1794, June 16, 1795, MS. coll., NYHS.
42. *Conn. Col. Recs.*, V, 233; *Pa. Stat. at L.*, IV, 61.
43. Massachusetts Archives, IX, 152–53, MS. coll., MSL.
44. *Smith* v. *Hoff*, I Cowen's New York Reports 127 (New York Supreme Court, 1823).

dom at the time stipulated unless the master could prove that the slave had not lived up to the terms of the agreement.[45]

Legal technicalities caused even more uncertainty in the case of testamentary manumissions. One Massachusetts slave freed by will had to raise his own security bond in order to make the manumission effective.[46] Another slave in New York lost a grant of freedom when his master's executor refused to post the necessary security.[47] Moreover, a testamentary manumission might be canceled at any time during the life of the master. Since a will created only contingent rights, nothing could prevent the master from reneging on his promise even though the slave had performed his part of the bargain. If the master sold the slave, the sale revoked the manumission and the slave remained permanently in bondage.[48] Only a deed of emancipation that became effective at the master's death provided an irrevocable grant of freedom. The sale of such a slave did not impair the grant, for the deed brought automatic freedom at the grantor's death. All that the buyer obtained was the right to the slave's services during the lifetime of the manumitter.[49]

The greatest thrust for Negro freedom came during the Revolutionary era. Public opinion veered sharply against slavery almost in direct proportion to the deterioration of relations with England. White militants demanding political freedom for themselves found it difficult to justify chattel bondage for Americans of darker pigmentation.[50] For the most part they did not try, not even in the Southern colonies where slavery was inextricably part of the social structure.[51] Everywhere the natural rights doctrine espoused by the patriot party forced a change in attitudes about

45. *Kettletas* v. *Fleet,* I Anthon's Nisi Prius Reports 36 (New York, 1808).

46. *Journals of the House of Representatives of Massachusetts, 1715–1764,* 40 vols. (Cambridge, Mass.: Massachusetts Historical Society, 1919–70), XV, 172, 174–75.

47. E. B. O'Callaghan and Berthold Fernow, eds., *Documents Relative to the Colonial History of the State of New York,* 15 vols. (Albany: Weed, Parsons, 1856–87), V, 461, hereafter cited as *N.Y. Col. Docs.*

48. *In re Michel,* 14 Johnson's Reports 324 (New York Supreme Court, 1817).

49. *In re Tom,* 5 Johnson's Reports 365 (New York Supreme Court, 1810).

50. Arthur Zilversmit, *The First Emancipation: The Abolition of Slavery in the North* (Chicago: University of Chicago Press, 1967), p. 109.

51. John W. Cromwell, *The Negro in American History* (Washington, D.C.: The American Negro Academy, 1914), p. 10.

the Negro and his place in American life. When James Otis denounced British tyranny in 1765, he felt constrained to speak for blacks as well as whites, reminding the patriots that both were British subjects "and entitled to all the essential civil rights of such."[52]

Editorial attacks on slavery became increasingly common in the Northern press. The March 24, 1760, edition of the *New York Weekly Post-Boy* described the victims of the slave trade as "poor pagans whom Christians have thought fit to consider cattle," and the *Pennsylvania Chronicle* declared on October 11, 1773, that "while we persist in the practice of enslaving the Africans, our mouths ought to be shut entirely as to any duties or taxes which Great Britain may see cause to lay upon us." The newspapers also printed excerpts from the antislavery pamphlets of Bishop Warburton, who warned that "the infamous traffic for slaves directly infringes both divine and human law."[53] These attacks often appeared with reports of Negroes who had performed heroic acts or who had in some way struck a blow for freedom.[54] The *Pennsylvania Chronicle* reported approvingly in its November 29, 1773, edition that a Virginia slave had killed his master and then himself in order to save a fellow slave from a brutal beating. "What in a European would be called a glorious struggling for liberty," the paper reminded its readers, could also move blacks to make the ultimate sacrifice in resisting tyranny.

Since England had a large stake in the slave trade, proposals to restrict the traffic fitted neatly into the American strategy of economic pressures and boycotts. A Massachusetts law to bar the importation of slaves from Africa failed in 1771 only because Governor Hutchinson interposed his veto.[55] In 1773 Pennsylvania doubled its slave tariff in a move to make the importation of Negroes prohibitive.[56] The following year the Continental Congress

52. James Otis, *The Rights of the British Colonies Asserted and Proved* (Boston, 1765), p. 37, cited in Zilversmit, *The First Emancipation*, p. 98.

53. Bishop William Warburton, *A Sermon Preached before the Incorporated Society for the Propagation of the Gospel in Foreign Parts* (London: E. Owen & T. Harrison, 1766), excerpted in the *Pennsylvania Chronicle*, March 23, 1767.

54. *New York Weekly Post-Boy*, December 15, 1763; *Pennsylvania Chronicle*, November 29, 1773.

55. George H. Moore, *Notes on the History of Slavery in Massachusetts* (New York: Appleton, 1866), pp. 130–32.

56. *Pa. Stat. at L.*, VIII, 330–32.

voted to discontinue the trade completely and ordered a boycott of those who continued to import Negroes.[57] The *New York Weekly Mercury* on November 4, 1774, reported that the distillers of New York City had pledged themselves not to distill molasses or syrup for use by slave traders. Both Connecticut and Rhode Island outlawed the traffic. The Rhode Island prohibition noted that "those who are desirous of enjoying all the advantages of liberty themselves should be willing to extend personal liberty to others."[58]

So general was the reaction against slavery that abolitionists caught the first glimpse of ultimate success. Quakers long active in the fight now redoubled their efforts in order to make the most of the shift in public opinion. To present a united front they moved vigorously to purge their own ranks of any connection with slavery. The Pennsylvania and New Jersey congregations insisted that their members have nothing to do with the buying and selling of Negroes.[59] Even the conservative New York Yearly Meeting set up freedom committees to urge Friends to manumit their slaves as soon as possible.[60] The New England Yearly Meeting appointed a committee to visit such members "as are concerned in keeping slaves & endeavour to dissuade them from that practice." The committee reported back that it had visited Quaker slaveholders and "labored with them respecting setting such at liberty that were suitable for freedom."[61]

The shots fired at Concord and Lexington impelled all opponents of slavery to greater militancy. Demanding an immediate ban on advertisements for the sale of slaves, the Reverend William Gordon of Massachusetts admonished newspaper printers that such notices "in the present season are peculiarly shocking."[62] Everywhere abolitionists warned the patriots that to ignore the plight of Negroes would expose their own struggle for freedom to

57. Worthington C. Ford and Gaillard Hunt, eds., *Journals of the Continental Congress*, 24 vols. (Washington, D.C.: G. P. O., 1904–37), I, 77.
58. *Conn. Col. Recs.*, XIV, 329; *R.I. Col. Recs.*, VII, 251–53.
59. Drake, *Quakers and Slavery in America*, p. 71.
60. Minutes of the New York Yearly Meeting (1746–1800), pp. 64, 94, MS. coll., Haviland Records Room, Friends Seminary, New York City.
61. Minutes of the New England Yearly Meeting (1683–1782), p. 292, MS. coll., RIHS.
62. Quoted in Moore, *Notes on the History of Slavery in Massachusetts*, p. 179.

the charge of hypocrisy. "The man who only abhors tyranny when it points at himself," the November 8, 1780, edition of the *New Jersey Gazette* declared, "is altogether unworthy of the esteem of the virtuous, and can never . . . merit the confidence of a free people." The Reverend Samuel Hopkins of Newport saw the war as a mark of divine displeasure with slavery. "If we continue in this evil practice," he warned, "have we any reason to expect deliverance from the calamities we are under?"[63]

Blacks also served notice on their masters that the right to liberty could not be limited by pigmentation. In 1773 a group of Boston Negroes petitioned the general court that they expected "great things from men who made such a noble stand against the designs of their *fellow-men* to enslave them." In another petition they tied their demand for freedom directly to the natural rights doctrine and asked the lawmakers to emancipate all slave children at the age of twenty-one.[64] Others sought freedom through the courts by attacking defects in title deeds and in some cases challenging the legality of slavery itself.[65] These suits not only kept the issue before the public but also emboldened the slaves to press for freedom on their own account. One Negro suing for his liberty in 1780 ran newspaper notices in the February 2, 9, and 16 editions of the *New Jersey Gazette* to warn prospective buyers that he expected "freedom, justice and protection . . . by the laws of the state."

The bargaining power of slaves grew tremendously during the war, and masters found themselves under heavy pressure to make concessions in order to obtain loyal service. Numerous deeds were recorded giving slaves freedom after a stipulated period of time.[66] Indeed, buyers of slaves sometimes preferred Negroes who could be depended upon for limited service to those who could not be relied upon at all. One advertisement for "a good Negro wench" informed prospective sellers that "if to be sold on terms of free-

63. [Samuel Hopkins], *A Dialogue Concerning the Slavery of the Africans* (Norwich, Conn.: Spooner, 1776), pp. 50–51.
64. Quoted in Zilversmit, *The First Emancipation*, pp. 101–102.
65. Nathan Dane, *A General Abridgement and Digest of American Law with Occasional Notes and Comments*, 9 vols. (Boston: Cummings, Hilliard, 1823–29), II, 426–27.
66. Records of the Pennsylvania Society for Promoting the Abolition of Slavery, I, 27–43, 69, 72, 79, MS. coll., HSP; Register of Manumissions, pp. 63, 65–66, MS. coll., MCNY.

dom by far the most agreeable."[67] The privilege of choosing between buyers also became more general, thereby enabling many
slaves to obtain promises of freedom before accepting a new
master.[68]

Frequently slaves took advantage of wartime dislocations that
occurred when their masters fled the enemy forces.[69] Some owners
had to leave their slaves behind to shift for themselves. One slave
woman fled from Rhode Island in 1777 with a pass giving her permission "to go where she thought proper to get her living."[70] Many
slaves did not wait for such permission but took their chances that
the wartime movement of people would provide cover for getting
away. The number of runaways rose so sharply after 1775 that
there can be no doubt that the machinery of control no longer
functioned effectively.[71] Fugitives often fled to the opposing armies to seek freedom in return for military service. A New Jersey
master reported in 1778 that his runaway had "gone to join the
enemy," and another advertised that his Negro would probably
"endeavor to get . . . to the American camp, as he is fond of
soldiery."[72]

The British deliberately encouraged slave defections by advertising offers of freedom to runaways who took refuge with the
army.[73] They also made it clear that blacks who supported the
patriot cause could expect harsh treatment. During a raid into
northern New Jersey in 1779 British troops killed two Negro
women for "endeavoring to drive off some cattle belonging to
their masters."[74] On the other hand, slaves who responded to the
offer of asylum found employment and safety with the British
forces in New York.[75] So many crossed the lines from New Jersey

67. *Pennsylvania Packet*, August 22, 1778, cited in Turner, *The Negro in Pennsylvania*, p. 63n.
68. Register of Manumissions, pp. 43, 45, 171, MS. coll., MCNY.
69. Jacob E. Mallmann, ed., *Historical Papers on Shelter Island and Its Presby-terian Church* (New York: Bustard, 1899), p. 67.
70. Nicholas Cooke, certificate to a Negro woman, March 28, 1778, MS. coll., JCBL.
71. *Boston News Letter*, 1775–76; *New Jersey Gazette*, 1778–81; *Pennsylvania Gazette*, 1775–83; *Pennsylvania Journal*, 1775–83; *Pennsylvania Packet*, 1778–83; Rivington's *Royal Gazette*, 1778–81; *New York Weekly Mercury*, 1775–83.
72. *New Jersey Gazette*, January 7, September 23, 1778.
73. Rivington's *Royal Gazette*, July 3, 1779.
74. *New Jersey Gazette*, May 26, 1779.
75. "Proceedings of a Board of General Officers of the British Army at New

that the authorities took special precautions to contain the problem. "It may be dangerous to the community to permit such Negroes to reside near enemy lines," the New Jersey legislature concluded in voting to remove slaves "to some more remote or interior parts of the state."[76]

Defections to the British compelled the Americans to compete for the loyalty of the slaves by offering freedom in return for military service. Some blacks needed little urging to support the American cause: Crispus Attucks was among the first to fall at the Boston Massacre, and Peter Salem distinguished himself at the Battle of Bunker Hill. Enlistment opportunities for the blacks increased as the war dragged on, for the states found it difficult to make up troop quotas by relying on white volunteers.[77] New Hampshire awarded bounties to slaveholders who manumitted black recruits, and Massachusetts authorized the recruitment of blacks in regular troop levies.[78] Connecticut encouraged slave enlistments by granting exemptions from service to every two men who could procure one substitute. Moreover, manumission was made easier to make sure that black substitutes would be available. A wartime rule was adopted that any slave certified as healthy could be freed without bond if the town selectmen found that the manumission was in the slave's best interests.[79] By the end of the war several hundred blacks had gained freedom by serving as substitutes for whites in Connecticut's armed forces.[80]

Rhode Island and New York had to pass slave enlistment laws in order to make up critical troop shortages. By 1778 Rhode Island's two battalions in the Continental army had become so

York, 1781," in NYHS *Colls.*, XLIX (1916), 112, 118, 125–26, 130–31, 134, 136–37, 139, 141–42, 174, 210. See Thomas Jones, *History of New York during the Revolutionary War*, 2 vols. (New York: New-York Historical Society, 1879), I, 334.

76. *New Jersey Gazette*, January 5, 1780.

77. Benjamin Quarles, *The Negro in the American Revolution* (Chapel Hill: University of North Carolina Press, 1961), pp. 51–52.

78. Jeremy Belknap, "Queries Respecting the Slavery and Emancipation of Negroes in Massachusetts," in MHS *Colls.*, 1st ser., IV (1795), 203; Quarles, *The Negro in the American Revolution*, pp. 54–55.

79. Charles J. Hoadly and Leonard W. Labaree, eds., *Public Records of the State of Connecticut*, 9 vols. (Hartford: Lockwood & Brainard, 1894–1953), I, 415–16.

80. Zilversmit, *The First Emancipation*, pp. 122–23.

depleted that a plan was adopted for filling up the ranks with slave recruits.[81] The masters were to be compensated up to a value of £20, but they could not prevent a slave from enlisting. Although the plan was condemned by some as confiscatory, the scarcity of white recruits left the legislature no alternative. Every slave who enlisted for the duration received automatic freedom "as though he had never been encumbered with any kind of servitude or slavery."[82] In 1781 a similar law was passed by New York granting freedom to any slaves who enlisted for three years with the master's consent. The owners were reimbursed with five hundred acres of land for every slave allowed to join the armed forces.[83]

Slaves who traded military service for freedom contributed vitally to the American war effort. By the end of the war more than four thousand blacks had served in the Continental army and thousands more in the state militia.[84] One Rhode Island regiment enrolled more than two hundred Negroes, and those too young for combat were used as orderlies and drummers.[85] Indeed, the heavy reliance upon black manpower aroused the apprehensions of some military officials. "Is it consistent with the Sons of Liberty," General Philip Schuyler wondered during the Saratoga campaign, "to trust their all to be defended by slaves?"[86] General William Heath conceded that his Negro troops "were generally able-bodied," but nevertheless complained that he was "never pleased to see them mixed with white men."[87] On the other hand, General Horatio Gates had only gratitude and praise for slaves

81. *R.I. Col. Recs.*, VIII, 640–41.
82. *Ibid.*, pp. 359–61. See Sidney S. Rider, "An Historical Inquiry Concerning the Attempts to Raise a Regiment of Slaves in Rhode Island," *Rhode Island Historical Tracts*, X (1880), 9–22.
83. *Laws of New York, 1781*, XXXII.
84. W. E. Hartgrove, "The Negro Soldier in the American Revolution," *JNH*, I (1916), 113–19.
85. Lorenzo J. Greene, "Some Observations on the Black Regiment of Rhode Island in the American Revolution," *JNH*, XXVII (1952), 165; Quarles, *The Negro in the American Revolution*, p. 72; "Journal of Lieutenant Charles Philip von Krafft, of the Regiment of Von Bose, 1776–1784," in NYHS Colls., XL (1882), 183.
86. "Heath Papers," in MHS *Colls.*, 7th ser., IV (1904), 135–36, cited in Quarles, *The Negro in the American Revolution*, p. 72.
87. "Heath Papers," in MHS *Colls.*, 7th ser., IV, 148.

"permitted to assist us in securing our freedom at the risk of their own lives."[88]

Although some blacks served in local militia units, most were to be found in the line regiments which bore the brunt of the fighting.[89] During the Rhode Island campaign in 1778, Colonel Christopher Greene's Negro regiment repulsed waves of Hessian troops in one of the bloodiest local actions of the war.[90] Jack Sisson, one of the black soldiers in this regiment, also participated in the raid that captured a British commander, General Prescott.[91] When the American army retreated at Brandywine in 1777, a Negro in the Third Pennsylvania Artillery fought off the enemy with abandoned weapons until he could bring his ammunition wagon to safety.[92] In 1781 black troops participated in the fierce defense of Fort Griswold in Connecticut, and one of them gave his life avenging the murder of the commander when the fort finally fell.[93]

British commanders recognized the usefulness of blacks to the American war effort. A Hessian officer serving with General Burgoyne in 1777 noted that no American regiment "is to be seen in which there are not Negroes in abundance; and among them are able-bodied, strong, and brave fellows."[94] Sir Henry Clinton believed that the enlistment of blacks by the Americans deprived the British of "another principle of support" by reducing the rate of slave defections.[95] Indeed, Clinton justified his proclamation granting asylum to runaways as a countermeasure against the enlistment of slaves by the Americans.[96] Moreover, the offer of asylum was coupled with a warning in the *New York Weekly*

88. General Horatio Gates to the Massachusetts Council, July 2, 1779. Massachusetts Archives, CCI, 140, MS. coll., MSL.
89. Quarles, *The Negro in the American Revolution*, pp. 71–72.
90. George H. Moore, *Historical Notes on the Employment of Negroes in the American Army of the Revolution* (New York: Charles T. Evans, 1862), p. 19.
91. J. Lewis Diman, "The Capture of Prescott," *Rhode Island Historical Tracts*, I (1877), 11–44.
92. Quarles, *The Negro in the American Revolution*, pp. 74–75.
93. Frederick C. Norton, "Negro Slavery in Connecticut," *Connecticut Magazine*, No. 6, V (1899), 324. See Charles Allyn, *The Battle of Groton Heights* (New London, Conn.: Allyn, 1882), pp. 91–92.
94. August Schlozer, *Briefwechsel*, 10 vols. (Göttingen, 1780–82), IV, 365.
95. *New Jersey Gazette*, April 12, 1780.
96. Quarles, *The Negro in the American Revolution*, pp. 113–14.

Mercury, July 5, 1779, that Negroes captured with rebel forces would be sold into slavery regardless of their legal status. Thus free blacks who could not be persuaded to join the British felt heavy pressure to remain neutral if they valued their liberty.

Both sides made good on their promises of freedom, for otherwise black recruits might have gone over to the enemy. "Non-emancipated soldiers," the *Boston Gazette* warned on October 13, 1777, "are irresistibly tempted to defect to our foes."[97] New York and Rhode Island freed slaves outright in return for military service, and in other states the same result was obtained by postwar statutes and judicial decisions.[98] In 1784 the New Jersey legislature freed a slave who had enlisted with the Americans after his master had joined the British, and two years later the lawmakers freed another black veteran who "had shown himself entitled to their favorable notice."[99] Although no freedom statutes were passed by Connecticut, the courts ruled that enlistment with the master's consent brought automatic freedom. When Thomas Ivers of New Haven tried to re-enslave a Negro after the war, the superior court ruled that the slave had become "a free man, absolutely manumitted from his master by enlisting and serving in the army."[100]

Thousands of slaves likewise found freedom with the British. General Cornwallis would not allow runaways to be taken from his camp, even when their owners had no ties with the enemy. Sir Guy Carleton also kept faith with the refugees in his plans for the evacuation of New York at the end of the war. He adopted the policy that Negroes who had crossed the lines before the signing of the provisional peace treaty were to be free; only those who came over subsequently were to be returned to their masters.[101] Since it was difficult to determine exactly when slaves had passed through the lines, his policy favored the fugitives. Despite heavy pressure from the Americans for the return of all runaways, Carleton refused to break the promises of freedom that had been

97. *Ibid.,* pp. 79–80.
98. *Laws of New York, 1781,* XXXII; *R.I. Col. Recs.,* VIII, 359–61.
99. *Laws of New Jersey* (1784), p. 110; (1786), p. 368. Cited in Marion T. Wright, "New Jersey Laws and the Negro," *JNH,* XXVIII (1943), 173.
100. *Jack Arabas* v. *Thomas Ivers,* I Root 19 (Connecticut Superior Court, 1784).
101. Quarles, *The Negro in the American Revolution,* pp. 131–32, 171.

made during the war. To do so, he declared, would be "a dishonorable violation of the public faith." Altogether, about three thousand Negroes left with the British besides hundreds more who got away unrecorded in private vessels.[102]

The Revolution fatally undermined Northern slavery. While ideology weakened the resolve of whites to defend the system, military operations ended the automatic subordination of blacks. Slaves could take advantage of the war by supporting one side or the other in order to achieve their own goal of freedom. Many earned manumission in the Revolutionary armies, and others who sided with the British gained freedom in exile when the war was over. Some who left with the Hessian forces ended up in central Europe, but they arrived there with few regrets.[103] All that mattered was that the break in the white hegemony had opened the way to freedom. The thousands who seized the opportunity regardless of risk served notice on the whites that the slave regime would never be the same.

---

102. *Ibid.*, pp. 168, 172.
103. "The Brunswick Contingent in America, 1776–1783," *PMHB*, XV (1891), 224.

10

The Politics of Abolition

Attacks on slavery as a legal institution began during the first year of the Revolution. In 1775 Pennsylvania's Provincial Congress called upon the colonies to prohibit the importation of slaves, and the Chester County Committee of Correspondence endorsed the principle of gradual emancipation.[1] Two years later the newly organized State of Vermont outlawed slavery under a constitution declaring that no one "ought to be holden by law to serve any person as a servant, slave, or apprentice after he arrives at the age of twenty-one years."[2] A vigorous campaign against slavery at New York's Constitutional Convention culminated in a resolution endorsing the proposition that "every human being who breathes the air of the state" should enjoy the privileges of freedom.[3] In 1779 Rhode Island prohibited the export of Negroes held in slavery "until some favorable occasion may offer for its total abolition."[4]

But while the war continued, practical measures for Negro emancipation were politically unfeasible. Defenders of the status

1. Arthur Zilversmit, *The First Emancipation: The Abolition of Slavery in the North* (Chicago: University of Chicago Press, 1967), pp. 125–26.
2. *Vermont Constitution of 1777*, Article I, in John C. Hurd, *The Law of Freedom and Bondage in the United States*, 2 vols. (Boston: Little, Brown, 1858–62), II, 36–37.
3. *Journals of the New York Provincial Congress*, 2 vols. (Albany: Weed, 1842), I, 887–89.
4. *Acts and Resolves at the General Assembly of the Governor and Company of the State of Rhode Island and Providence Plantation*, October, 1779, p. 6, hereafter cited as *R.I. Acts and Resolves*.

quo argued forcefully that abolition might disturb the unity of
the states, particularly in the South, and thereby weaken the war
effort.[5] Thus the Massachusetts House of Representatives refused
to pass legislation against slavery because of "apprehension that
our brethren in the other colonies should conceive there was an
impropriety."[6] In 1778 the New Jersey assembly persuaded Governor William Livingston to withdraw an antislavery message on
the grounds that the country was in "too critical a situation to enter on the consideration of it at that time."[7] When some New
Hampshire Negroes presented a freedom petition in 1780, the
legislature voted that "further consideration and determination of
the matter be postponed till a more convenient opportunity."[8]

The separation of the three Delaware counties from Pennsylvania in 1776 accelerated the emancipation movement. These
counties contained a heavy concentration of slaves and their de-
tachment as an independent state shifted the balance of forces
toward freedom. According to the first federal census, Pennsylvania had only 3,761 slaves in a population of 435,150; Delaware,
with fewer than 60,000 people had nearly 9,000 slaves.[9] In February of 1780, after nearly a year of public debate, Pennsylvania
became the first state to pass a gradual abolition law.[10] The law
emancipated Negro children born after February, but provided
that they should remain in service until the age of twenty-eight
in order to reimburse their masters for raising them.[11] To prevent

5. *Journals of the House of Representatives of the Commonwealth of Pennsylvania, 1776–1781* (Philadelphia, 1782), p. 436, hereafter cited as *Pa. H. of R.
Journals, 1776–1781.*
6. "Letter Reported to the Massachusetts House of Representatives in 1777
Respecting the Freeing of Negroes," MHS *Proceedings,* X (1867-69), 332–33.
7. William Livingston to Samuel Allinson, July 25, 1778, Allinson Letters, MS.
coll., Rutgers University Library, quoted in Zilversmit, *The First Emancipation,*
p. 140. See Henry S. Cooley, *A Study of Slavery in New Jersey* (Baltimore: The
Johns Hopkins Press, 1896), p. 23.
8. Nathaniel Bouton, ed., *Documents and Records Relating to the State of New
Hampshire during the Period of the American Revolution, from 1776 to1783* (Concord: Jenks, 1874), pp. 861–62. See Isaac W. Hammond, "Slavery in New
Hampshire in the Olden Time," *Granite Monthly,* IV (1880), 110.
9. Evarts B. Greene and Virginia D. Harrington, *American Population before
the Federal Census of 1790* (New York: Columbia University Press, 1932), pp.
120–21.
10. *Pa. H. of R. Journals, 1776–1781,* p. 435. See Zilversmit, *The First Emancipation,* pp. 124–31.
11. James T. Mitchell and Henry Flanders, comps., *The Statutes at Large of*

evasions, every slaveholder was required to register his slaves by November, and any Negroes who remained unregistered after that date became legally emancipated. The law also abolished the colonial system of special courts and punishments for blacks, repealed the prohibition on interracial marriage, and allowed free Negroes to testify against whites in all the courts of the state.[12]

The early victory of antislavery in Pennsylvania can partly be credited to the long campaign of moral suasion waged by the Quakers. Almost from the beginning of the Revolution, a powerful ground swell for Negro freedom appeared throughout the state. Moreover, moral arguments against slavery were buttressed by the practical consideration that slaves no longer played an important role in the economy. By the time emancipation was enacted, the proportion of slaves in the general population had reached its lowest point in half a century. In 1730 the ratio was about 1 to 11, whereas in 1779 it was no more than 1 to 30.[13] Thus when legal abolition was finally proposed, there was virtually no economic or party interest left to organize an opposition.

Nevertheless, resistance to the law surfaced almost immediately. Although gradual emancipation was generally accepted, social conservatives recoiled at the prospect of legal equality between the races. What bothered them were the political and social implications of the law rather than abolition itself. Twenty-three members of the House of Representatives joined in a petition against some of the key civil rights provisions. To give every black the right to vote and hold public office, they warned, was socially unsound and politically dangerous. They predicted ruin if Negroes became citizens "in so extensive a manner as this law proposes," and declared that civil rights should be withheld until the blacks became "more civilized and better qualified to receive them."[14]

Pennsylvania from 1682–1801, 16 vols. (Harrisburg: State Printer, 1896–1911), X, 67–69, 72, hereafter cited as Pa. Stat. at L.

12. Ibid., pp. 70–73.

13. In 1775 Governor John Penn put the ratio at 1 to 150, but this estimate is probably much too low. Extrapolating from the federal census of 1790, it is likely that the proportion of slaves to free men was more on the order of 1 to 30. Greene and Harrington American Population before the Federal Census of 1790, pp. 114, 116, 120.

14. One member of the House of Representatives who had voted against the

Some of the opposition came from slaveowners who had failed to register their Negroes before the November deadline.[15] "Christians have reason to complain," a dissident declared in the *Pennsylvania Journal*, February 21, 1781, "when their servants are forced from them without sufficient compensation." Defenders of the law, however, realizing that any concessions would encourage further attacks on Negro freedom, resisted proposals to waive registration.[16] The September 21, 1781, edition of the *Freeman's Journal* (Philadelphia) quoted one unregistered black as preferring death to a return to slavery, "for many of our masters would treat us with unheard of barbarity for daring to take advantage (as we have done) of the law made in our favour." In the end, an attempt to waive registration was defeated, and the legislature made only minor revisions allowing the residents of Washington and Westmoreland counties (previously under the jurisdiction of Virginia) additional time to register their slaves.[17] Although individual slaveholders continued to petition for relief, resistance to the law virtually vanished as a political issue.[18]

Success in Pennsylvania encouraged antislavery in other states. In Massachusetts, Negroes carried their fight for freedom into the courts, sometimes invoking Revolutionary ideology to argue that slavery violated the rights of humanity.[19] So pervasive was the sentiment for liberty that many of these freedom suits went virtually undefended. To contest such a suit, usually before a hostile jury, must have seemed pointless to many masters. "The defence of the master was faintly made," Chief Justice Parsons commented on these cases, "for such was the temper of the times that a restless, discontented slave was worth little."[20] Moreover, when a

bill did not join in the protest, whereas three members not recorded on the bill signed the petition. *Pa. H. of R. Journals, 1776–1781*, pp. 424–25, 436.

15. Robert L. Brunhouse, *The Counter-Revolution in Pennsylvania, 1776–1790* (Harrisburg: Pennsylvania Historical Commission, 1942), p. 102.

16. Zilversmit, *The First Emancipation*, pp. 133–36.

17. *Pa. Stat. at L.*, X, 367–68, 463.

18. Zilversmit, *The First Emancipation*, pp. 136–37.

19. "Queries Respecting the Slavery and Emancipation of Negroes in Massachusetts," in MHS *Colls.*, 1st ser., IV (1795), 202–203; Emory Washburn, "The Extinction of Slavery in Massachusetts," in MHS *Colls.*, 4th ser., IV (1858), 334–35; "Letters and Documents Relating to Slavery in Massachusetts," in MHS *Colls.*, 5th ser., III (1877), 401.

20. *Inhabitants of Winchendon v. Inhabitants of Hatfield*, 4 Tyng 128 (Mass. Supreme Judicial Court, 1808).

slave gained freedom through the courts, the owner had no liability for his future support. Thus masters frequently rid themselves of troublesome, litigious slaves by turning freedom suits
into manumissions by legal default.[21]

The willingness of the Massachusetts courts to move against
slavery contrasts sharply with the inaction of the legislature. In
1777 the lawmakers tabled a proposal for gradual emancipation
and voted instead to appoint a committee to ascertain whether
such a measure would disturb the wartime unity of the states.[22]
However, the report of this committee was also tabled, so no further action was taken on the proposal.[23] Nor was any progress
made in 1778 when the legislature drafted a constitution for the
state. Not only was slavery recognized as a legal institution, but
free Negroes were specifically excluded from voting.[24] But this
was too reactionary for the times, and the constitution was overwhelmingly rejected at the polls.[25] Two years later the people rati-
fied a more liberal constitution that contained a bill of rights declaring that "all men are born free and equal, and have . . . the
right of enjoying and defending their lives and liberty."[26]

This declaration of rights became the basis of a freedom suit
that judicially abolished slavery. The case involved a slave named
Quork Walker, his master Nathaniel Jennison, and John and Seth
Caldwell, who had hired Walker as a free worker. In 1781 Walker,

21. Nathan Dane, A General Abridgement and Digest of American Law with
Occasional Notes and Comments, 9 vols. (Boston: Cummings, Hilliard, 1823–29),
II, 426–27. See Washburn, The "Extinction of Slavery in Massachusetts," in MHS
Colls., 4th ser., IV (1858), pp. 334–35.
22. A Journal of the Honourable House of Representatives of the State of
Massachusetts Bay in New England (Boston:Thomas & John Fleet, 1777), p. 25.
23. George H. Moore, Notes on the History of Slavery in Massachusetts (New
York: Appleton, 1866), pp. 181–82.
24. Journal of the Convention for Framing a Constitution of Government for
the State of Massachusetts Bay, September 1, 1779 to June 16, 1780 (Boston,
1832), p. 257.
25. Since the entire constitution was defeated, there is no way to ascertain how
much the provision concerning slavery had to do with its rejection. The absence
of a bill of rights for whites may have had as much to do with its defeat as its
provisions regarding Negroes. See Washburn, "The Extinction of Slavery in
Massachusetts," in MHS Colls., 4th ser., IV (1858), p. 339; Moore, Notes on the
History of Slavery in Massachusetts, pp. 186–94; Hurd, The Law of Freedom and
Bondage, II, 28n.
26. Francis N. Thorpe, ed., The Federal and State Constitutions, Colonial
Charters and Other Organic Laws, 7 vols. (Washington, D.C., G. P. O., 1909),
III, 1889.

who had been beaten by Jennison for running away, brought suit for assault and battery; Jennison, in turn, sued the Caldwells for enticing Walker to run away. The technical legal issue was whether a promise of freedom made by a previous owner had given Walker a right to freedom. Both Walker and the Caldwells were represented by Levi Lincoln, who was not content to try the case on narrow technical grounds. Lincoln argued forcefully that slavery was contrary to the natural law and that it specifically violated the declaration of rights in the new constitution.[27] Jennison lost both suits, and was also convicted in a criminal proceeding for assaulting Walker.[28] Chief Justice Cushing's charge to the jury in the latter case left no doubt about the future of slavery in Massachusetts. "The idea of slavery," he ruled, "is inconsistent with our own conduct and constitution . . . and there can be no such thing as perpetual servitude of a rational creature."[29]

Defeated in the courts, Jennison petitioned the legislature for relief. "Your memorialist having been possessed of ten Negro servants," he appealed, "is now informed that . . . the Bill of Rights is so to be construed as to operate to the total discharge and manumission of all Negro servants whatsoever."[30] What Jennison wanted was a legislative declaration reversing the courts or, failing that, compensation and a release from liability for his lost slaves. Accordingly, the House of Representatives drafted a compromise bill declaring that "there never were *legal* slaves" in Massachusetts, and providing an indemnity for "all masters who have held slaves *in fact*."[31] Such a bill was passed in February, 1783, but died in the senate after only one reading.[32] The upper house apparently concluded that it would be politic as well as economic

27. "Letters and Documents Relating to Slavery in Massachusetts," in MHS *Colls.*, 5th ser., III (1877), 438–42.

28. William O'Brien, S.J., "Did the Jennison Case Outlaw Slavery in Massachusetts?" *WMQ*, 3d ser., XVII (1960), 225–26. See Washburn, "The Extinction of Slavery in Massachusetts," in MHS *Colls.*, 4th ser., IV (1858), pp. 336–37.

29. "Minutes of Chief Justice Cushing in the Case of the Commonwealth vs. Jennison," MHS *Proceedings*, XIII (1875), 294.

30. Quoted in Moore, *Notes on the History of Slavery in Massachusetts*, p. 218.

31. Journal of the Massachusetts House of Representatives, III (1782–83), 444, MS. coll., MSL.

32. Journal of the Massachusetts Senate, III (1782–83), 413, MS. coll., MSL. See O'Brien, "Did the Jennison Case Outlaw Slavery in Massachusetts?" *WMQ*, 3d ser., XVII, 235–41.

merely to accept judicial abolition as a *fait accompli*. No further attempt was made to reimburse slaveholders or to interfere with the court decisions.[33]

Some historians and legal scholars have questioned the immediate legal effect of the Jennison decisions. If, as the decisions seem to indicate, Walker became free under his previous master's promise of manumission, then all the rulings on the constitutionality of slavery were merely dicta. Technically only the *ratio decidendi* of the case would be binding, and if Walker had become free *ex contractu*, the legal status of slavery was not a justiciable issue. However, in a practical sense the constitutional rulings were decisive, for they served notice on how the courts would resolve the issue if it came before them. Negroes could thereafter sue for freedom confident that they would not be returned to slavery. The masters could be equally sure that to resist such suits would be an expensive exercise in futility.[34]

That judicial emancipation encountered so little opposition owed more to economic conditions than to Revolutionary ideology. By the time the Jennison cases were decided, the role of slavery in Massachusetts had been sharply reduced. A comparison of population trends between 1763 and 1784 strikingly reveals the decline of the system, as shown in Table 1.[35] Moreover, the concomitant growth of a white working force made slavery vulnerable to political attack. White workers understandably opposed slave competition for the jobs they needed to earn a livelihood. "If the gentlemen had been permitted by law to hold slaves," John Adams observed, "the common people would have put the Negroes to death, and their masters too, perhaps."[36] Thus the Jennison deci-

33. Failure to resolve the question of financial responsibility for indigent freedmen resulted in decades of litigation between the towns and former slaveholders. See Helen T. Catterall, ed., *Judicial Cases Concerning American Slavery and the Negro*, 5 vols. (Washington, D.C.: Carnegie Institute, 1926–37), IV, 482–91, 493–97.

34. John D. Cushing, "The Cushing Court and the Abolition of Slavery in Massachusetts: More Notes on the 'Quock Walker Case,'" *American Journal of Legal History*, V (1961), 118–44; O'Brien, "Did the Jennison Case Outlaw Slavery in Massachusetts?" *WMQ*, 3d ser., XVII, 219–41; Zilversmit, *The First Emancipation*, p. 115.

35. Statistics compiled by Jeremy Belknap in MHS *colls.*, 1st ser., IV (1795), 198.

36. "Letters and Documents Relating to Slavery in Massachusetts," in MHS *Colls.*, 5th ser., III (1877), 401–402.

TABLE 1

Year	Whites	Blacks	Proportion of Whites to Blacks
1763	235,810	5,214	45:1
1776	343,845	5,249	65:1
1784	353,133	4,377	80:1

sions legitimated a process of extinction that had already begun. By the time of the first federal census in 1790 Massachusetts could report that no slaves remained in the state.[37]

Slavery in New Hampshire succumbed to a similar process of wartime attrition. Between 1773 and 1786 the number of slaves declined from 674 to only 46, most of whom were concentrated in Rockingham County.[38] Many obtained their freedom by serving in the armed forces, others by running away or deserting to the British.[39] Prince Whipple, a militant Negro belonging to a Continental army officer, shamed his master into freeing him by pointing out the hypocrisy of maintaining slavery during a war for liberty.[40] In 1779 Whipple and eighteen other blacks sent a petition to the legislature for Negro emancipation. Declaring slavery to be incompatible with "justice, humanity, and the rights of mankind," they demanded "such laws . . . whereby we may regain our liberty."[41]

But no progress toward abolition was made until the adoption in 1783 of a constitution declaring that "all men are born equal and independent," with natural rights, "among which are enjoying and defending life and liberty."[42] The precise legal effect of this declaration remains obscure, for no judicial records of how the courts construed the clause have survived. Some writers insist

37. Greene and Harrington, *American Population before the Federal Census of 1790*, p. 46.
38. *Ibid.*, pp. 73–74.
39. Benjamin Quarles, *The Negro in the American Revolution* (Chapel Hill: University of North Carolina Press, 1961), pp. 53–54.
40. Zilversmit, *The First Emancipation*, p. 118.
41. Quoted by Hammond, "Slavery in New Hampshire," *Granite Monthly*, IV (1880), 108–10.
42. Hurd, *The Law of Freedom and Bondage*, II, 35.

that the provision abolished slavery prospectively, while others believe that it ended the institution immediately and completely. "The construction there put on his clause," Jeremy Belknap wrote in 1795, "is that all who have been born since the constitution are free."[43] On the other hand, Nathaniel Bouton contended that the clause abolished slavery absolutely, and that by the end of the decade "slaves ceased to be known and held as property in New Hampshire."[44] However ambiguous its legal import, the freedom clause speeded the extinction of slavery. Slaves were removed from the rolls of taxable property in 1789, and by 1800 only eight of them remained in the state.[45]

Antislavery made rapid progress in Rhode Island during the final year of the Revolution. In October, 1783, Moses Brown and five other Quakers presented an emancipation petition to the assembly. The lawmakers responded by drafting a bill to provide for gradual abolition and to prohibit citizens of the state from participating in the slave trade. The bill was printed and referred to the next session of the legislature in order to allow time for public consideration. Although Brown worked hard to swing public opinion behind the bill, Newport's shipping interests worked equally hard to protect the slave trade.[46] In February of 1784 the legislature passed a compromise measure that provided for gradual emancipation without disturbing the overseas slave trade. All slave children born after March 1 became apprentices, the girls becoming unconditionally free at the age of eighteen and the boys at twenty-one. Until then, they were to be supported by their respective towns. The law also allowed the masters to manumit any adult slave under the age of forty without giving security that he would not become a public charge.[47]

43. "Queries Respecting the Slavery and Emancipation of Negroes in Massachusetts," in MHS *Colls.*, 1st ser., IV (1795), 204.
44. Nathaniel Bouton, ed., *Town Papers: Documents and Records Relating to Towns in New Hampshire* (Concord: Pearson, 1875), pp. 897–98n.
45. Emma L. Thornbrough, "Negro Slavery in the North: Its Legal and Constitutional Aspects," unpublished Ph.D. dissertation (University of Michigan, 1946), pp. 110–11; U.S. Census Office, *Second Census of the United States, 1800* (Washington, D.C., 1801), p. 7.
46. Mack Thompson, *Moses Brown* (Chapel Hill: University of North Carolina Press, 1962), pp. 177–82.
47. *R.I. Acts and Resolves*, February, 1784, pp. 6–7.

There was virtually no resistance to the law. Wartime manumissions had already reduced the slave force, and an increase in the supply of free labor had undercut the role of slavery in the state's economy. In 1749 the proportion of Negroes to whites was about 1 to 14, whereas by 1783 it had dropped to less than 1 to 22.[48] Moreover, the law carefully protected existing property interests. No slaves were emancipated outright; the foreign slave trade was left undisturbed; and the masters were relieved of the expense of raising children who became free. Indeed, in 1785 the masters were given the right to the services of these children during their statutory apprenticeships. Although they also became responsible for raising such children, the services they received should have covered whatever expense was involved. But if the arrangement proved to be burdensome or costly, the master could rid himself of the children completely by manumitting their mother.[49]

The Revolution put heavy pressure on slavery in Connecticut. From 1777 onward hundreds of slaves enrolled in the armed forces, thereby gaining freedom for themselves and underscoring the plight of blacks in general. "We are endowed with the same faculties with our masters," the Negroes of Stratford and Fairfield petitioned the legislature in 1779, "and the more we consider the matter, the more we are convinced of our right to be free."[50] Later in the year several slaves belonging to a Tory master also petitioned for freedom. They argued forcefully that they hoped "the free State of Connecticut, engaged in a war with tyranny, will not sell good honest Whigs . . . because the Whigs ought to be *free*, and the *Tories* should be sold."[51]

Connecticut's lawmakers were extremely cautious about moving against slavery. Negroes were more numerous in the state than in the rest of New England combined, and racial anxieties were

48. Greene and Harrington, *American Population before the Federal Census of 1790*, pp. 66, 69–70.

49. John R. Bartlett, ed., *Records of the Colony of Rhode Island and Providence Plantations in New England, 1636–1792*, 10 vols. (Providence: Greene, 1856–65), X, 132.

50. Gwendolyn Evans Logan, "The Slave in Connecticut during the American Revolution," CHS *Bulletin*, XXX (1965), 77.

51. Quoted in George Livermore, *An Historical Research Respecting the Opinions of the Founders of the Republic on Negroes as Slaves, as Citizens, and as Soldiers* (Boston: Williams, 1863), p. 116.

correspondingly more acute. When emancipation bills were rejected in 1777, 1779, and 1780, abolitionists realized that emancipation could not be enacted without substantial concessions.[52] The next emancipation bill brought before the assembly was reported in 1784 as part of a general statute codifying colonial race controls. Only after these regulations had been recapitulated in detail did the bill finally declare that "sound public policy" required the abolition of slavery. Almost as a postscript the bill provided that Negro and mulatto children born after March 1 would become free at the age of twenty-five years.[53] Although lacking in libertarian spirit, the strategy proved so effective that no votes were cast in opposition.[54]

Success in New England shifted the focus of abolition to New Jersey and New York. Except for the laws emancipating blacks who had served in the armed forces, the slave system remained as firmly entrenched in both states after the Revolution as before. New Jersey defenders of the status quo not only invoked the property rights of the masters but used racist arguments as well to justify Negro bondage.[55] One proponent of slavery argued in the *New Jersey Journal* (Chatham), November 29, 1780, that the Negro's "deep wrought disposition to indolence" and "want of judgment" made him generally unsuitable for freedom. Although such arguments were seldom heard in New York, defenders of slavery asserted that emancipation was not in the public interest. In 1777 the Provincial Congress refused to endorse a statement of principles condemning slavery as a violation of basic human rights. The congress also rejected a vague proposal for eventual emancipation on the grounds that "it would be highly inexpedient to proceed to the liberation of slaves within this state in the present situation."[56]

The end of the Revolution deprived proslavery men of the

52. Jeffrey R. Brackett, "The Status of the Slave, 1775–1789," in J. Franklin Jameson, ed., *Essays in the Constitutional History of the United States in the Formative Period, 1775–1789* (Boston: Houghton, Mifflin, 1889), p. 296; Zilvermit, *The First Emancipation*, p. 123.

53. Hurd, *The Law of Freedom and Bondage*, II, 41–42.

54. Professor Arthur Zilversmit speculates that some of the lawmakers may not have realized that they were voting for emancipation. See Zilversmit, *The First Emancipation*, pp. 123–24.

55. *Ibid.*, pp. 139–40, 142–46.

56. *Journals of the New York Provincial Congress*, I, 887–89.

argument that emancipation might weaken the war effort. Thus in 1785 the New York assembly reported a bill granting freedom to Negro children after a limited period of service. Before the bill came to a vote, however, Aaron Burr proposed an amendment for the immediate and unconditional abolition of slavery. Realizing that such a proposal would be too radical for public acceptance, the antislavery forces defeated the amendment and rallied behind the original bill.[57] But they failed to hold their ranks against amendments limiting the civil rights of Negroes. The emancipation bill that finally emerged from the assembly prohibited intermarriage, denied blacks the right to vote or hold public office, and disqualified them as witnesses against whites in all the courts of the state.[58]

This attempt to relegate Negroes to second-class citizenship met strong resistance in the senate. The upper house feared that racial restrictions might lead to disorders, and so it deleted the discriminatory amendments before returning the bill to the assembly for reconsideration. Although the assembly was willing to waive the restrictions on intermarriage, office-holding, and the qualification of witnesses, it refused to give way on the issue of voting. Blacks could have freedom, but they were not to have political power. Accordingly, the revised version of the bill reaffirmed the ban on Negro voting.[59] Since it was now clear that there would be no emancipation law without the voting proviso, the senate reluctantly passed the assembly's version and sent it on to the council of revision for approval.[60]

The council of revision, however, vetoed the bill and returned it to the upper house with a message condemning the voting proviso as dangerous and unjust.[61] Although the senate agreed in

57. *Journal of the Assembly of the State of New York* (New York, 1785), February 25, 1785, hereafter cited as *N.Y. Assembly Journal*. Most of the members supporting Burr's amendment were bent on political sabotage. Ten of the thirteen assemblymen who voted for the amendment subsequently voted against the emancipation bill itself. *Ibid.*, March 1, 1785. See Zilversmit, *The First Emancipation*, p. 148.

58. *N.Y. Assembly Journal*, March 1, 1785.

59. *Ibid.*, March 9, 12, 1785.

60. *Journal of the Senate of the State of New York* (New York, 1785), March 12, 1785, hereafter cited as *N.Y. Senate Journal*.

61. Alfred B. Street, *The Council of Revision of the State of New York*

principle with the council, a majority wanted action on emancipation regardless of the price. They overrode the veto and sent the bill back to the assembly, expecting that similar action would be taken there.[62] But the assembly by now had become confused and uncertain. The majority agreed that racial disfranchisement was dangerous; yet they refused to vote for emancipation without it. Given the choice between a bad bill or no bill at all, they chose the latter and voted to sustain the council's veto.[63] In the final analysis, emancipation was blocked by a majority that feared Negro power more than it desired Negro freedom.

Antislavery made limited progress on other fronts. In 1785 the New York legislature prohibited the importation of slaves for sale within the state. The law also allowed slaveholders to grant manumission without posting bond if the overseers of the poor certified that the slave was capable of self-support.[64] The following year similar measures were passed in New Jersey. Persons guilty of "the barbarous custom of bringing the unoffending Africans from their native country . . . into a state of slavery" were subject to a fine of £50, and a £20 fine was imposed on those who imported Negroes from other states. The law also sought to remove "every unnecessary obstruction in the way of freeing slaves." The masters could henceforth manumit any bondsman between the ages of twenty-one and thirty-five without giving security that he would not become a public charge.[65]

Newspaper attacks on slavery kept the issue before the public and increased the pressure for emancipation. "Slavery is worse than death," a letter in the September 20, 1780, edition of the *New Jersey Gazette* declared, and anyone "who enslaves his fellow creature must, in our esteem, be worse than he who takes his life." Abuse was heaped upon defenders of the status quo. Denouncing the rejection of emancipation by New York's assembly in 1785, a writer to the *New York Packet* urged voters not to support slaveholders for public office, "for those who make slaves of

(Albany: Gould, 1859), p. 268; *N.Y. Senate Journal*, March 12, 1785; *N.Y. Assembly Journal*, March 26, 1785.

62. *N.Y. Senate Journal*, March 21, 1785.
63. *N.Y. Assembly Journal*, March 26, 1785.
64. *Laws of New York, 1785*, LXVIII.
65. *Acts of the General Assembly of the State of New Jersey, 1786* (10th sess.), pp. 239–40, hereafter cited as *N.J. Assembly Acts*.

the blacks . . . will likewise of the whites."[66] An attack on slave-holders in the *New York Journal,* June 22, 1786, declared that the masters deserved to be "plundered, tormented, and even massacred by the avenging hands of their purchased slaves."

The rapid growth of antislavery sentiment brought sweeping reforms in the slave controls. In 1788 New Jersey abolished special punishments for slave offenses; henceforth crimes by slaves were to be "adjudged, corrected and punished in like manner as the criminal offenses of the other inhabitants of this state."[67] New York also revised its slave code to give slaves the right to a jury trial for crimes involving the death penalty. Terroristic punishments were abolished, and slaves charged with serious offenses were brought under the same penalties prescribed by law for white offenders.[68] The net result in both states was a uniform system of justice for whites and blacks alike.

Repeal of the colonial codes made slavery more humane. So pervasive was the sentiment against brutality that some masters chose to manumit unruly slaves rather than risk social opprobrium by punishing them severely.[69] The judicial climate also improved as the courts gave increasingly liberal interpretations to the laws governing manumission.[70] In 1795 the New Jersey supreme court ruled that a mere promise of manumission, though unsupported by legal consideration, created a valid claim to freedom. "It is far better to adopt this rule," the court declared, "than to suffer promises thus made . . . to be violated or retracted at pleasure."[71]

The most powerful thrust for Negro freedom came from the state abolition societies. By the 1790s these organizations had raised constituencies that gave the movement a formidable political base. The New York Manumission Society counted among its members such influential men as John Jay, Alexander Hamil-

66. *New York Packet,* March 31, 1785, cited in Zilversmit, *The First Emancipation,* pp. 149–50.
67. *N.J. Assembly Acts, 1788* (13th sess.), p. 488. See Brackett, in Jameson, *Essays in the Constitutional History of the United States,* p. 300.
68. *Laws of New York, 1788,* XL.
69. Edward A. Collier, *A History of Old Kinderhook* (New York: Putnam's, 1914), p. 210.
70. Catterall, *Judicial Cases Concerning Slavery,* IV, 321–27, 357, 360–61.
71. *State v. M'Donald and Armstrong,* 1 Coxe 334–35 (N.J. Supreme Court, 1795).

ton, Melancton Smith, St. John de Crèvecoeur, Philip Schuyler, James Duane, and Robert R. Livingston.[72] The society waged a constant campaign by circulating petitions, sponsoring lectures and debates, awarding prizes for antislavery articles, and printing and distributing large quantities of abolition literature.[73] The New Jersey Society for Promoting the Abolition of Slavery generally followed the same strategy. Numerous petitions were sent to the legislature and heavy pressure was put on state officials to protect the rights of Negroes.[74] These organizations were the heart of the antislavery movement. They provided legal counsel for slaves bringing freedom suits, and in some cases they helped Negroes to recover damages from the masters.[75]

The New York Manumission Society organized boycotts against the slave trade. Vendue houses and newspapers were put on notice that any participation in the buying and selling of slaves would bring reprisals.[76] Indeed, whether the antislavery letters and articles that appeared in the press sprang from the conviction that slavery was wrong or from economic intimidation is an open question. A standing committee of the society visited newspaper offices from time to time and admonished publishers against accepting advertisements for the purchase or sale of slaves. Another committee kept track of persons involved in the overseas slave trade.[77] Lists were compiled, and the public was urged not to patronize businesses that had any connection with the traffic. Ships known to engage in the trade were kept under surveillance, and the authorities were informed of violations of the state's trading laws.[78] Such tactics helped to convince the business class that any involvement in slavery would be costly.

72. Minutes of the New York Manumission Society, February 4, 1785, MS. coll., NYHS.
73. Ibid., February 15, 1787; September 24, 1788; August 20, 1789; May 15, 1792. New York Gazetteer, February 18, 1785; January 15, 1787. New York Journal, or the Weekly Register, October 26, November 9, 1786.
74. Marion T. Wright, "New Jersey Laws and the Negro," JNH, XXVIII (1943), 175–76.
75. Minutes of the New York Manumission Society, April 16, 1795; Cooley, Study of Slavery in New Jersey, pp. 23–24.
76. Minutes of the New York Manumission Society, November 20, 1788; August 18, 1795.
77. Ibid., May 18, August 18, 1790.
78. Ibid., June 22, 1792; January 11, 1793.

Since the rest of the North had accepted emancipation, it was not difficult for abolitionists to drive slavery into social disrepute. Writing in 1797, the New York City diarist William Dunlap observed that "within 20 years the opinion of the injustice of slaveholding has become almost universal."[79] After 1790 slave auctions practically disappeared, and the few that were held attracted more critics than buyers. A public sale of Negroes in New York was attacked in Frothingham's Long Island Herald, January 11, 1796, as "disgraceful to humanity," and readers were urged to protest against the "outrage" by sending petitions to the legislature. The bias against slaveholding extended to the courts. Slaveholders in New Jersey were reviled by the judges as "speculators in human flesh," while abolitionists were praised as "laudable and humane" for their efforts on behalf of Negroes.[80] So hostile were some of the judges that the slaveholders petitioned the legislature for the right of jury trial in all freedom suits.[81]

Demographic changes played a crucial role in promoting antislavery. The white population in New York and New Jersey had a high birth rate during the last half of the eighteenth century, and there was a concomitant influx of settlers from other states.[82] By 1771 the ratio of blacks to whites in New York reached its lowest point in almost seventy years, as shown in Table 2.[83] During the next fifteen years whites increased by about 50 percent while Negroes, as can be seen in Table 3,[84] declined by almost 5 percent. Although migration from other states increased New Jersey's black population during the Revolution, the white population grew even more rapidly. Moreover, the latter continued to increase after the war, while the ban on slave imports in 1786 ended the influx of

79. "William Dunlap's Diary, 1776–1839," in NYHS Colls., LXII–LXIV (3 vols., 1929–31), I, 119.

80. State v. M'Donald and Armstrong, 1 Coxe 334 (N.J. Supreme Court, 1795); State v. Frees, I Coxe 259 (N.J. Supreme Court, 1794).

81. Wright, "New Jersey Laws and the Negro," JNH, XXVIII, 175–76. The usual suit for freedom in New Jersey was by habeas corpus, a proceeding which did not require a jury. See State v. Farlee, 1 Coxe 41 (N.J. Supreme Court, 1790).

82. E. Wilder Spaulding, New York in the Critical Period (New York: Columbia University Press, 1932), pp. 30–31; Cooley, Study of Slavery in New Jersey, p. 31n.

83. Statistics compiled from Greene and Harrington, American Population before the Federal Census of 1790, pp. 95–102.

84. Ibid., pp. 102–103.

TABLE 2

Year	Percent Slave	Year	Percent Slave
1703	11.5	1746	14.8
1723	14.8	1749	14.4
1731	14.3	1756	14.0
1737	14.7	1771	11.8

TABLE 3

Year	Whites	Slaves	Percent Slave
1771	148,124	19,883	11.8
1786	219,996	18,889	7.9

TABLE 4

	1786	1800	Percent Increase
White	139,934	211,949	52.2
Slave	10,501	12,422	8.6

Negroes. Between 1786 and 1800 whites increased at six times the rate of blacks, and by the end of the century the proportion of slaves in the general population had become negligible, as shown in Table 4.[85]

The growing availability of white workers undermined the slave economy. Slave costs were relatively high both from the standpoint of capital invested and the expense of maintaining slaves during periods of unemployment. As the supply of free workers increased and the wage rate fell, slavery became obsolete

85. Statistics compiled from U.S. Census Office, *Second Census of the United States, 1800*, p. 34; Greene and Harrington, *American Population before the Federal Census of 1790*, p. 108.

as a system of labor. Newspaper advertisements indicate that after 1780 blacks were more in demand as hired workers than as purchased slaves.[86] In 1797 the New York Manumission Society estimated that at least two thousand free Negroes were employed at wage labor in New York City alone.[87] These changes gave impetus to the antislavery movement. The ideal of freedom was a powerful motive force, but the steady erosion of slave profits was an important factor in its widespread acceptance.

So rapidly did the slave interest decline in New York that the legislature again took up the question of Negro emancipation. In 1799 a bill was proposed to emancipate Negro children born after July 4, the boys to become absolutely free at the age of twenty-eight and girls at the age of twenty-five. Slaveowners were required to register all slave births within nine months, and failure to do so would result in automatic emancipation. Properly registered children might be held to service until they reached freedom age in order to reimburse the masters. The latter could rid themselves of all responsibility for such children by assigning them to the overseers of the poor.[88] These proposals, most of which had already been enacted in other states, encountered little opposition. The bill passed both houses easily, by a vote of 68 to 23 in the assembly and 22 to 10 in the senate.[89]

New York proponents of emancipation astutely avoided the racial issues that had deadlocked the legislature fourteen years before. The qualification of Negroes as witnesses was not debated, nor did their eligibility to vote or hold public office become an issue. Moreover, the provision allowing assignment of Negro children to the overseers of the poor contained a hidden subsidy for the slaveowners. Such children were to be bound out to service

86. *New York Weekly Mercury*, May 27, 1782; June 30, 1783. Rivington's *Royal Gazette*, July 13, August 21, 1782. *The Independent Journal* (New York), May 19, 1784. *New York Journal & Patriotic Register*, April 6, December 21, 1799.

87. *Minutes of the Proceedings of the Fourth Convention of Delegates from the Abolition Societies Established in Different Parts of the United States Assembled at Philadelphia on the Third Day of May, One Thousand Seven Hundred and Ninety-seven, and Continued, by Appointments, until the Ninth Day of the Same Month, Inclusive* (Philadelphia, 1797), pp. 29–31.

88. *Laws of New York, 1799,* LXII.

89. *N.Y. Assembly Journal,* March 28, 1799; *N.Y. Senate Journal,* March 25, 27, 1799.

by the overseers with an allowance of $3.50 per month for their support. Since the law did not prohibit binding out a child to the person who had technically abandoned him, slaveowners were able to collect an indirect bonus for every child emancipated.[90] There was also a provision that permitted owners to manumit slaves regardless of age or physical condition.[91] These generous concessions virtually guaranteed that abolition would have wide public acceptance.

Success in New York made emancipation inevitable in neighboring New Jersey. Antislavery petitions had flooded the legislature during the 1790s, and by the end of the century it was clear that the institution was marked for extinction.[92] In 1804 the legislature passed a law that emancipated Negro children born after July 4, the boys to be free at the age of twenty-five and the girls at the age of twenty-one. Slaveowners were required to register all births with the clerks of their respective counties as evidence of the age at which the children became free. Properly registered children would remain in service until the freedom age in order to reimburse the masters for raising them. However, the owners could rid themselves of this responsibility by assigning them to the overseers of the poor.[93] These concessions virtually disarmed the opposition. The law passed both houses overwhelmingly, by a vote of 34 to 4 in the assembly and 12 to 1 in the council.[94]

New Jersey's emancipation law carefully protected existing property rights. No one lost a single slave, and the right to the services of young Negroes was fully protected. Moreover, the courts ruled that the right was a "species of property," transferable "from one citizen to another like other personal property."[95] The law also granted slaveowners an indirect subsidy under the clause allowing them to assign slave children to the overseers of the poor. Such children could be reassigned back to the masters

90. Zilversmit, *The First Emancipation*, p. 182.
91. *Laws of New York, 1799*, LXII.
92. Cooley, *Study of Slavery in New Jersey*, pp. 25–26.
93. *N.J. Assembly Acts, 1804* (28th sess.), pp. 251–54.
94. *Votes and Proceedings of the Twenty-Eighth General Assembly of the State of New Jersey* (Trenton, 1805), February 11, 1804; *Journal of the Proceedings of the Legislative Council of the State of New Jersey* (Trenton, 1805), February 15, 1804.
95. *Ogden* v. *Price*, 4 Halsted 170 (N.J. Supreme Court, 1827).

with an allowance of $3.00 per month for their support.[96] By 1806 such disbursements amounted to one-third of all state expenditures, and three years later the "abandoned blacks" appropriation climbed to 40 percent of the budget.[97] This expense was borne by the entire state, whereas the windfall went to only a few slaveholding counties.[98] All in all, such concessions went far to reduce slaveholder resistance.

Although the North's abolition laws provided for only gradual emancipation, the commitment to freedom was complete and irreversible. In 1810 the federal census for New England reported 418 slaves out of a black population of almost 20,000, and ten years later only 145 Negroes remained in bondage. By 1810 New Jersey, Pennsylvania, and New York had fewer than 18,000 slaves, only about 0.6 percent of the total population.[99] This progress toward freedom had implications for the entire nation. It marked the point at which North and South diverged to pursue separate goals: the one with a commitment, however inchoate, to freedom and equality; the other to a way of life dependent upon slavery and repression.[100] That these goals would surely clash meant that white Americans could expect neither peace nor national unity while black Americans remained in bondage.

96. *N.J. Assembly Acts, 1804* (28th sess.), pp. 252–53.
97. *Votes and Proceedings of the General Assembly of the State of New Jersey*, November 5, 1806; November 2–21, 1809. See Cooley, *Study of Slavery in New Jersey*, p. 27.
98. According to the federal census of 1800, Burlington, Gloucester, and Salem counties had 334 slaves in a population of over 49,000; Bergen and Somerset counties, with fewer than 28,000 people, had 4,688 slaves. U.S. Census Office, *Second Census of the United States, 1800*, p. 34.
99. U.S. Census Office, *Third Census of the United States, 1810* (Washington, D.C., 1811), p. 1; U.S. Census Office, *Fourth Census of the United States, 1820* (Washington, D.C., 1821), p. 21.
100. Zilversmit, *The First Emancipation*, p. 200.

11

A Different Bondage

Emancipation did not mean that blacks would automatically enjoy the same rights and privileges as the white population. Many whites who opposed slavery as an institution were nevertheless unwilling to relinquish their racial prerogatives. Frequently white support of abolition owed more to immediate self-interest than to any concern for the welfare of blacks. Indeed, much of the working-class opposition to slavery was motivated primarily by the desire to eliminate slave competition. "The common people," John Adams observed, "would not suffer the labour, by which alone they could obtain a subsistence, to be done by slaves."[1] Some of the self-serving character of the abolition movement can be discerned in the early laws against slavery. Connecticut prohibited the slaves trade on the grounds that "the increase of slaves is injurious to the poor," and New Jersey outlawed the importation of slaves "in order that white labor may be protected."[2]

Concern for racial justice played only a minor role in the politics of abolition. Too often intrigue and compromise prevailed over the moral issue as the price of political acceptability. Massachusetts abolished slavery indirectly by court decisions, New Hampshire by an ambiguous constitutional provision, and Con-

1. "Letters and Documents Relating to Slavery in Massachusetts," in MHS *Colls.*, 5th ser., III (1877), 402.
2. *Acts and Laws of Connecticut, 1784*, pp. 233–34; *Acts of the General Assembly of the State of New Jersey, 1786* (10th sess.), p. 239. Hereafter cited as Conn. *Laws* and *N.J. Assembly Acts.*

necticut by what amounted to a legislative coup. Only Rhode Island, New York, Pennsylvania, and New Jersey faced the issue squarely and abolished slavery by statute after full debate. But no state provided for immediate emancipation, and none of the statutes interfered with existing property interests. Although New York and Connecticut finally abolished slavery completely in 1827 and 1848 respectively, the rest of the North settled for gradualism.[3] New Jersey retained slaveholding without technically remaining a slave state by reclassifying its slaves as apprentices for life.[4] Blacks remained in apprentice bondage there as late as 1860, and the federal census continued to list them as slaves.[5]

Gradual emancipation provided numerous opportunities to wring a final profit out of slavery. Some masters sent pregnant slave women out of the state so that their children could not claim freedom under the abolition statutes.[6] Somewhat riskier was the illegal export of Negroes to the South and the West Indies. This traffic attained such proportions that the New York Manumission Society appointed watchers throughout the state to report on unusual purchases of Negroes.[7] Some exporters evaded the law by leasing their slaves for long periods instead of selling them outright.[8] Others manumitted slaves under long indentures which could then be sold to buyers in other states. One of these technically free Negroes was exported from New Jersey under an indenture that bound him to ninety-nine years of service.[9]

Frequently free Negroes became the victims of unscrupulous traders. Blacks apprenticed to white artisans were sometimes sold as slaves despite the terms of their indentures. Others were enticed into debt at usurious rates and then sold into bondage when they were unable to pay.[10] According to the *Philadelphia Gazette*,

3. *Laws of New York, 1817*, CXXXVII; *Revised Statutes of the State of Connecticut, 1849*, p. 584.
4. John C. Hurd, *The Law of Freedom and Bondage in the United States*, 2 vols. (Boston, 1858–62), II, 67.
5. U.S. Census Bureau, *Negro Population, 1790–1915* (Washington, D.C.: G. P. O., 1918), p. 57.
6. Edward R. Turner, *The Negro in Pennsylvania* (Washington, D.C.: The American Historical Association, 1911), p. 80.
7. Minutes of the New York Manumission Society, June 22, 1792, January 11, 1793, MS. coll., NYHS.
8. *Sable* v. *Hitchcock*, 2 Johnson's Cases 79 (N.Y. Supreme Court, 1800).
9. Minutes of the New York Manumission Society, June 23, 1795.
10. *Ibid.*, February 11, June 20, August 28, 1794; April 20, May 25, 1797.

July 25, 1818, Negroes were sometimes seized on the streets and forcibly exported to the South.[11] Many were lured away by treachery or promises of employment and then sold to buyers in the slave states. One Philadelphia trader turned an infamous profit by marrying several mulatto women in order to sell them into slavery.[12] How many blacks were deprived of freedom by one ruse or another can never be estimated, but in just one year thirty-three cases of unlawful enslavement were uncovered in New York City alone.[13]

The sale of Negroes to the slave states cut deeply into the North's black population. Federal census returns reveal that during the period 1790–1830 the rate of growth of New York's black population declined from 2.13 percent to about 0.57 percent yearly. In 1790 Negroes accounted for 7.6 percent of all inhabitants; by 1830 they had decreased to only 2.3 percent of the total population. This decline had parallels in almost every Northern state. Connecticut's black population grew at an annual rate of only 0.6 percent between 1790 and 1850, and during the period 1840–50 actually declined by several hundreds.[14] Since there is no evidence of fewer births or greater mortality after 1800, it seems obvious that the black population was depleted by emigration. Nor is it likely that blacks left voluntarily, for their status in the North was infinitely better than in the South or the West Indies. It seems far more probable that they were the victims of a forced migration organized by kidnappers and criminals who dealt in human misery.

Although the demographic evidence strongly supports these conclusions, it would be an oversimplification to assume that kidnapping and smuggling tell the whole story. Some allowance must be made for the possibility that Northern census returns under-report the number of free blacks in the population. So long as blacks remained slaves, great care was taken to include them on the rolls of taxable property. But once they became free and ceased to be property, it was less important for census officials

11. See Turner, *The Negro in Pennsylvania*, pp. 115–16.
12. Jesse Torrey, Jr., *A Portraiture of Domestic Slavery in the United States* (Philadelphia: the Author, 1817), p. 57.
13. Minutes of the New York Manumission Society, March 21, 1797.
14. U.S. Census Bureau, *Negro Population, 1790–1915*, pp. 44–45.

to make precise counts. While this trend cannot be quantified, it perhaps contributed as much to the statistical decline of the North's black population as the illegal trade in Negroes.

Whatever the extent of this miserable traffic, public officials tried with mixed success to stamp it out. A New York law of 1801 provided that masters could not leave the state with slaves purchased less than one year before, and the period was later extended to ten years.[15] New York City denied the use of its jails for the detention of alleged runaways, for this had become a pretext for seizing and exporting free Negroes.[16] In 1818 New Jersey prohibited "the exportation of slaves or servants of color," and three years later Connecticut forbade resident slaveholders to send their Negroes out of the state for any reason.[17] Pennsylvania outlawed the export of slaves completely and prescribed heavy penalties for kidnapping. Any person convicted of selling or forcibly transporting a free Negro from the state was liable for $2,000 in fines and twenty-one years in prison.[18]

Although the North punished attempts to deprive blacks of their freedom, public policy otherwise promoted Negrophobia. That blacks were legally free did not prevent Massachusetts, Rhode Island, and Maine from prohibiting them to intermarry with whites. Such marriages were absolutely void in Rhode Island, and persons who performed them were subject to criminal penalties.[19] Several states enacted statutes to keep out nonresident blacks. In 1833 Connecticut passed a residency requirement for blacks seeking to attend free schools, declaring that open admissions "would tend to the great increase of the colored people of the state and thereby to the injury of the people."[20] New Jersey prohibited Negroes to enter for the purpose of settling, and Massachusetts prescribed flogging for nonresident blacks who remained for longer than two months.[21]

15. *Laws of New York, 1801*, pp. 548–49; *ibid.* (1807), pp. 92–93.
16. *Minutes of the Common Council, 1784–1831*, 19 vols. (New York: Brown, 1917), III, 691.
17. *N.J. Assembly Acts, 1818* (43d sess.), p. 3; *Conn. Laws, 1821*, p. 429.
18. *Acts of the Pennsylvania Assembly, 1820*, pp. 104–106.
19. *Massachusetts Acts and Laws, 1783–1789*, p. 439; *Rhode Island Public Laws, 1789*, p. 483; *Revised Statutes of Maine, 1821*, LXX.
20. *Revised Statutes of Connecticut, 1835*, Title 53.
21. *N.J. Assembly Acts, 1786* (10th sess.), p. 242; *Mass. Acts and Laws, 1788*, XXI.

By the 1830s it had become clear that nothing would be allowed to disturb the white hegemony. State after state passed laws disfranchising blacks and restricting their eligibility for public office. New Jersey led the way in 1807 with a law providing that no one should be eligible to vote "unless such person be a free, white, male citizen."[22] In 1814 Connecticut limited the suffrage to white male citizens, and four years later this restriction became part of the state's constitution.[23] Pennsylvania Negroes lost the suffrage by an 1837 state court decision that they were not "freemen" and therefore not eligible to vote.[24] The following year this decision was written into the state constitution under a provision specifically limiting the suffrage to white freemen.[25] Rhode Island achieved the same result by a statute barring Negroes from the freemanship needed to vote in local and state elections.[26] Though New York Negroes were not deprived of the franchise completely, they had to satisfy higher property qualifications than those prescribed for white voters.[27]

Far more damaging than these suffrage restrictions was the systematic exclusion of blacks from economic opportunities. Protests by white workers against Negro competition had occurred repeatedly in colonial times, but so long as slaveholders profited from their labor the place of blacks in the economy was fully protected. However, with the demise of slavery this protection vanished, and Negroes were pushed out of one line of work after another. Whites who had opposed slavery for keeping the wage rate down or for causing unemployment now made it clear that no form of black competition would be tolerated. As the working force grew larger through immigration, the pressure on whites became irresistible to protect their job opportunities at the expense of Negroes. "Every hour sees the black man elbowed out of employment," Frederick Douglass reported, "by some newly

22. *Compiled Laws of New Jersey, 1811*, p. 23; *Revised Laws of New Jersey, 1821*, p. 741.

23. *Conn. Laws, 1814*, p. 162; *Connecticut Constitution of 1818*, Article 6.

24. *Hobbs et al.* v. *Fogg*, 6 Watt's Cases 553 (Pa. Supreme Court, 1837).

25. Francis N. Thorpe, ed., *The Federal and State Constitutions, Colonial Charters and Other Organic Laws*, 7 vols. (Washington, D.C.: G. P. O., 1909), V, 3108.

26. *R.I. Public Laws, 1822*, pp. 89–90.

27. Thorpe, *Federal and State Constitutions*, V, 2643.

arrived immigrant, whose hunger and whose color are thought to give him better title."[28]

Cut off from economic opportunities, blacks entered a downward spiral of idleness, squalor, and disease. By 1838 many of Philadelphia's Negroes lived in grinding poverty, and in New York City the main employment open to blacks was domestic service.[29] Between 1830 and 1850 the percentage of deaf, dumb, blind, and insane among the blacks of New York City was twice that of the white population.[30] There was no opportunity for blacks to develop their talents or improve their condition. Those who sought employment in Boston were insulted, threatened, and even attacked on the streets by gangs of ruffians.[31] So miserable was their plight that Jeremy Belknap concluded that most of them had been better off in their former state of slavery.[32] They became pariahs in the North, isolated from the mainstream of life, economically proscribed, and subject everywhere to restrictions that mocked their alleged freedom.[33]

The loss of rights that protected others made the Negro a convenient public scapegoat. Blacks were pilloried by demagogs who found it safe and politically profitable to stir up racial antagonism. "Federalists with Blacks Unite" became the rallying cry of Republicans bidding for votes in New York during the campaign of

28. Philip S. Foner, ed., *The Life and Writings of Frederick Douglass*, 4 vols. (New York: International Publishers, 1950–55), II, 223–25. For similar economic pressures on blacks in the South during this period, see Richard C. Wade, *Slavery in the Cities* (New York: Oxford University Press, 1967), pp. 273–75.

29. Pennsylvania Society for Promoting the Abolition of Slavery, *The Present State and Condition of the Free People of Color in the City of Philadelphia* (Philadelphia, 1838), pp. 12–15; Henry Wansey, *The Journal of an Excursion to the United States of America in the Summer of 1794* (London, 1796), p. 227. See J. P. Brissot de Warville, *New Travels in the United States of America*, 2 vols. (London, 1794), I, 239–40.

30. J. D. B. De Bow, *Statistical View of the United States, Being a Compendium of the Seventh Census, 1850* (Washington, D.C.: Beverly Tucker, 1854), p. 113.

31. Lorenzo J. Greene, *The Negro in Colonial New England, 1620–1776* (New York: Columbia University Press, 1942), p. 304.

32. "Letters and Documents Relating to Slavery in Massachusetts," in MHS *Colls.*, 5th ser., III (1877), 402. Jupiter Hammon, New York's slave poet, conjectured in 1787 whether "it may be more to our comfort to remain as we are." Jupiter Hammon, *An Address to the Negroes of the State of New York* (New York: Carroll & Patterson, 1787), p. 13.

33. Austin Steward, *Twenty-Two Years a Slave and Forty Years a Freeman* (Rochester, N.Y.: William Alling, 1857), pp. 125, 167.

1808.[34] Racial polarization was also aggravated by scurrilous pamphleteers who flooded the North with hate sheets maligning Negroes as a subhuman species.[35] Such attacks poisoned the air and set the stage for violent confrontations. Philadelphia was racked by repeated disorders in which blacks were beaten, burned out of their homes, and sometimes killed by raging street gangs.[36] In 1834 the longest riot on record before the Civil War erupted in New York City. Hundreds of Negro homes were burned or destroyed, and order was not restored until the governor sent troops into the city.[37] Northern leaders either remained silent in the face of these outrages or else sought political gain by excusing and patronizing the perpetrators.

Sectional considerations contributed heavily to racist politics. With only three exceptions, every President during the period 1800–50 came from below the Mason-Dixon line. Because the main concern of the South was the protection of slavery, Northern party leaders could not afford to give any offense on this issue.[38] Some went even further than their patronage needs required and outdid their Southern allies in anti-Negro demagogy. Apologists for slavery printed articles and editorials defending the status quo and pledging solidarity with the South on racial issues.[39] The attorney general of Massachusetts cravenly excused the rioters who murdered the abolitionist editor Elijah Lovejoy, likening them to the "orderly mob" that staged the Boston Tea Party.[40] So "mercenary and unprincipled" were Northern defenders of the slave

34. Dixon Ryan Fox, "The Negro Vote in Old New York," *Political Science Quarterly*, XXXII (1917), 256–57.

35. For an example of racist pamphleteering at its worst, see John Jacobus Flournoy, *An Essay on the Origin, Habits, etc., of the African Race: Incidental to the Propriety of Having Nothing to Do with Negroes* (New York, 1835), pp. 2–7.

36. Leon F. Litwack, *North of Slavery: The Negro in the Free States, 1790–1860* (Chicago: University of Chicago Press, 1961), pp. 100–101. See Turner, *The Negro in Pennsylvania*, pp. 143–68.

37. Dwight Dumond, *Antislavery: The Crusade for Freedom in America* (Ann Arbor: University of Michigan Press, 1961), pp. 218–19. See Litwack, *North of Slavery*, p. 102.

38. Dumond, *Antislavery*, pp. 71–73.

39. *Sentinel of Freedom* (Newark), November 4, 1834; September 8, 1835, cited in Marion T. Wright, "New Jersey Laws and the Negro," *JNH*, XXVIII (1943), 183.

40. Louis Filler, *The Crusade against Slavery, 1830–1860* (New York: Harper, 1963), p. 80.

power, one of their critics charged, that "they could not have worked more heartily to carry out the wishes of their Southern masters."[41]

Politicians of both sections also joined hands to eliminate free Negroes by colonization. If Negroes developed colonies of their own in the Caribbean or in Africa, the argument ran, then the burden of prejudice would disappear and they would be free to work out their own destiny. No movement ostensibly organized to assist black people received such enthusiastic support from the white establishment. Congress appropriated $100,000 to transport free Negroes to Africa, and fourteen state legislatures instructed their congressmen to support the scheme.[42] Most Negroes, however, rejected the idea of colonization.[43] "We are natives of this country," a New York Negro leader declared, "we ask only to be treated as well as foreigners . . . to share equal privileges with those who came from distant lands."[44] So long as blacks continued to hope for equal treatment they would not leave the only land they knew.

What must have strained such hopes to the breaking point were the continuous reminders that blackness meant second-class citizenship. Negroes who refused to leave railroad cars reserved for whites were dragged from their seats and beaten by conductors and brakemen. The fact that they had paid full fare along with the whites did not protect them from insult and assault.[45] Frederick Douglass, who had few illusions about racial attitudes in the North, was nevertheless shocked by the "colorphobia" he encountered in New York City.[46] Even at concerts and lectures given by blacks racial lines were tightly drawn. When the black abolitionist Samuel Ringgold Ward spoke in Philadelphia in 1850,

41. Quoted in Joseph Atkinson, *The History of Newark, New Jersey* (Newark, N.J.: Guild, 1878), p. 239.

42. Filler, *The Crusade against Slavery*, pp. 20–21. See Early L. Fox, *The American Colonization Society, 1817–1840* (Baltimore: The Johns Hopkins Press, 1919), pp. 9–10, 64–65.

43. Louis R. Mehlinger, "The Attitude of the Free Negro toward African Colonization," *JNH*, I (1916), 276–301.

44. Address by Peter Williams, July 4, 1830, quoted in Carter G. Woodson, *Negro Orators and Their Orations* (Washington, D.C.: Associated Publishers, 1925), p. 80.

45. Foner, *The Life and Writings of Frederick Douglass*, I, 52–53.

46. *Ibid.*, pp. 384–87.

notices of the meeting announced that seats in the lower hall "will be appropriated exclusively to our white citizens."[47] By such acts of harassment and humiliation blacks were made to understand that while they were no longer slaves they had not yet achieved full freedom.

Emancipation freed Negroes from the control of individual masters but left them in bondage to white society. Long after slavery had been abolished in the North the doctrine of white superiority continued to provide a rationale for racial repression. That men should be subordinate simply because they were black had been a recurring justification of slavery from the beginning. The treatment accorded black prisoners of war in the eighteenth century is a sharp reminder of how color equated with status in colonial times. Nor could whites systematically exploit and brutalize blacks for nearly two centuries without internalizing the grossest racial conceits. Negroes did not become slaves by accident or bad luck, the argument ran, but because nature had made them an inferior people. This conception of race entered deeply into the consciousness of white Americans to poison the wellsprings of national life. Out of it came that fatal infatuation with color that has blighted countless lives and bequeathed to the present a legacy of racial discontent.

47. *Ibid.*, p. 96.

12

The North in Perspective

No regional study of slavery would be complete without considering the Western culture in which it existed. The North's slave system was part of a total colonial experience that modified the history of this hemisphere. Wherever the system of Negro slavery existed—whether in Pennsylvania, Virginia, of Brazil—it had a logic of its own that transcended differences in climate, geography, and nationality. Nothing was above or beyond it: not the law, which legitimated and defended slave relations; not religion, which tolerated or ignored its abuses; not even those members of the master class who had moral qualms.

The universal fact about American slavery was race—that blacks should be subject to whites because of their color. Wherever slavery existed, Negroes were forced to shape their behavior according to the expectations of a white hegemony. Although slaves in Cuba or Brazil might be technically protected by safeguards lacking in the English colonies, slavery everywhere rested upon the total subordination of blacks. Frank Tannenbaum and Stanley M. Elkins have argued persuasively that there was a great contrast between the English and the Hispano-Portuguese colonies, for the latter recognized the Negro's basic humanity while the former treated him as a chattel.[1] Yet there is no clear evidence that technical differences in status made the slightest practical

1. Frank Tannenbaum, *Slave and Citizen: The Negro in the Americas* (New York: Knopf, 1947): Stanley M. Elkins, *Slavery: A Problem in American Institutional and Intellectual Life* (New York: Grosset & Dunlap, 1961).

difference in the everyday life of the slave. David Brion Davis'
more recent study of slavery in Western culture reveals a picture
of widespread hatred and racial oppression in Latin America that
matches the worst barbarities of the English colonies.[2]

What happened to the Negro in the North occurred in every
colony where slavery struck roots. He was subject to a regime
that ground him down to whatever level of subordination was
needed to serve the interests of his masters. Neither law nor religion had much effect on the actual operation of the system. The
legal status of slaves differed greatly from colony to colony: In
Massachusetts they were listed on the tax rolls as personal property; in Virginia a statute classified them as reality; and in Latin
America they technically had the status of persons.[3] Yet these differences counted for little against the power of the master class.
In French Canada, where slave marriages were legally valid, small
children were sold at the will of the mother's owner and spouses
might be separated by sale at any time.[4] The torture of slaves was
forbidden in Brazil, yet in some districts fiendish punishments
were inflicted without any interference from the authorities.[5]

Much has been written about the concern of the Roman Catholic Church for saving black souls under slavery. Tannenbaum
believes that religious assimilation humanized Latin American
slavery, and Elkins argues that even if conversion did not always
improve the physical well-being of slaves, it did prevent their
definition solely as property.[6] "Whatever the formal relations between slave and master," Tannenbaum writes, "they must both
recognize their relationship to each other as moral human beings
and as brothers in Christ."[7] The same conclusion has been reached
by Robin Winks, who believes that the influence of the Catholic

2. David Brion Davis, *The Problem of Slavery in Western Culture* (Ithaca,
N.Y.: Cornell University Press, 1966), pp. 223–43.

3. Lorenzo J. Greene, *The Negro in Colonial New England 1620–1776* (New
York: Columbia University Press, 1942), p. 170; Helen T. Catterall, ed., *Judicial
Cases Concerning American Slavery and the Negro*, 5 vols. (Washington, D.C.:
Carnegie Institute, 1926–37), I, 269; Tannenbaum, *Slave and Citizen*, pp.
43–57.

4. Davis, *The Problem of Slavery in Western Culture*, p. 252.

5. *Ibid.*, pp. 235–36.

6. Tannenbaum, *Slave and Citizen*, pp. 62–65, 97–99; Elkins, *Slavery*, pp.
68–75.

7. Tannenbaum, *Slave and Citizen*, p. 63.

Church resulted in more humane slave laws and regulations in French Canada.[8]

However, Protestants also were concerned with the salvation of blacks, and systematic missionary efforts were made in several English colonies, including New York, Massachusetts, Rhode Island, Jamaica, and South Carolina.[9] If the results obtained were not always numerically impressive, it was not for lack of zeal or dedication.[10] By and large, Roman Catholic missionaries baptized Negroes after only perfunctory religious instruction; sometimes whole cargoes of slaves were baptized in Angola before leaving for America.[11] Protestant proselytizers, on the other hand, insisted upon rigorous indoctrination before admitting slaves to church membership. This meant that Protestant conversions were profoundly personal and therefore more difficult; it did not mean that Protestants had less concern for the souls of blacks. Nor were nominally Catholic slaves automatically recognized as "brothers in Christ" by their Catholic masters. There were planters in rural Brazil who insisted that blacks belonged to an inferior species which could be controlled only by brutal and continuous punishment.[12]

But religious comparisons lose much of their point when we consider the actual practices of slavery. There is no evidence that religion had the slightest effect on the quality of slave life. Every act of horror perpetrated in the English colonies had its counterpart in Latin America. Nor is Elkins' argument persuasive that the real contrast between the two systems was not in the slave's treatment but in the recognition of his basic humanity. A slave tortured to death in the backcountry of Brazil could take small comfort from the fact that society recognized his basic humanity. Barbarous punishments were common occurrences in some districts where Negroes were driven to almost ceaseless labor under

8. Robin Winks, *The Blacks in Canada* (New Haven: Yale University Press, 1971), pp. 12–14.

9. Davis, *The Problem of Slavery in Western Culture*, p. 252; Greene, *The Negro in Colonial New England*, pp. 257–89.

10. Frank Klingberg, *Anglican Humanitarianism in Colonial New York* (Philadelphia: The Church Historical Society, 1940), *passim*.

11. Henry Koster, *Travels in Brazil*, C. Harvey Gardiner, ed. (Carbondale: Southern Illinois University Press, 1966), p. 179.

12. Davis, *The Problem of Slavery in Western Culture*, pp. 235–36.

the lash.[13] Although these brutalities prove nothing about the moral status of slaves, the failure of the authorities to punish such abuses proves a great deal about the significance of moral status under a slave regime.

Nor was there any real difference between North and South America in the legal status of slaves. Although English colonial law classed slaves with various types of property, the purpose of such classification was not to dehumanize the slave but to define certain property aspects of slaveholding. The Massachusetts law that classified slaves as chattels was a tax measure designed to reach into the pockets of the masters.[14] Similarly, Virginia classified slaves as realty in order to define the conditions under which they might be transferred or sold to satisfy the claims of creditors.[15] But each colony also had laws that recognized the basic humanity of the slaves. The killing or mutilation of a slave was everywhere a crime, and some statutes prescribed the death penalty for whites guilty of murdering a slave.[16]

But the legal categorization of slaves as persons had virtually no effect on their actual treatment. In every colony slaves were systematically brutalized with almost no interference from the authorities. Despite numerous cases of outright murder, no master was put to death in the English colonies for killing a slave. Killing and mutilation likewise went unpunished in Latin America, where the law supposedly provided better safeguards. In point of fact, the Spanish model law, *las Siete Partidas,* actually gave owners the right to kill slaves under certain conditions.[17] In the rural districts of Brazil, Portuguese masters had the power of life and death over their slaves. The masters in Minas Gerais posted the heads of fugitives along the roadside in order to deter slaves from running away.[18]

The prevalence of racial intermixture in the Hispano-Portuguese colonies has sometimes been cited as evidence that slavery was not intrinsically tied to socio-racial prejudice. According to

13. *Ibid.*
14. Greene, *The Negro in Colonial New England,* p. 170.
15. John C. Hurd, *The Law of Freedom and Bondage in the United States,* 2 vols. (Boston: Little, Brown, 1858–62), I, 239.
16. *Ibid.,* p. 267.
17. Davis, *The Problem of Slavery in Western Culture,* p. 234.
18. *Ibid.,* p. 237.

Tannenbaum, in Latin America "the dynamics of race contact and sex interest were stronger than prejudice, theory, law, or belief."[19] Latin American society allegedly accepted interracial sexual relations as a matter of course, and masters felt free to acknowledge their mistresses and grant them special privileges.[20] Whites could also legitimize their mixed offspring without fear of ostracism or social pressure. The Brazilian sociologist Gilberto Freyre has described racial mobility in his own country in tones of national pride, as a process that broke through the barriers of race and slavery to produce a fluid, humane society.[21]

The English colonies, on the other hand, were seemingly obsessed by the desire to maintain racial purity. Sexual contacts between the races were forbidden by law and condemned by society. Massachusetts, Pennsylvania, Virginia, and Maryland punished both races for miscegenation, and in the other colonies the strongest social pressures were exerted against such relationships. The texts of some of the laws and court decisions punishing miscegenation provide undeniable evidence of racial prejudice. In 1630 Virginia ordered a white man "to be soundly whipped before an assembly of Negroes and others for abusing himself . . . by defiling his body in lying with a Negro."[22] The Massachusetts law of 1705 against interracial sexual contacts was specifically enacted "for the better preventing of a spurious and mixt issue."[23] So pervasive was the derogation of such contacts that racial intermixture virtually equated with racial contamination.

Yet, too much can be made of differing attitudes toward miscegenation. By and large, the prevalence of racial intermixture in Latin America stemmed not from the acceptance of other races but from a demographic imbalance that left whites with no choice except to seek sexual partners among Indians and blacks.[24] Frequently these relations were authoritarian and brutal, for the de-

19. Tannenbaum, *Slave and Citizen*, p. 121.
20. Davis, *The Problem of Slavery in Western Culture*, p. 275.
21. Gilberto Freyre, *The Mansions and the Shanties: The Making of Modern Brazil* (New York: Knopf, 1963), pp. 400–31.
22. Hurd, *The Law of Freedom and Bondage*, I, 229. See Wilbert E. Moore, "Slave Law and the Social Structure," *JNH*, XXVI (1941), 179–80.
23. Hurd, *The Law of Freedom and Bondage*, I, 263.
24. Magnus Mörner, *Race Mixture in the History of Latin America* (Boston: Little, Brown, 1967), pp. 21–23, 73.

fenseless condition of the slave women invited sexual exploitation. There is no clear evidence that binding ties of loyalty and
affection were formed or that the children of mixed parentage
could look forward to eventual freedom. In some areas of Brazil,
wealthy planters apparently thought nothing of selling their illegitimate children to slave traders.[25] It is difficult to believe that
masters who sold their own mulatto offspring into slavery could
have felt racial respect for their sexual partners.

Miscegenation in Latin America seems to have exaggerated
rather than muted racial distinctions. The complex and confusing
classifications that sprang up to describe every conceivable racial
intermixture reveal an almost pathological compulsion to sort people out by color. Many of these bewildering terminologies, as
Magnus Mörner correctly points out, cannot be taken as a reflec-
tion of social reality; rather, they are attributable to an intense
contemporary interest in genealogical nomenclature.[26] Nevertheless, the nature of the classifications indicates quite clearly that
racial preoccupations were capable of resisting the dissolving
power of white blood. These preoccupations crop up repeatedly
in colonial statutes and administrative codes.[27] Venezuela prohibited marriage between whites and free Negroes, and in every
colony there were laws that fixed status according to pigmentation.[28] Santo Domingo severely punished Negroes and mulattoes
who threatened whites, and the penalties were apportioned according to the lightness of the offender's skin.[29]

The racial intermixture that occurred in Latin America had
its counterpart wherever a population imbalance existed between
the sexes. In Massachusetts and Connecticut, where there were
fewer white men than women, the latter found sexual partners
among the blacks.[30] Such connections became so prevalent in sev-

25. Davis, The Problem of Slavery in Western Culture, p. 235.
26. Magnus Mörner, "The History of Race Relations in Latin America: Some
Comments on the State of Research," Latin American Research Review, I (1966),
24–27.
27. Charles R. Boxer, The Golden Age of Brazil, 1690–1750: Growing Pains of
a Colonial Society (Berkeley: University of California Press, 1962), pp. 17–18.
28. Davis, The Problem of Slavery in Western Culture, pp. 274–75; William H.
Dusenberry, "Discriminatory Aspects of Legislation in Colonial Mexico," JNH,
XXXIII (1948), 284–302.
29. Davis, The Problem of Slavery in Western Culture, pp. 240–41.
30. "Letters and Documents Relating to Slavery in Massachusetts," in MHS

enteenth-century Maryland that for a time the colony adopted the rule of *partus sequitur patrem,* under which a child took the status of its father.[31] There was of course a double standard: where there was a surplus of white men, the law and mores tended to be more tolerant. Winthrop Jordan has shown that Barbados, which had the strictest prohibitions against racial intermixture, also had a surplus of white females. Jamaica, on the other hand, where white males outnumbered females by about two to one, had a much more liberal attitude toward mixed bloods.[32]

The amount of racial intermixture that occurred in the colonies seemingly had less to do with national and cultural differences than with the sex ratio and proportion of slaves in the population. In many areas of Latin America Negro slaves heavily outnumbered a predominantly male white population.[33] That this should quickly dilute the genetic pool of both races had nothing to do with toleration. Indeed, Fernando Romero argues persuasively that racial prejudices actually promoted miscegenation in Latin America. Since every admixture of white blood was an automatic promotion in status, there was heavy pressure on blacks to amalgamate with the masters.[34] This fact, combined with heavy demographic imbalances in the Hispano-Portuguese colonies, set the stage for a rapid proliferation of racial diversity.

Recent comparative studies indicate that basic similarities existed between the slave systems of North and South America.[35] Wherever slavery took root blacks were bought and sold like chattels, their families disrupted at the whim of the masters, and their race derogated as a badge of inferiority. The slave systems of

Colls., 5th ser., III (1877), 386; Greene, *The Negro in Colonial New England,* pp. 201–202.

31. Hurd, *The Law of Freedom and Bondage,* I, 249.

32. Winthrop Jordan, "American Chiaroscuro: The Status and Definition of Mulattoes in the British Colonies," *WMQ,* 3d ser., XIX (1962), 197–99.

33. James F. King, "The Negro in Continental Spanish America: A Select Bibliography," *Hispanic American Historical Review,* XXIV (1944), 548; Oriol Pi-Sunyer, "Historical Background to the Negro in Mexico," *JNH,* XLII (1957), 239–42. Cited in Davis, *The Problem of Slavery in Western Culture,* p. 129n.

34. Fernando Romero, "The Slave Trade and the Negro in South America," *Hispanic American Historical Review,* XXIV (1944), 374, cited in Davis, *The Problem of Slavery in Western Culture,* p. 275n.

35. Carl N. Degler, *Neither Black nor White: Slavery and Race Relations in Brazil and the United States* (New York: Macmillan, 1971), p. 43; Arnold A. Sio, "Interpretations of Slavery: The Slave Status in the Americas," *Comparative Studies in Society and History,* VII (1965), 289–308.

Brazil and Mexico were no different in their racial premises than slavery in Pennsylvania or Virginia. The subordination of all blacks to whites was the heart of American slavery. Free Negroes suffered discrimination in every colony, and they were generally classed with slaves in the regulatory codes. Colonies as different in environment and social institutions as Brazil and New Jersey prevented free Negroes from acquiring possessions which might raise them to the level of whites.[36] The maintenance and defense of white dominance everywhere prevailed over national and cultural differences.

But if such differences counted for little in the treatment of slaves, what then made the difference? Why were some treated better, enjoying economic leverage and personal privileges, while others were brutalized and destroyed by the system? The answer has less to do with the institutions of a particular slave society than with the sort of work blacks performed under slavery. Slaves possessing special skills giving them leverage with the masters naturally enjoyed a privileged position within the system. Black artisans in Massachusetts and New York were treated better than rural slaves in Brazil, and town and household slaves in Brazil were better off than plantation slaves in Virginia. This is not to say that slaves fared better under any of these systems, but that their treatment under all systems varied according to their economic relationships.

The gradual abolition of slavery in the North brought into sharper focus the economic determinants of the system. When white workers in Boston and New York City took over the jobs of Negro slaves, they also displaced blacks from skills and occupations they had long practiced under slavery. The bitter paradox of emancipation in the North is that it excluded blacks from the economic opportunities needed to make a go of freedom.[37] Even the physical presence of Negroes tended to be negated by census takers who underreported the black population. Significantly, the

36. Boxer, *The Golden Age of Brazil,* pp. 17–18; Hurd, *The Law of Freedom and Bondage,* I, 284.

37. In Cuba, on the other hand, where the pressure of an expanding white working force, primarily peasant, was not so great, free blacks managed to retain the skilled occupations they had worked at under slavery. See Herbert S. Klein, *Slavery in the Americas: A Comparative Study of Virginia and Cuba* (Chicago: University of Chicago Press, 1967), pp. 186–87, 191–92.

same tendency in Latin America resulted in a paucity of information about the Negro after emancipation. Historical interest in blacks comes to an abrupt halt with emancipation, as though, with slavery gone, Negroes no longer counted as part of society.[38]

The fact that Northern emancipation took the form of economic displacement made it easier for whites to accept the idea of legal freedom for blacks. There were no great social or economic interests to be defended, as on the *fazendas* of Brazil or the plantations of Virginia. Northern slaveowners lost nothing when their slaves became free, and the system of public compensation adopted by some states actually provided the masters with a windfall.[39] Emancipation in some ways strengthened the tyranny of race by imposing on blacks new forms of subordination that better served the economic interests of the whites. The historical reality of race relations in the Americas is that whites have never altered their institutions primarily for the benefit of blacks. Whether in the backcountry of Brazil or in the urban ghettos of New York, the hopes for racial justice have always depended upon the blacks themselves. Only black hands and the black determination to be truly free have managed to shape a future for black Americans out of the tragic shambles of the black past.

38. Mörner, "The History of Race Relations in Latin America," *Latin American Research Review*, I (1966), 33–34.
39. Arthur Zilversmit, *The First Emancipation: The Abolition of Slavery in the North* (Chicago: University of Chicago Press, 1967), pp. 181–82, 194–96.

Appendix

Unless otherwise indicated, the statistics on northern population in this appendix have been compiled from Evarts B. Greene and Virginia D. Harrington, *American Population before the Federal Census of 1790*. Colonial census returns generally used the words *Negroes, blacks,* and *slaves* interchangeably. Thus the occasional inclusion of freedmen tends to overestimate somewhat the actual number of bondsmen. On the other hand, in colonies where slaves were taxed as polls or personalty, the masters were likely to underreport their holdings. All figures are therefore approximate, providing estimates of population trends rather than precise counts. Where arithmetical errors occur in the sources, the correct totals are indicated in brackets.

MASSACHUSETTS

| | Census of 1754–55[1] | | 1764[2] | | |
| | Negroes | | Negroes and Mulattoes | | Whites |
Counties	Male	Female	Male	Female	
Suffolk	792	423	814	537	34,987
Middlesex	216	123	485	375	22,827
Essex	178	184	624	446	42,665
Worcester	40	22	138	114	30,126
Hampshire	56	18	121	73	17,051
Plymouth	69	52	243	219	21,571
Bristol	39	22	165	128	17,683
Barnstable	36	30	135	96	11,717
Dukes	3	4	25	21	2,360
York	75	41	120	105	10,419
Cumberland	—	—	55	40	7,359
Lincoln	—	—	17	7	3,620
Nantucket	—	—	24	20	3,333
Berks	—	—	50	38	2,941
	1,504	919	3,016	2,219	238,659
	Total: 2,423		Total: 243,894		

1. "Number of Negro Slaves in the Province of the Massachusetts Bay, Sixteen Years Old and Upward," MHS *Colls.*, 2d ser., III (1815), 95–97.
2. W. A. Rossiter, ed., *A Century of Population Growth in the United States, 1790–1900* (Washington, D.C., 1909), pp. 158–61.

MASSACHUSETTS (continued)

Counties	1776 White	1776 Negroes	1790 Free Whites	1790 Other Free
Barnstable	12,936	171	16,982	372
Berkshire	17,952	216	30,168	323
Bristol	24,916	585	30,980	729
Dukes	2,822	59	3,232	33
Essex	50,923	1,049	56,033	880
Hampshire	32,701	245	59,230	451
Middlesex	40,121	702	42,140	597
Nantucket	4,412	133	4,510	110
Plymouth	26,906	487	29,032	503
Suffolk	27,419	682	43,819	1,056
Worcester	45,031	432	56,398	409
Cumberland	14,110	162	25,404	156
Hancock	—	—	9,511	38
Lincoln	15,546	85	29,572	151
Washington	—	—	2,739	20
York	17,623	241	29,023	155
	333,418	5,249	475,756	5,983
	Total: 338,667		Total: 481,739	

NEW HAMPSHIRE

Counties	Census of 1773 Whites	Census of 1773 Slaves Male	Census of 1773 Slaves Female	1775 Total Inhabitants	1775 Negroes
Rockingham	34,707	260	206	37,850	435
Strafford	10,826	64	38	12,713	103
Hillsborough	13,514	39	38	15,948	87
Cheshire	9,496	7	2	10,659	7
Grafton	3,549	9	11	3,880	24
	72,092	379	295	81,050	656
	Total: 72,766				

NEW HAMPSHIRE (continued)

1786

Counties	Free Inhabitants	Slaves	Others
Rockingham	32,138	21	185
Strafford	13,877	9	8
Hillsborough	25,933	9	48
Cheshire	15,160	7	54
Grafton	8,344	0	56
	95,452	46	351

Total: 95,849

1790

Counties	Free Whites	Other Free	Slaves
Rockingham	42,796	292	97
Strafford	23,524	64	21
Hillsborough	32,705	176	—
Cheshire	28,665	70	18
Grafton	13,419	28	21
	141,109	630	157

Total: 141,896

RHODE ISLAND

Towns	Census of 1708		1748–49	
	Total Inhabitants	Blacks	Whites	Negroes
Newport	2,203	220	5,335	110
Providence	1,446	7	3,177	225
Portsmouth	628	40	807	134
Warwick	480	10	1,513	176
Westerly	570	20	1,701	59
New Shoreham	208	6	260	20
North Kingston ⎱	1,200	85	1,665	184
South Kingston ⎰			1,405	380
Greenwich	240	6	956	61
Jamestown	206	32	284	110
Smithfield	—	—	400	30
Scituate	—	—	1,210	16
Gloucester	—	—	1,194	8
Charlestown	—	—	641	58
West Greenwich	—	—	757	8
Coventry	—	—	769	16
Exeter	—	—	1,103	63
Middletown	—	—	586	76
Bristol	—	—	928	128
Tiverton	—	—	842	99
Little Compton	—	—	1,004	62
Warren	—	—	600	50
Cumberland	—	—	802	4
Richmond	—	—	500	5
	7,181	426	28,439	2,082

Total: 30,521

RHODE ISLAND (continued)

1755

Towns	Whites	Blacks	
		Male	Female
Newport	5,519	648	586
Providence	2,897	123	139
Portsmouth	1,172	101	90
Warwick	1,684	109	118
Westerly	2,177	58	56
New Shoreham	264	51	63
North Kingston	1,820	142	147
South Kingston	1,397	282	234
East Greenwich	1,040	71	56
Jamestown	361	78	78
Smithfield	1,854	37	30
Scituate	1,795	11	7
Gloucester	1,504	5	2
Charlestown	712	201	217
West Greenwich	1,204	20	22
Coventry	1,162	8	8
Exeter	1,321	39	44
Middletown	681	48	49
Bristol	966	78	56
Tiverton	1,095	102	128
Little Compton	1,142	57	73
Warren	827	51	47
Cumberland	1,070	8	5
Richmond	803	11	15
Cranston	1,372	48	40
	35,839	2,387	2,310

Total: 40,536

RHODE ISLAND (continued)

Towns	1783		
	Whites	Mulattoes	Blacks
Newport	4,914	51	549
Providence	4,015	33	252
Portsmouth	1,266	11	67
Warwick	1,951	36	100
Westerly	1,667	36	28
North Kingston	2,110	22	188
South Kingston	2,190	38	415
East Greenwich	1,529	17	53
Jamestown	270	—	65
Smithfield	2,158	7	40
Scituate	1,613	19	3
Gloucester	2,769	—	22
Charlestown	1,204	9	30
West Greenwich	1,677	7	14
Coventry	2,093	3	9
Exeter	1,946	7	87
Middletown	646	4	29
Bristol	954	13	63
Tiverton	1,792	44	93
Little Compton	1,294	—	34
Warren	867	5	30
Cumberland	1,537	2	9
Richmond	1,061	15	17
Cranston	1,508	17	50
Hopkinton	1,677	11	17
Johnston	928	37	28
North Providence	676	—	17
Barrington	488	20	26
Foster	1,756	—	7
	48,556	464	2,342

Total: 51,362

RHODE ISLAND (continued)

Counties	1790			1800[3]	
	Whites	Other Free Persons	Slaves	Total Population	Slaves
Bristol	3,021	92	98	3,801	46
Kent	8,434	351	63	8,487	20
Newport	13,120	814	366	14,845	185
Providence	23,531	778	82	25,854	5
Washington	16,634	1,372	339	16,135	124
	64,470	3,407	948	69,122	380

Total: 68,825

CONNECTICUT

Counties	Census of 1756		1774	
	Whites	Blacks	Whites	Blacks
Hartford	35,714	854	50,675	1,215
New Haven	17,955	226	25,896	923
New London	22,015	829	31,542	2,036
Fairfield	18,849	711	28,936	1,214
Windham	19,670	345	27,494	634
Litchfield	11,773	54	26,905	440
	125,976	3,019	191,448	6,462

Total: 128,995   Total: 197,910

3. U.S. Census Office, *Second Census of the United States, 1800* (Washington, D.C., 1801), p. 26.

CONNECTICUT (continued)

Counties	1782		1790		
	Whites	Negroes & Indians	Whites	Other Free Persons	Slaves
Fairfield	29,722	1,134	35,126	327	795
Hartford	55,647	1,320	37,436	430	263
Litchfield	33,127	529	38,199	323	233
Middlesex	—	—	18,578	144	216
New Haven	25,092	885	29,972	425	433
New London	31,131	1,920	31,885	729	586
Tolland	—	—	12,965	94	47
Windham	28,185	485	28,397	340	184
	202,904	6,273	232,558	2,812	2,757
	Total: 209,177		Total: 238,127		

1800[4]

Counties	Total Population	Slaves
Fairfield	38,208	276
Hartford	42,147	67
Litchfield	41,214	47
Middlesex	19,874	72
New Haven	32,162	236
New London	34,888	209
Tolland	14,319	9
Windham	28,222	35
	251,002	951
	[251,034]	

4. *Ibid.*, p. 20.

PENNSYLVANIA

Counties	Census of 1790[5]			1800[6]	
	Free Whites	Other Free	Slaves	Total Population	Slaves
Allegheny	10,151	12	159	15,087	79
Bedford	13,044	34	46	12,039	5
Berks	29,913	201	65	32,407	19
Bucks	24,559	581	261	27,496	59
Chester	27,251	543	145	32,093	46
Cumberland	17,814	206	223	25,386	228
Dauphin	18,709	57	238	22,270	93
Delaware	9,133	289	50	12,809	7
Fayette	12,995	48	282	20,159	92
Franklin	15,052	273	330	19,638	181
Huntingdon	7,498	24	43	13,008	32
Lancaster	35,254	545	348	43,403	178
Luzerne	4,880	13	11	12,839	18
Mifflin	7,461	42	59	13,609	23
Montgomery	22,371	441	113	24,150	33
Northampton	24,064	133	23	30,062	8
Northumberland	16,963	109	89	27,797	29
Philadelphia	51,851	2,101	384	81,009	85
Washington	23,624	12	265	28,298	84
Westmoreland	15,851	39	128	22,726	136
York	36,411	837	499	25,643	77
(formed after 1790)					
Wayne	—	—	—	2,562	1
Adams	—	—	—	13,172	114
Armstrong	—	—	—	2,399	1
Beaver	—	—	—	5,776	4
Butler	—	—	—	3,916	1
Crawford	—	—	—	2,346	5
Green	—	—	—	8,605	22
Lycoming	—	—	—	5,414	39
Mercer	—	—	—	3,228	5
Somerset	—	—	—	10,188	—
Venango	—	—	—	1,130	—
Warren	—	—	—	230	—
Erie	—	—	—	1,468	2
	424,849	6,540	3,761	602,362	1,706

Total: 435,150

5. Population data for Pennsylvania before 1790 are fragmentary and unreliable.
6. U.S. Census Office, *Second Census of the United States, 1800*, pp. 2C, 2F.

NEW YORK

Counties	Census of 1698		1703	
	Whites	Negroes	Whites	Negroes
Albany	1,453	23	2,015	200
Ulster and Dutchess	1,228	156	1,481	145
Orange	200	19	230	33
New York	4,237	700	3,745	630
Richmond	654	73	407	97
Westchester	917	146	1,709	198
Suffolk	2,321	558	3,158	188
Kings	1,721	296	1,569	343
Queens	3,366	199	3,968	424
	15,897	2,170	18,282	2,258
	Total: 18,067		Total: 20,540[7]	

Counties	1723		1731	
	Whites	Negroes	Whites	Negroes
New York	5,886	1,362	7,045	1,577
Richmond	1,251	255	1,513	304
Kings	1,774	444	1,658	492
Queens	6,068	1,123	6,731	1,264
Suffolk	5,266	975	7,074	601
Westchester	3,961	448	5,341	692
Orange	1,097	147	1,785	184
Dutchess	1,040	43	1,612	112
Ulster	2,357	566	2,996	732
Albany	5,693	808	7,300	1,273
	34,393	6,171	43,055	7,231
	Total: 40,564		Total: 50,286	

7. Plus 125 persons over the age of 60 unclassified by race.

NEW YORK (continued)

Counties	1737		1746	
	Whites	Negroes	Whites	Negroes
New York	8,945	1,719	9,273	2,444
Albany	9,051	1,630	—	—
Westchester	5,894	851	8,563	672
Orange	2,547	293	2,958	310
Ulster	3,998	872	4,154	1,111
Dutchess	3,156	262	8,306	500
Richmond	1,540	349	1,691	382
Kings	1,784	564	1,686	645
Queens	7,748	1,311	7,996	1,644
Suffolk	6,833	1,090	7,855	1,399
	51,496	8,941	52,482	9,107
	Total: 60,437		Total: 61,589	

Counties	1749		1756	
	Whites	Negroes	Whites	Negroes
New York	10,926	2,368	10,768	2,278
Kings	1,500	783	1,862	845
Albany	9,154	1,480	14,805	2,619
Queens	6,617	1,323	8,617	2,169
Dutchess	7,491	421	13,298	859
Suffolk	8,098	1,286	9,245	1,045
Richmond	1,745	409	1,667	465
Orange	3,874	360	4,456	430
Westchester	9,547	1,156	11,919	1,338
Ulster	3,804	1,006	6,605	1,500
	62,756	10,592	83,242	13,548
	Total: 73,384		Total: 96,790	

NEW YORK (continued)

1771

Counties	Whites	Blacks	
		Male	Female
New York	18,726	1,500	1,637
Albany	38,829	2,226	1,651
Ulster	11,996	1,091	863
Dutchess	21,044	750	610
Orange	9,430	368	294
Westchester	18,315	1,777	1,653
Kings	2,461	606	556
Queens	8,744	1,156	1,080
Suffolk	11,676	798	654
Richmond	2,253	351	243
Cumberland	3,935	7	5
Gloucester	715	6	1
	148,124	10,636	9,247

Total: 168,007

1786

Counties	Total Population	Blacks	
		Male	Female
New York	23,614	896	1,207
Albany	72,360	2,335	2,355
Ulster	22,143	1,353	1,309
Dutchess	32,636	830	815
Orange	14,062	442	416
Westchester	20,554	649	601
Kings	3,986	695	622
Queens	13,084	1,160	1,023
Suffolk	13,793	567	501
Richmond	3,152	369	324
Montgomery	15,057	217	188
Washington	20,554	8	7
	238,897	9,521	9,368

NEW YORK (continued)

Counties	1790 Total Population	1790 Slave	1800[8] Total Population	1800[8] Slave
Albany	75,921	3,929	34,043	1,808
Clinton and Essex	1,614	17	8,514	58
Columbia	27,732	1,623	35,322	1,471
Dutchess	45,266	1,856	47,775	—
Kings	4,495	1,432	5,740	1,479
Montgomery	28,893	588	21,700	466
New York	33,131	2,369	60,489	2,868
Ontario	1,075	11	15,218	57
Orange	18,478	966	29,355	—
Queens	16,014	2,309	16,893	1,528
Richmond	3,835	759	4,563	675
Suffolk	16,440	1,098	19,464	886
Ulster	29,397	2,906	24,855	—
Washington	14,033	47	35,574	80
Westchester	23,941	1,419	27,423	1,259
(formed after 1790)				
Rockland	—	—	6,353	551
Rensselaer	—	—	30,442	890
Green	—	—	12,584	520
Tioga	—	—	6,889	17
Steuben	—	—	1,788	22
Cayuga	—	—	15,871	53
Onondaga	—	—	7,406	11
Saratoga	—	—	24,483	358
Otsego	—	—	21,636	46
Delaware	—	—	10,228	16
Herkimer	—	—	14,479	61
Oneida	—	—	22,047	50
Chenango	—	—	15,666	16
Schohary	—	—	9,808	354
	345,312	22,306	591,619	20,613

8. U.S. Census Office, *Second Census of the United States, 1800*, p. 32.

NEW JERSEY

Census of 1726

Counties	Whites	Blacks	
		Male	Female
Middlesex	3,706	163	140
Essex	3,922	162	146
Monmouth	4,446	258	175
Somerset	1,892	213	166
Bergen	2,181	273	219
Burlington	3,872	139	118
Hunterdon	3,236	75	66
Gloucester	2,125	56	48
Salem	3,827	87	63
Cape May	654	9	5
	29,861	1,435	1,146

Total: 32,442

1738

Counties	Whites	Negroes and Other Slaves	
		Male	Female
Middlesex	4,261	305	198
Essex	5,951	198	177
Monmouth	5,431	362	293
Somerset	3,773	425	307
Bergen	3,289	443	363
Burlington	4,895	192	151
Hunterdon	5,288	124	95
Gloucester	3,145	74	48
Salem	5,700	97	87
Cape May	962	21	21
	42,695	2,241	1,740

Total: 46,676

NEW JERSEY (continued)

1745

Counties	Total Population	Slaves	
		Male	Female
Morris	4,436	57	36
Hunterdon	9,151	244	216
Burlington	6,803	233	197
Gloucester	3,506	121	81
Salem	6,847	90	97
Cape May	1,188	30	22
Bergen	3,006	379	237
Essex	6,988	244	201
Middlesex	7,612	483	396
Monmouth	8,627	513	386
Somerset	3,239	194	149
	61,403	2,588	2,018

1772 (incomplete)

Counties	Whites	Negroes	
		Male	Female
Morris	11,168	211	156
Hunterdon	14,510	586	509
Burlington	12,393	411	320
Gloucester	8,438	178	138
Salem	5,662	169	129
Cape May	1,648	59	52
Sussex	8,944	154	131
Cumberland	4,949	66	44
	67,712	1,834	1,479

Total: 71,025

NEW JERSEY (continued)

Counties	1790[9] Total Population	Slaves	1800[10] Total Population	Slaves
Hunterdon	20,253*	1,301	21,261	1,220
Sussex	19,500	439	22,534	514
Burlington	18,095	227	21,521	188
Essex	17,785	1,171	22,269	1,521
Monmouth	16,918	1,596	19,872	1,633
Morris	16,216	636	17,750	775
Middlesex	15,956	1,318	17,890	1,564
Gloucester	13,363	191	16,115	61
Bergen	12,601	2,301	15,156	2,825
Somerset	12,296	1,810	12,815	1,863
Salem	10,437	172	11,371	85
Cumberland	8,248	120	9,529	75
Cape May	2,571	141	3,066	98
	184,139	11,423	211,149	12,422

* [20,153]
9. U.S. Census Office, *First Census of the United States, 1790* (Philadelphia, 1791), pp. 42–44.
10. U.S. Census Office, *Second Census of the United States, 1800*, p. 34.

Bibliographical Essay

Most of the unpublished sources used in this volume are widely scattered in collections that seldom relate to slavery directly yet contain valuable information on the social and economic organization of the system. The ledgers, diaries, business records, and personal correspondence cited in the notes are a mine of information on the management of slaves, the cost of their maintenance, hiring rates, and slave relations in general. A comparatively large proportion of this material is in the manuscript collections of the Rhode Island Historical Society, the Newport Historical Society, the John Carter Brown Library in Providence, the Massachusetts State Library, the Connecticut State Library, the New-York Historical Society, the American Philosophical Society, and the Historical Society of Pennsylvania. The Museum of the City of New York, the East Hampton Free Library of Long Island, and the University of Pennsylvania Library have useful information on the buying and selling of slaves, the assessment and taxation of slave property, and the conditions under which slaves were manumitted. Valuable material on slave controls and judicial procedures, much of it recently assembled and cataloged, can be found in the Historical Documents Collection at Queens College of the City University of New York.

The Library of Congress transcripts and photocopies of the records of the Society for the Propagation of the Gospel in Foreign Parts (SPG) provide information on the proselytization of slaves and on Anglican humanitarianism in general. Supplementing the SPG records, and important for the religious and ideological origins of antislavery, are the records of the Society of Friends. Much of this material is in the minutes of the Pennsylvania Monthly and Yearly Meetings, in the Friends Historical Library of Swarthmore College; the minutes of the New England Yearly Meeting, in the Rhode Island Historical Society; and the minutes of the New York Yearly Meeting, in the Friends Seminary, New York City. Also important, particularly for information on the organization and tactics of the emancipation movement, are the minutes of the New York Manumission Society, in the New-York Historical Society, and the records of the Pennsylvania Society for Promoting the Abolition of Slavery, in the Historical Society of Pennsylvania. These records reveal more clearly than any other sources the moral dilemma posed by slavery and are besides a storehouse of information about the Negro.

Newspapers were indispensable for this study. Advertisements of slaves for sale or hire and runaway notices contain useful information on slave prices and wage rates, the occupational range of slavery, and master-slave relationships. Moreover, news reports of shipping and the slave trade often

215

reveal significant data not available in other sources. Of the newspapers cited, the following are the most important: *The Boston News Letter*, 1704–76; *Boston Gazette*, 1719–98; *New England Weekly Journal*, Boston, 1727–41; *Essex Gazette*, Salem, 1768–75; *Connecticut Courant*, Hartford, 1764–94; *Providence Gazette*, 1762–94; Bradford's *New York Gazette*, 1726–43; *New York Weekly Journal*, 1733–51; *New York Weekly Post-Boy*, 1743–73; *New York Mercury*, 1742–68; Weymann's *New York Gazette*, 1759–67; Rivington's *Royal Gazette*, New York, 1773–83; *New Jersey Gazette*, Trenton, 1777–86; *Centinel of Freedom*, Newark, 1796–1805; *American Weekly Mercury*, Philadelphia, 1719–46; *Pennsylvania Gazette*, Philadelphia, 1735–80; *Pennsylvania Chronicle*, Philadelphia, 1767–74; and *The Freeman's Journal*, Philadelphia, 1781–85. The files of these newspapers are an inexhaustible mine of information about slavery.

Most of the public records relating to slavery in New England are available in printed collections. The most useful are: Nathaniel Bouton, ed., *Provincial Papers: Documents and Records Relating to the Province of New Hampshire, from the Earliest Period of Its Settlement, 1623–1776*, 7 vols. (Concord and Nashua: Jenks, 1867–73); Nathaniel B. Shurtleff and David Pulsifer, eds., *Records of the Colony of New Plymouth, in New England*, 12 vols. (Boston: White, 1855–61); and Nathaniel B. Shurtleff, ed., *Records of the Governor and Company of the Massachusetts Bay in New England, 1628–1674*, 5 vols. (Boston: White, 1853–54). The latter contains valuable information on the slave trade and on the legal status of slaves and servants in early Massachusetts. Also important are: Gertrude Kimball, ed., *Correspondence of the Colonial Governors of Rhode Island, 1723–1775*, 2 vols. (Boston: Houghton, Mifflin, 1902–1903); John R. Bartlett, ed., *Records of the Colony of Rhode Island and Providence Plantations in New England*, 10 vols. (Providence: Greene, 1856–65), which contains bills of sale, indentures, and other documents relating to slavery; J. Hammond Trumbull and Charles J. Hoadly, eds., *The Public Records of the Colony of Connecticut*, 15 vols. (Hartford: Lockwood & Brainard, 1850–90); and Charles J. Hoadly and Leonard W. Labaree, eds., *The Public Records of the State of Connecticut*, 9 vols. (Hartford: Lockwood & Brainard, 1894–1953). The latter contains information on the security measures taken by the Council of Safety during the Revolutionary War.

The laws of New England on slavery can be found in the following: *Acts and Resolves, Public and Private, of the Province of the Massachusetts Bay*, 5 vols. (Boston: Wright & Potter, 1869–86), valuable for material on racial regulations in the eighteenth century; William H. Whitmore, ed., *The Colonial Laws of Massachusetts* [1641–72] (Boston: Rockwell & Churchill, 1889); Whitmore, ed., *The Colonial Laws of Massachusetts* [1672–86] (Boston: Rockwell & Churchill, 1890); and *Journals of the House of Representatives of Massachusetts 1715–1764*, 40 vols. (Cambridge, Mass.: Massachusetts Historical Society, 1919–70). The latter contains useful information on proposals for taxing the slave trade. Also important are: *Acts and Laws,*

Passed by the General Court or Assembly of His Majesty's Province of New Hampshire in New England with Sundry Acts of Parliament (Portsmouth, N.H.: Fowle, 1771); *Acts and Laws Passed by the General Court or Assembly of His Majesty's Colony of Connecticut in New England* (New London: Timothy Greene, 1729); Trumbull and Hoadly, eds., *Public Records of the Colony of Connecticut,* already cited; *Acts and Laws of His Majesty's Colony of Rhode Island and Providence Plantations in America* (Newport: James Franklin, 1730); and *Charter and the Acts and Laws of His Majesty's Colony of Rhode Island and Providence Plantations in America* (Providence: Sidney & Burnett Rider, 1858), which contains material on the slave controls and the regulation of Negroes in general.

Documentary material for the Middle colonies can be found in E. B. O'Callaghan and Berthold Fernow, eds., *Documents Relative to the Colonial History of the State of New York,* 15 vols. (Albany: Weed, Parsons, 1856–87); E. B. O'Callaghan, ed., *Calendar of Historical Manuscripts in the Office of the Secretary of State,* 2 vols. (Albany: Weed, Parsons, 1866); and Berthold Fernow, ed., *Records of New Amsterdam, 1653–1674,* 7 vols. (New York: The Knickerbocker Press, 1897), indispensable for information on slavery during the New Netherland period. Valuable data on slave ownership and testamentary manumission are in "Abstracts of Wills on File in the Surrogate's Office, City of New York," in New-York Historical Society *Collections,* XXV–XLI (17 vols., 1893–1913). *Documents Relating to the Colonial, Revolutionary, and Post-Revolutionary History of the State of New Jersey,* 42 vols. (Newark: New Jersey Historical Society, 1900–49), cited as *New Jersey Archives* (binder's title) in the notes, contains useful information on slave occupations. Miscellaneous material on slavery can be found in John B. Linn and W. H. Egle, eds., *Pennsylvania Archives,* 2d ser., 19 vols. (Harrisburg: State Printer, 1878–96) and George E. Reed, ed., *Pennsylvania Archives,* 4th ser., 12 vols. (Harrisburg: State Printer, 1900–1902). The "Minutes of the Provincial Council of Pennsylvania," in Samuel Hazard, ed., *Colonial Records of Pennsylvania,* 16 vols. (Philadelphia: J. Severns, 1852), is an important source for proposals to tax the slave trade.

The statutes and ordinances of the Middle colonies relating to slavery can be found in the following: E. B. O'Callaghan, ed., *Laws and Ordinances of New Netherland, 1638–1674* (Albany: Weed, Parsons, 1868); *Colonial Laws of New York from 1664 to the Revolution,* 5 vols. (Albany: James B. Lyon, 1894); *Journal of the Legislative Council of the Colony of New York, 1691–1775* (Albany: Weed, 1861); and *Journals of the New York Provincial Congress,* 2 vols. (Albany, 1842). The latter contains material on legislative proposals for emancipation. Aaron Leaming and Jacob Spicer, eds., *The Grants, Concessions, and Original Constitutions of the Province of New Jersey* (Somerville, N.J.: Honeyman, 1881), Samuel Nevill, comp., *The Acts of the General Assembly of the Province of New Jersey,* 2 vols. (Philadelphia and Woodbridge, N.J., 1752–61), and Samuel Allinson, comp., *Acts of the General Assembly of the Province of New Jersey* (Burlington, N.J.:

Isaac Collins, 1776), contain information on every aspect of slave control. By far the best source for Pennsylvania is James T. Mitchell and Henry Flanders, eds., *The Statutes at Large of Pennsylvania from 1682–1801*, 16 vols. (Harrisburg: State Printer, 1896–1911), which contains a complete index and legislative history of the slave code. Other useful sources are the *Journals of the House of Representatives of the Commonwealth of Pennsylvania, 1776–1781* (Philadelphia, 1782), invaluable for information on emancipation, and *Laws of the Government of New-Castle, Kent, and Sussex upon Delaware*, 2 vols. (Philadelphia, 1763–75), which contains material on the Delaware counties.

Judicial proceedings and court records cover the whole range of slavery, from litigation among the masters to the resistance of blacks to the system. The following are indispensable: Helen T. Catterall, ed., *Judicial Cases Concerning American Slavery and the Negro*, 5 vols. (Washington, D.C.: Carnegie Institute, 1926–37); John B. Noble, ed., *Records of the Court of Assistants of the Massachusetts Bay, 1630–1692*, 3 vols. (Boston: Pub. by Suffolk County, 1901–1908); George F. Dow, ed., *Records and Files of the Quarterly Courts of Essex County, Massachusetts*, 8 vols. (Salem, Mass.: Essex Institute, 1911–21); and Samuel E. Morison, ed., "Records of the Suffolk County Court, 1671–1680," in Colonial Society of Massachusetts *Collections*, XXIX–XXX (2 vols., 1933), which contains records of the punishments imposed on slave offenders. The court records of New Netherland can be found in the following collections: Berthold Fernow, ed., *Minutes of the Orphanmasters Court of New Amsterdam*, 2 vols. (New York: Francis P. Harper, 1907); A. J. F. Van Laer, ed., *Minutes of the Court of Fort Orange and Beverwyck, 1652–1660*, 2 vols. (Albany: State University of New York, 1920–23); Van Laer, ed., *Minutes of the Court of Rensselaerswyck, 1648–1652* (Albany, 1908); and Fernow, ed., *Records of New Amsterdam*, already cited. The latter contains the minutes of the Court of Burgomasters and Schepens from 1653 to 1674. Useful for the period after 1674 are "Minutes of the Supreme Court of Judicature, 1673–1701," New-York Historical Society *Collections*, XLV (1912), and Richard B. Morris, ed., *Select Cases of the Mayor's Court of New York City, 1674–1784* (Washington, D.C.: The American Historical Association, 1935), which includes records of the litigation concerning the purchase and sale of slaves.

Town and county records relating to slavery can be found in the following: *A Report of the Record Commissioners of the City of Boston*, 39 vols. (Boston: Rockwell & Churchill, 1881–1909); *Records of the Town of Plymouth, 1636–1742*, 2 vols. (Plymouth, Mass.: Avery & Doten, 1889–92); Clarence S. Brigham, ed., *The Early Records of Portsmouth* (Providence: E. L. Freeman, 1901); and *The Early Records of the Town of Providence*, 20 vols. (Providence: Snow & Fornbrow, 1892–1909). The latter contains information on testamentary manumissions, the ownership of slaves, and the status of Negroes in general. The *Minutes of the Common Council of the City of New York, 1675–1776*, 8 vols. (New York: Dodd, Mead, 1905) and *Minutes of the Common Council of the City of Philadelphia, 1704–1776* (Philadelphia: Crissy & Markley, 1847) contain material on the problems of slave control in the commercial centers. The translated records of New Netherland can be found in the following: A. J. F. Van Laer and Jonathan Pearson, eds., *Early Records of the City and County of Albany and Colony of Rensselaerswyck,* 4 vols. (Albany: State University of New York, 1915–19); Berthold Fernow, ed., *Records of New Amsterdam,* already cited; and A. J. F. Van Laer, ed., *The Van Rensselaer Bowier Manuscripts* (Albany: State University of New York, 1908), which contains information on the use of slaves by the Dutch patroons. Other local material for New York is in the published records of Southold, Oyster Bay, East Hampton, Jamaica, Smithtown, and Huntington, which are cited in the notes.

Documentary material on the slave trade can be found in W. Noel Sainsbury, *et al.,* eds., *Calendar of State Papers: Colonial Series, America and West Indies,* 42 vols. (London: H.M.S.O., 1860–1953), indispensable for official British sources; W. L. Grant and James Munro, eds., *Acts of the Privy Council: Colonial Series, 1613–1783,* 6 vols. (London: Wyman, 1908–12); and Elizabeth Donnan, ed., *Documents Illustrative of the History of the Slave Trade to America,* 3 vols. (Washington, D.C.: Carnegie Institute, 1930–35). Much useful information on the Dutch slave trade is in E. B. O'Callaghan, ed., *Voyage of the Slavers St. John and Arms of Amsterdam* (Albany: Munsell, 1867). Vice-admiralty proceedings relating to slavery can be found in Charles M. Hough, ed., *Reports of Cases in the Vice Admiralty of the Province of New York and the Court of Admiralty of the State of New York, 1715–1788* (New Haven: Yale University Press, 1925). The "Letter Book of John Watts, 1762–1765," New-York Historical Society *Collections,* LXI (1928), and *The Letter Book of James Browne of Providence: Merchant, 1735–1738* (Providence: Rhode Island Historical Society, 1929) contain information on the business practices of slave traders. Valuable material on the importation, price range, and marketing of slaves can be found in the newspaper files of Boston, Philadelphia, and New York City.

Contemporary accounts and journals provide a great deal of information about slavery. The most useful are: John Josselyn, "An Account of Two Voyages to New England," Massachusetts Historical Society *Collections,* 3d ser., III (1833), and John Winthrop, *History of New England, 1630–1649,* ed. by James K. Hosmer, 2 vols. (New York: Scribner's, 1908), which contain material on the origins of slavery in New England; Peter Kalm, *Travels into North America,* trans. by John R. Forster, 3 vols. (London: Eyres, 1770–71); J. Hector St. John Crèvecoeur, *Letters from an American Farmer* (London: Davies, 1783), valuable for master-slave relations; and Sarah Kemble Knight, *The Journals of Madam Knight* (New York: Smith, 1935), an account by a traveler from Boston to New York in 1704. Anne Grant, *Memoirs of an American Lady,* 2 vols. (New York: Dodd, Mead, 1901) describes slave life in Albany County, New York. Daniel Horsmanden, *The New York Conspiracy, History of the Negro Plot, 1741–1742* (New York:

Southwick & Pelsue, 1810), is a contemporary account of the affair by a judge who presided at the trials. Though biased and self-serving throughout, it conveys convincingly the fear and tension that gripped the province. A firsthand account of slavery and freedom by a former slave can be found in Austin Steward, *Twenty-Two Years a Slave and Forty Years a Freeman* (Rochester, N.Y.: William Alling, 1857). Henry Wansey, *The Journal of an Excursion to the United States of America in the Summer of 1794* (London, 1796) and J. P. Brissot de Warville, *New Travels in the United States of America*, 2 vols. (London, 1794) contain material for New York and Pennsylvania. Information on religious proselytization can be found in Cotton Mather, *The Negro Christianized* (Boston, 1706), which reveals Puritan attitudes, and David Humphreys, *An Account of the Endeavours Used by the Society for the Propagation of the Gospel in Foreign Parts to Instruct the Negro Slaves in New York* (London, 1730), useful for the Anglican missionary effort.

There is no general history of slavery in the North, but regional and state studies contain a wealth of material on the subject. The best of these is Lorenzo J. Greene's classic *The Negro in Colonial New England, 1620–1776* (New York: Columbia University Press, 1942), a gold mine of information about slavery in the Puritan colonies; it is the starting point for any study of the Northern slave system. Other studies useful for local coverage are George H. Moore, *Notes on the History of Slavery in Massachusetts* (New York: Appleton, 1866); William Johnston, *Slavery in Rhode Island, 1755–1776* (Providence: Rhode Island Historical Society, 1894); Bernard Steiner, *History of Slavery in Connecticut* (Baltimore: The Johns Hopkins Press, 1893); Edgar J. McManus, *A History of Negro Slavery in New York* (Syracuse, N.Y.: Syracuse University Press, 1966), which covers both the Dutch and English periods; Henry S. Cooley, *A Study of Slavery in New Jersey* (Baltimore: The Johns Hopkins Press, 1896), a loose conspectus not commensurate with the importance of the subject; and Edward R. Turner, *The Negro in Pennsylvania* (Washington, D.C.: The American Historical Association, 1911). The latter is the standard work on slavery in Pennsylvania and covers the history of the Negro until 1861. Much valuable information can also be found in Darold D. Wax's unpublished doctoral dissertation, "The Negro Slave Trade in Colonial Pennsylvania" (University of Washington, 1962).

Journal articles and monographs contain a wide variety of topical material. The most useful are: Winthrop D. Jordan, "The Influence of the West Indies on the Origins of New England Slavery," *William and Mary Quarterly*, 3d ser., XVIII (1961); Robert C. Twombly and Robert H. Moore, "Black Puritan: The Negro in Seventeenth-Century Massachusetts," *William and Mary Quarterly*, 3d ser., XXIV (1967); Milton Cantor, "The Image of the Negro in Colonial Literature," *New England Quarterly*, XXXVI (1963); Jordan, "American Chiaroscuro: The Status and Definition of Mulattoes in the British Colonies," *William and Mary Quarterly*, 3d ser., XXIX (1962); Benjamin Quarles, "The Colonial Militia and Negro Manpower," *Mississippi*

Valley Historical Review, XLV (1959); Leonard P. Stavisky, "Negro Crafts-manship in Early America," *American Historical Review*, LIV (1949); Darold D. Wax, "The Demand for Slave Labor in Colonial Pennsylvania," *Pennsylvania History*, XXXIV (1967); Edwin Olson, "Social Aspects of Slave Life in New York," *Journal of Negro History*, XXVI (1941); and Kenneth W. Porter, "Relations between Negroes and Indians within the Present Limits of the United States," *Journal of Negro History*, XVII (1932), which contains information on fugitive slaves. For the slave trade, the best secondary source is still W. E. B. DuBois, *The Suppression of the African Slave Trade to the United States of America, 1638–1870* (New York: Long-mans, Green, 1896); also useful are John H. Spears, *The American Slave Trade* (New York: Scribner's, 1901); Kenneth G. Davies, *The Royal African Company* (New York: Longmans, Green, 1957); and Eric Williams, *Capital-ism and Slavery* (Chapel Hill: University of North Carolina Press, 1944), which traces the connection between British capitalism and the slave trade. George F. Dow, *Slave Ships and Slaving* (Salem, Mass.: Marine Research Society, 1927) contains material on the New England slave trade, and Darold D. Wax's dissertation, already cited, is valuable for Pennsylvania's traffic in slaves.

There are several useful studies of the efforts to Christianize the slaves. The best summary is by Marcus W. Jernegan, "Slavery and Conversion in the American Colonies," *American Historical Review*, XXI (1916). For Anglican proselytization, Frank J. Klingberg, *Anglican Humanitarianism in Colonial New York* (Philadelphia: The Church Historical Society, 1940) is a highly readable, thoroughly documented work, based primarily on manu-script sources of the SPG. Also valuable are articles by C. E. Pierre, "The Work of the Society for the Propagation of the Gospel in Foreign Parts among the Negroes of the Colonies," *Journal of Negro History*, I (1916); Klingberg, "The SPG Program for Negroes in Colonial New York," *Histori-cal Magazine of the Protestant Episcopal Church*, VIII (1939); Klingberg, "The African Immigrant in Colonial Pennsylvania and Delaware," *Historical Magazine of the Protestant Episcopal Church*, XI (1942); and Edgar L. Pennington, "The Work of the Bray Associates in Pennsylvania," *Pennsyl-vania Magazine of History*, LVIII (1934), which contains material on Negro education. A good deal of interesting information can be found in Morgan Dix, *A History of the Parish of Trinity Church in the City of New York*, 5 vols. (New York: vols. I–IV, The Knickerbocker Press; vol. V, Columbia University Press, 1898–1950). Two early works that continue to be useful are Ernest Hawkins, *Historical Notices of the Church of England in the American Colonies* (London: Fellowes, 1845) and Charles F. Pascoe, *Two Hundred Years of the SPG, An Historical Account of the Society for the Propagation of the Gospel in Foreign Parts, 1701–1900*, 2 vols. (London: The Society, 1901), both of which are based on the society's manuscript records.

Among the general works on slave law and judicial procedures, John C. Hurd, *The Law of Freedom and Bondage in the United States*, 2 vols.

(Boston: Little, Brown, 1858–62), which contains abstracts of the slave code of every colony, and Thomas R. R. Cobb, *An Inquiry into the Law of Slavery in the United States of America* (Philadelphia: Johnson, 1858) have never been superseded. Also useful are William Goodell, *The American Slave Code* (New York: The American and Foreign Anti-Slavery Society, 1853); George M. Stroud, *A Sketch of the Laws in Relation to Slavery in the United States of America* (Philadelphia: Kimber & Sharpless, 1827); and Jacob D. Wheeler, *Practical Treatise on the Law of Slavery* (New York, 1837). Articles by Edwin Olson, "The Slave Code in Colonial New York," *Journal of Negro History,* XXIX (1944), and Marion T. Wright, "New Jersey Laws and the Negro," *Journal of Negro History,* XXVIII (1943), describe two of the most rigorous slave codes enacted in colonial times. Wilbert E. Moore, "Slave Law and the Social Structure," *Journal of Negro History,* XXVI (1941), explores the social context of the slave controls. A complete survey of slave legislation and the legal status of Negroes can be found in Emma L. Thornbrough's unpublished doctoral dissertation, "Negro Slavery in the North: Its Legal and Constitutional Aspects" (University of Michigan, 1946).

The best study of black resistance to slavery is Herbert Aptheker, *American Negro Slave Revolts* (New York: Columbia University Press, 1943). Also useful are Joshua Coffin, *An Account of Some of the Principal Slave Insurrections in the United States and Elsewhere* (New York: The American and Foreign Anti-Slavery Society, 1860) and Joseph C. Carroll, *Slave Insurrections in the United States, 1800–1865* (Boston: Chapman & Grimes, 1938). An excellent article by Kenneth Scott, "The Slave Insurrection in New-York in 1712," *New-York Historical Society Quarterly,* XLV (1961), based primarily on manuscript sources, definitively describes the uprising. For the impact of the Revolutionary War on slavery the study by Benjamin Quarles, *The Negro in the American Revolution* (Chapel Hill: University of North Carolina Press, 1961), is indispensable. Much useful information, some of it documentary, can be found in the following articles: W. E. Hartgrove, "The Negro Soldier in the American Revolution," *Journal of Negro History,* I (1916); Lorenzo J. Greene, "Some Observations on the Black Regiment of Rhode Island in the American Revolution," *Journal of Negro History,* XXVII (1952); and Sidney S. Rider, "An Historical Inquiry Concerning the Attempts to Raise a Regiment of Slaves in Rhode Island," *Rhode Island Historical Tracts,* X (1880). Gwendolyn Evans Logan's brief but thoroughly researched article, "The Slave in Connecticut during the American Revolution," *Connecticut Historical Society Bulletin,* XXX (1965), is a fine local study.

Arthur Zilversmit's excellent book, *The First Emancipation* (Chicago: University of Chicago Press, 1967), is the best general account of abolition in the North. An earlier work by Mary S. Locke, *Anti-Slavery in America* (Boston: Ginn, 1901), continues to be useful for the colonial origins of the antislavery movement. Material on abolition in individual states can be found in articles by Edward R. Turner, "The Abolition of Slavery in Pennsylvania," *Pennsylvania Magazine of History and Biography*, XXXVI (1912); Edgar J. McManus, "Antislavery Legislation in New York," *Journal of Negro History*, XLVI (1961); Emory Washburn, "The Extinction of Slavery in Massachusetts," Massachusetts Historical Society *Collections*, 4th ser., IV (1858); William O'Brien, S.J., "Did the Jennison Case Outlaw Slavery in Massachusetts?" *William and Mary Quarterly*, 3d ser., XVII (1960); and John D. Cushing, "The Cushing Court and the Abolition of Slavery in Massachusetts: More Notes on the 'Quock Walker Case,'" *American Journal of Legal History*, V (1961). What happened to Northern blacks after emancipation is described in Leon F. Litwack, *North of Slavery* (Chicago: University of Chicago Press, 1961). Additional information on the failure of abolition to bring real freedom can be found in articles by James T. Adams, "Disfranchisement of Negroes in New England," *American Historical Review*, XXX (1925); Herman D. Block, "The New York Negro's Battle for Political Rights," *International Review of Social History*, IX (1964); and Charles W. Wesley, "Negro Suffrage in the Period of Constitution-Making, 1787–1865," *Journal of Negro History*, XXX (1947).

For general background, Kenneth M. Stampp, *The Peculiar Institution* (New York: Knopf, 1956) is indispensable. Also useful, though flawed by its racial preconceptions, is Ulrich B. Phillips, *American Negro Slavery* (New York: Appleton, 1918). Additional perspective can be obtained from John Hope Franklin, *From Slavery to Freedom* (New York: Knopf, 1963), a work of meticulous scholarship with information of every kind about the Negro; David B. Davis, *The Problem of Slavery in Western Culture* (Ithaca, N.Y.: Cornell University Press, 1966), which traces the philosophical and intellectual premises of Western slavery from ancient to modern times; and Winthrop D. Jordan, *White over Black* (Chapel Hill: University of North Carolina Press, 1968), an encyclopedic, insightful study of racial attitudes from colonial times to the nineteenth century. Two excellent comparative studies are Herbert S. Klein, *Slavery in the Americas: A Comparative Study of Virginia and Cuba* (Chicago: University of Chicago Press, 1967), which contrasts the pattern of slavery in the mixed economy of Cuba with that of the plantation economy of colonial Virginia, and Carl N. Degler, *Neither Black nor White: Slavery and Race Relations in Brazil and the United States* (New York: Macmillan, 1971), which provides useful insights into the operation of the two largest slave societies in the Western hemisphere.

Valuable information on the complexity of Southern slavery can be found in Robert S. Starobin, *Industrial Slavery in the Old South* (New York: Oxford University Press, 1970) and Richard C. Wade, *Slavery in the Cities* (New York: Oxford University Press, 1967). The provocative study by Stanley M. Elkins, *Slavery: A Problem in American Institutional and Intellectual Life* (New York: Grosset & Dunlap, 1961), uses the methods of modern psychology and sociology to illuminate the historical experience of slavery. Finally, Eugene D. Genovese, *The World the Slaveholders Made* (New York: Pantheon Books, 1969), is a disciplined dialectical treatment of the significance of economic classes in a slave regime.

Index

Abolition: measures proposed, 160; in Vermont, 160; reasons for delaying, 160–61; opposition to, 160–61, 162–63, 170; in Pennsylvania, 161–62; in Massachusetts, 164–67; in New Hampshire, 167–68; in Rhode Island, 168; in Connecticut, 169–70; in New York, 171–72, 177; work of societies for, 174; protects property rights of slaveholders, 177–79, 197; in New Jersey, 178–79; national implications of, 179; supported by white workers, 180; evasion of laws for, 181; displaces blacks economically, 196–97

Abolition societies: activities of, 173–74

Acadia: French exiles from, 126

Acrelius, Israel: on Pennsylvania iron industry, 43

Adams, Abigail: reports conspiracy rumor, 140

Adams, John: on communication between slaves, 140; on abolition in Massachusetts, 166; on working class opposition to slavery, 180

Africa: demand for slaves from, 20–22; effect of slave raids on, 23; price of slaves in, 23, 50; duties on slaves from, 31–34

Albany: slaves forbidden to carry weapons in, 69; restricts slave gatherings, 81; fear of slave subversion in, 141

Albany Committee of Safety: retains militia to guard against insurrection, 141

Allen, Joseph: on illegal enslavement of Negro, 149

American Revolution: slaves gain freedom during, 123–24; effect on slavery, 124, 150–59; undermines slave discipline, 139–40, 141–42; military service by Negroes in, 155–58

American Weekly Mercury (Philadel-phia): slave advertisements in, 26–27, 111; arrest of runaways reported in, 115

Anglicans. *See* Church of England

Angola: slaves imported from, 3; trade encouraged with, 7–8

Antigua: slaves imported from, 20

Antislavery. *See* Abolition

Apprenticeship: limited to fixed periods, 11–12

Articles of Capitulation: transfer New Netherland to England, 11; confirm Dutch slave titles, 11, 59–60

Articles of Confederation: extradition of fugitives under, 124

Assiento: revocation of, 22

Attucks, Crispus: killed in Boston Massacre, 155

Auchmuty, Rev. Samuel: on slave converts, 103

Baptists: accept black converts, 101

Barbados: slaves imported from, 20; prohibits miscegenation, 195

Battle of Bunker Hill, 155

Baxter, Richard, 66

Beckwith, Rev. George: vindicates condemned slave, 87

Beekman, Adrian: killed during slave uprising, 129

Belcher, Andrew, 34

Belcher, Jonathan: governor of Massachusetts, 11; slave merchant, 11, 18

Belknap, Jeremy: on abolition in New Hampshire, 168; on plight of free Negroes, 185

Bellomont, Richard Coote, Lord: governor of New York, 17; on importance of black labor, 17; on bill to promote slave conversions, 101

Benezet, Anthony: opens school for slaves, 100